Becoming
Willa Cather

Becoming Willa Cather

Creation and Career

DARYL W. PALMER

UNIVERSITY OF NEVADA PRESS *Reno & Las Vegas*

University of Nevada Press | Reno, Nevada 89557 USA
www.unpress.nevada.edu

Cover design by Rebecca Lown
Cover photographs courtesy of © Shutterstock Images

Library of Congress Cataloging-in-Publication Data
Names: Palmer, Daryl W., author.
Title: Becoming Willa Cather : creation and career / Daryl W. Palmer.
Description: Reno ; Las Vegas : University of Nevada Press, 2019. | Includes bibliographical references and index. | Summary: "Willa Cather has long been admired for O Pioneers! (1913), Song of the Lark (1915), and My Ántonia (1918), the so-called "prairie novels" that launched her career; but the author's admirers have struggled to explain how a writer growing up in a small town in Nebraska in the late nineteenth century could have transformed what she remembered into literary greatness. To Cather's first critics, men such as Carl Van Doren and T. K. Whipple, her success had something to do with her native Nebraska. But what, exactly? Van Doren praised Cather for confronting the "clumsy towns, obese vulgarity, the uniform of monotonous standardization." In Whipple's view, Cather had managed to "triumph over Nebraska." A century later, scholars acknowledge Cather's place in the canon of American literature and continue to explore her relationship with the West, while often remaining puzzled by, even suspicious of, the author's Nebraskan roots. How could Cather's deep attachment to the region produce such impressive fiction? Drawing on original archival research and paying unprecedented attention to the author's early short stories, Daryl W. Palmer offers a ground-breaking account of Cather's evolution as a writer, demonstrating that her relationship with Nebraska in the years leading up to O Pioneers! is more dynamic than critics and scholars have supposed. Imbued with what the author calls an older "territorial imagination," the Nebraska of Cather's youth was a kind of laboratory for the future author, who delighted in reading, townmaking, newspapering, notoriety, make-believe, masculine attire, elocution, cycling, and even the occasional dissection. Readers will encounter a surprisingly adventurous young author, embracing a predilection for experimentation--in life and art--that resulted in her emergence as a major novelist intent on reimagining the American West"-- Provided by publisher.
Identifiers: LCCN 2019023209 (print) | LCCN 2019023210 (ebook) | ISBN 9781948908276 (cloth) | ISBN 9781948908283 (ebook)
Subjects: LCSH: Cather, Willa, 1873-1947--Childhood and youth. | Cather, Willa, 1873-1947--Criticism and interpretation. | Nebraska--Biography.
Classification: LCC PS3505.A87 Z754 2019 (print) | LCC PS3505.A87 (ebook) | DDC 813/.52 [B]--dc23
LC record available at https://lccn.loc.gov/2019023209
LC ebook record available at https://lccn.loc.gov/2019023210

The paper used in this book meets the requirements of American National Standard for Information Sciences—Permanence of Paper for Printed Library Materials, ANSI/NISO Z39.48-1992 (R2002).

First Printing

Manufactured in the United States of America

For Nina.

Table of Contents

Introduction

Next to writing I love to prowl around the Western country,
seeing little towns and how people live in them.
To me the real West begins with the Missouri [River].[1]
—Willa Cather

Still, if I had my choice, I would rather be
mayor of Sandy Point than Doge of Venice.[2]
—Willa Cather

Mention Willa Cather and Nebraska, and most people will think of pioneers and prairies. Many will have read at least one book in the so-called Prairie Trilogy of *O Pioneers!, The Song of the Lark,* and *My Ántonia.* Readers familiar with the latter novel will conjure up Cather's image of the plow against the setting sun. Loyal fans will summon pictures of Cather's hometown of Red Cloud along the Republican River. I see a woman on a wheel.

Envision, for a moment, a dusty road on a summer day in Nebraska. Contrary to popular opinion, the country in this part of the state is anything but flat. In fact, one might call it downright *hilly* as it "climbs from the river bottoms up to the Big Divide by a steady up grade, running white and hot through the scorched corn fields and grazing lands where the long-horned Texan cattle browse about in the old buffalo wallows."[3]

The year is 1895. Grover Cleveland is president. In England, Oscar Wilde has been convicted of "gross indecency." The penny-farthing, or high-bicycle, has been replaced by the safety bicycle, and women all across the United States have begun to ride, many identifying with the ideals of the New Woman.[4] Frances Willard, president of the Women's Christian Temperance Union, has published *How I Learned to Ride a Bicycle.* She describes her relationship with *Gladys,* her bicycle, and affirms her commitment to "momentum."[5] Back in Nebraska, after years of little rainfall and scorching heat, the country has nearly dried up, but motion is in the air.

Now envision "a grizzled old man with a long lean neck and a foolish sort of beard, like a goat's" heading downhill on this hot and dusty road in his rattling farm-wagon.[6] The pace is slow, and the dust makes him sneeze. Wiping his eyes, he looks up and blinks. For a moment, he thinks he sees a rider on a miniature pony. He rubs his eyes again and realizes it is no pony. It is some silly young fellow on a whatchamacallit. Then, as the figure comes up faster than the old man could have imagined, he recognizes the rider. It is Willa Cather, and the old man does not know what to think.

The young woman with the strong jaw pedals past without a glance. She knows what to think as she steers the device she calls her "wheel." The open spaces of Nebraska can intimidate her and the confines of the prairie town can make her feel claustrophobic, but now she remains intent on her own momentum, her own locomotion through a world that rarely comprehends her.

Moving forward under her own power, aware of her youth and of a certain masculine prowess, she hums the famous "Anvil Chorus" from Giuseppe Verdi's *Il Trovatore,* recalling the performance of the Tavary Opera Company in Lincoln the previous December. In the afternoon sunshine, she notices golden coreopsis and remembers a lecture given by botanist Charles E. Bessey at the university in Lincoln.[7] The sight of a winding draw leaves her feeling sentimental. She remembers a line from Virgil . . . *Optima dies* . . . that she once translated with William Ducker back in Red Cloud.

She sorts ideas for future contributions to the Lincoln newspapers. "All our makers of literature are asleep or playful," she muses (*WP Vol.1*, 274). "Woman may be man's inferior but she makes him pay for it," she says aloud in order to hear how it sounds (*WP Vol.1*, 127).

Heading north toward the territory where the French Canadians settled, she recites passages from French literature. She recalls the words of Michelet that she learned while studying in her neighbors' library: "Le but n'est rien; le chemin, c'est tout" (The end is nothing; the road is all). Exertion. Momentum. A cascade of ideas and experiments unrolling along a dusty road through the prairie landscape in which they first took root. The uncomprehending gaze of casual observers. And, most of all, youth striving, with each passing moment, to discover a remarkable destiny.

In this moment of frozen time, Willa Cather is not a famous author, but she is a rather well-known newspaper columnist, in Nebraska at least. Too old to be jejune and too young to be completely convincing, she is confused, confident, childlike, wired for self-preservation, skeptical, prone to fits of

Mary Miner, Willa Cather, and Douglass Cather with their wheels, c. 1895.
Source: Nebraska State Historical Society.

exertion and bouts of exhaustion, pragmatic, sarcastic, hyperbolic, and romantic. She holds on to her childhood friends and her fascination with various forms of bloodletting, particularly vivisection. She can be alternately charming and distant, faithful and vengeful. Both male and female admirers can capture her imagination. And it is imagination, above all else, that flows through her interior life like electricity. In this reverie, Cather is twenty-one years old, eighteen years away from the publication of *O Pioneers!*.

Nebraska is twenty-eight years old. In Cather's mind, the name refers to a territory, a people, a period in Western civilization, and much more. In her evolving imagination, Nebraska is flora, fauna, counties, churches, schools, banks, newspapers, drugstores, farms, and ranches. It is rivers, creeks, streams, bluffs, sandbars, roads, sidewalks, electric lights, ravines, railroad tracks, and bridges. It is wind, blizzards, thunderstorms, dust storms, droughts, floods and fires. It is weddings, funerals, elections, government scandals, opera house performances, recitals, fancy dances, murders, picnics, and ice-cream socials. It is, over and over again, the Divide, that real and symbolic boundary line between two watersheds, the southern flowing into the Republican River, the northern flowing into the Little Blue River.

For me, the story of how Willa Cather became a great American writer must begin with this woman on the wheel, riding through Nebraska, ready for trial and error, large and small, intent on being recognized for her work. Simpler, less-evocative images have filled the popular imagination. In 1920, Sinclair Lewis told an audience in Omaha that "'Miss Cather is Nebraska's foremost citizen. The United States knows Nebraska because of Willa Cather's books'" (qtd. in *WCLL*, 319). A year later, a reporter for the *Omaha World-Herald* explained that Cather's "pen has given Nebraska prairies a place in literature along with the far west of Bret Harte and the New England of a dozen writers of that region" (*WCP*, 28–29). In 1962, a reporter in the July 1 *Beatrice Sun* explained that Cather, having lived in Nebraska for only a "few years," was "both the product of her Nebraska experience and the great literary interpreter of the state and region" (6). It is safe to say that, in the American imagination, Cather and Nebraska go together like Shakespeare and Stratford or Hemingway and Key West. All this sounds triumphant, but it means that it has become increasingly easy to use shorthand while talking about Cather and Nebraska. With the best intentions, we can slip into the language of commemoration.

By starting with the woman on the wheel, I remind myself that nothing in Cather's career was certain, especially her relationship with Nebraska, even though it has often seemed so in retrospect. I remember to look for Cather in motion on her road, in moments of creation and desperation, assaying options and taking chances. As Cather herself observed, this sort of approach makes for a better sort of story. In her preface to the 1937 edition of *The Song of the Lark,* she declared, "The life of a successful artist in the full tide of achievement is not so interesting as the life of a talented girl 'fighting her way,' as we say. Success is never so interesting as struggle—not even to the successful."

Some years ago, Sharon O'Brien described this "struggle" as *emergence* in a groundbreaking book that continues to influence discussions of Cather. With unprecedented frankness, O'Brien appealed to contemporary psychoanalytic theory in order to offer compelling insights into the author's maturation. In many ways, my own thinking in this book is an extension of O'Brien's work, and I shared the scholar's realization that "the story of her [Cather's] artistic emergence was important enough to merit a volume of its own" (*WCEV*, 3). Call it growth, maturation, or becoming. In a metaphorical mood, call it germination and flowering. Invoke Aristotle's four causes and his notions of *energeia* and *entelechy.* Follow Henri Bergson, as Cather did, and talk about *creative evolution.* Tell it as a *Bildungsroman* or a *Künstlerroman.*

I think we should return to the creator of O'Brien's term. Two years after Cather was born, G. H. Lewes (partner of the novelist George Eliot) described the existence of "emergents," which occur "when, instead of adding measurable motion to measurable motion, or things of one kind to other individuals of their kind, there is a co-operation of things of unlike kinds. The emergent is unlike its components insofar as these are incommensurable, and it cannot be reduced to their sum or their difference."[8] Lewes had identified one of the great paradoxes in the cosmos. Somehow the combination of incommensurable ingredients could, on occasion, transcend the predictable outcome. A so-called theory of emergence was born, and no other notion I know of so perfectly names the magic of Cather's life, career, and craft. In fact, no other theory points, so precisely, to the author's mercurial and alchemical relationship to the American West.

When Cather's first critics began to ponder this emergence, they got stuck on the incommensurable components of her Nebraska roots.[9] An oft-quoted anonymous review in the *Nation* from 1920 declared: "Miss Willa Cather has worked at herself and her art. Today the product is finished and represents the triumph of mind over Nebraska."[10] Echoing this view, Carl Van Doren announced that Cather was part of a larger "revolt from the village."[11] In 1928, T. K. Whipple attempted to justify this revolt, arguing that Cather "shows us communities of people who are little and petty but withal complacent and self-satisfied, who are intolerant and contemptuous of what differs from themselves."[12] Invoking the language of the reviewer in the *Nation,* the critic concluded, "Her triumph over Nebraska implies that Miss Cather has also conquered the Nebraska in herself."[13] Nebraska, in this vision, was a kind of geographical malady.

We need not follow these early critics in order to discover the reasonable question behind their condemnations of Nebraska. How, we ought to ask, does a girl raised on the Great Plains at the end of the nineteenth century become a major author in the canon of American literature? Scholars have often asked these kinds of questions about artists. How did a man with William Shakespeare's background write *Hamlet* and *King Lear?* How did Mozart write "The Magic Flute?" In the case of Willa Cather, the questioning must center on her mercurial and experimental relationship with Nebraska. In ways Cather never stopped probing and in ways we have only begun to appreciate fully, author and state *emerged* together.

In the chapters that follow, I explore this symbiosis by focusing on Cather's experimental approach to life and art. When the Pittsburgh *Leader* offered her a position as telegraph editor in 1897, she embraced the "experiment."[14] When she looked back at her reading during the first decade of her career, she recalled favoring French writers over English writers because "they experimented more often and had a wider range of variety."[15] Cather preferred to follow suit. In fact, as Jo Ann Middleton and Merrill Skaggs have pointed out, Cather was experimenting with every book she wrote.[16] The same thing could be said about every decade of her early life.

Three crucial elements—memory, imagination, and craft—were at the heart of all this experimentation. Over and over again, in much of what she wrote, the author returned to memories. She recalled arriving in Nebraska, the color of the tall grass, scandals, and long days exploring the sandbars of the Republican River. But recollection alone would never have been enough to drive the kind of emergence I trace in this book: memory had to be transformed by imagination *and* craft.

From the first, the woman on the wheel in the 1890s understood intuitively that the past held keys to her emergence as an artist. Her first stories announce her commitment to Western memories, some quite personal, the kind of recollections that biographers trace to letters, some the result of a youth spent closely observing sunflowers and sandbars. Other memories were in many ways "public." As I have suggested elsewhere, "Cather, as she composed fiction about Nebraska, was always recomposing an archive of 'memories' preserved" in the newspapers of her youth in Red Cloud.[17] Other crucial parts of what I would call this matrix memory are the stories Cather gleaned from older settlers, including members of her own family, particularly Cather's Aunt Franc and Uncle George, who had gone West in 1873.[18]

Knowing this, Cather scholars regularly turn to *A Reader's Companion to the Fiction of Willa Cather* compiled by John March and edited by Marilyn Arnold. The volume (which runs to well over eight hundred pages) provides detailed information about real people, real places, texts, music, animals, plants, and so on that Cather either refers to directly or transforms in her fiction. A little time spent with this wonderful reference tool will help any reader appreciate Cather's explanation to Elizabeth Shepley Sergeant: "'Life began for me . . . when I ceased to admire and began to remember.'"[19]

Eventually, while working on *O Pioneers!,* Cather discovered a powerful affirmation of her instinctual emphasis on memory in Henri Bergson's *Creative Evolution,* first published in French in 1907 and translated into English in 1911. According to Bergson, we are all "artisans," moving through our daily lives moment by moment, "creating ourselves continually."[20] Our creating is an organic process, the philosopher explained, that looks a lot like emergence: "our personality shoots, grows, and ripens without ceasing. Each of its moments is something new added to what was before. We may go further: it is not only something new, but something unforeseeable."[21] The past, according to Bergson, informs all this "unforeseeable" growth: "all that we have felt, thought and willed from our earliest infancy is there, leaning over the present which is about to join it."[22] Cather was clearly inspired. As Tom Quirk explains, Cather found in Bergson's philosophy "a way to use her own best talents in the service of an art that was significantly more subtle and confident than that of her apprentice years."[23]

Cather certainly owed something to Bergson, but she owed even more to her near obsession with imaginative trial and error, a disposition rooted in her DNA but also in the American West. Indeed, I believe that Cather's youth in Webster County informed her imagination in countless ways we have yet to appreciate. For instance, I think we can say that the author inherited a distinctly *territorial imagination,* a living *poiesis* rooted in the colorful vicissitudes of the recent territorial past that had enveloped Cather from the moment she set foot in the region.[24] Although it is still valuable to follow Susan J. Rosowski and think of Cather's "foreground" beginning with the Homestead Act of 1862,[25] I think we gain insight by tracing the author's early influences back to 1854 and the birth of the territory with the Kansas-Nebraska Act.

More than anything else, the territorial imagination encouraged people to think big, take chances, and imagine the world and themselves—*otherwise.* Growing up in a country town on the Great Plains in the 1880s, Cather inherited this bold disposition. At first glance, the writers of the so-called local color movement—such as Rose Terry Cooke, Bret Harte, E. W. Howe, Sarah Orne Jewett, and Harriet Beecher Stowe—seem to have much in common with our author, but the territorial inheritance made Cather unique. Where the local colorists stuck to conventional literary forms, Cather liked to envision things otherwise.

A less disciplined author might have dithered with such a recipe, but early on in her career the woman on the wheel declared her devotion to what she called "the mighty craft": "In the kingdom of art there is no God, but one God, and his service is so exacting that there are few men born of woman who are strong enough to take the vows."[26] If art originated in the abstract realms of memory and imagination, it was made in the studio and the workshop, where experimental techniques and conventions could be refined through exacting service. As Bernice Slote and M. Catherine Downs have argued so convincingly, the nineteenth-century newspaper office was Cather's first workshop.[27] After writing and editing for Red Cloud newspapers in high school, Cather went on to refine her craft in Lincoln and Pittsburgh. "I found," she once explained, "that newspaper writing did a great deal of good for me in working off the purple flurry of my early writing" (*WCP,* 12). Of course, it should be pointed out that while Cather was "working off" bad habits, she was also assimilating newspapering techniques that came to permeate her evolving imagination. Nevertheless, as the years went by, she became convinced that journalism was undermining her literary craft. When I think of Willa Cather's emergence, I think of the author *working through* challenges formed out of memory, imagination, and craft on a long road from her arrival on the Great Plains in 1883 to the publication of *O Pioneers!* in 1913.

It goes without saying that I am hardly the first, or even the hundredth, person to study Cather's relationship to Nebraska and her place in the American West. Serious scholarly interest in the relationship began with *The World of Willa Cather,* Mildred Bennett's detailed study of Cather's Nebraska, first published in 1951.[28] A new era of literary criticism rooted in the American West was signaled in 1989 by Robert Thacker's *The Great Prairie Fact,* which remains the definitive study of literary imagination and the prairie, with Cather very much at its center. More recently, Rosowski and Janis Stout have announced approaches to gender and imagination in the West that will continue to inspire new interpretations of Cather's work.[29] Indeed, over the years, many other gifted scholars have contributed to the evolving conversation and their voices appear throughout this book.

That said, a knowledgeable reader could be forgiven for feeling that Willa Cather's relationship with the West, like the land itself, was largely settled some time ago. In fact, Cather's West has always been, to borrow a term from historian Elliott West, *contested*—by its inhabitants, historians, Cather's readers, and (of course) by the author herself.[30] It would, I believe, be a serious mistake to suppose that Cather ever "solved" her roots, any more than she resolved her ambivalence over her sexuality and identity.[31] As Ann Romines has pointed out, much remains to be said about the way Cather's Virginian origins matter to her life and career.[32] Meanwhile, anyone familiar with Cather's attachment to the Southwest will read the chapters that follow and realize that I have only begun to engage the author's relationship with that particular part of the American West. Needless to say, Cather's geographical imagination will always inspire fresh commentary and new paradigms.

Any explanation of this radical energy probably begins by acknowledging that the West may be the greatest paradox of all in Cather's writings. Adapting the author's language from her famous essay "The Novel Démeublé,"[33] I would put it this way. In Cather's poetry and fiction, *the West is the thing constantly named that suggests more than it names.* For Cather, the West is an inexplicable excess implying a verbal mood and an emotional aura that no writer before Cather had imagined possible on the Great Plains.

The author acknowledged some of this complexity when talking about her work. "As everyone knows," she wrote in a famous little essay, "Nebraska is distinctly déclassé as a literary background; its very name throws the delicately atuned *[sic]* critic into a clammy shiver of embarrassment."[34] The year was 1931, and Cather was in a magisterial mood, ready to shape the story of her emergence once and for all. The acclaimed author of *O Pioneers!, My Ántonia, The Song of the Lark,* and *A Lost Lady* could acknowledge what "everyone knows" and know more. She could even bend literary history to her will. Her first novel? *Alexander's Bridge* (1912), of course. But she decreed that there were two. *O Pioneers!* (1913) was the real beginning "because it had to do with a kind of country I loved" (*WCW,* 93). Cather's own public manifesto is clear: her artistic emergence was rooted in Nebraska. If only the author's relationship with the region were so simple. . . .

Although critics often refer to Cather's "Midwestern" home, the author was adamant that Nebraska was located in the West.[35] As a child in Virginia, she would have heard her father tell of the bears and wolves he saw while tramping about the West before he was married.[36] In Nebraska, newspapers of the time encouraged her vision by promoting "live western towns" in the state.[37] In her early cycling story "Tommy, the Unsentimental" (1896), Cather claims her region as the heroine surveys the eligible bachelors in a town modeled on Red Cloud: "She knew plenty of active young business men and sturdy ranchers," the narrator confides, "such as one meets about live western towns" (*CSF,* 474). In Cather's version of history, she had lived on a "ranch" and came from one of these towns.[38] Writing to Ellen Gere on July 27, 1896, about this time in her life, she describes spending happy moments with James Axtell's boy "Philly": "Because I come from the West he expected me to tell him Indian stories, and I fulfill my role in a way that would convulse you could you hear me" (*SLWC,* 37). In the famous interview of 1913 published in the *Philadelphia Record,* she explains, "When I was eight years old, my father moved from the Shenandoah Valley in Virginia to that Western country" (*WCP,* 9). In 1925, the novelist reported, "Next to writing I love to prowl around the Western country, seeing little towns and how people live in them. To me the real West begins with the Missouri [River]" (*WCP,* 76).

Cather had good reasons to think about Nebraska in this way.[39] Her reference to the Missouri River is precise. It was the body of water that marked old and new for the Kansas-Nebraska Territory in 1854. Pioneers headed for the Great Plains, for Utah and California, thought of the Missouri as their embarkation point. West of this boundary, rainfall diminished in dramatic fashion.[40] Grass dominated the region, running from tallgrass prairie through an ecotone of mixed-grass prairie to shortgrass prairie and then mountains. This was the land of bison, cowboys, forts, trading posts, wind, and sky. Identifying with this territorial realm of adventure and possibility, Cather liked to remind her readers that she came from "the real West."[41]

In claiming this "genuine" region, the author was participating in the ongoing competition for the "authentic" in Western writing that stretched all the way back to the expedition into present-day Kansas led by Francisco Vásquez de Coronado in 1541. Although the idea can still cause an academic ruckus, most serious readers will acknowledge that the "real West," like the "true West," is a fiction, part of a larger rhetorical project that has always invoked notions of "truth" and "authenticity" based on firsthand experience.[42] Cather clearly understood this rhetoric and took care to capitalize on it while maintaining her own sophisticated sense of irony. As William R. Handley observes, "In that ironic gap between representation and experience, or between romance and realism, Cather's art achieves at once a sense of historical authenticity and aesthetic duplicity."[43]

It was a prescient stance for a writer who would one day claim a spot in the canon of American literature. As Rosowski has pointed out, "From the beginning of discussions about American literature, writers identified its 'Americanness' with the West."[44] Cather recognized early on that her emergence as an American author depended on this vision of the West. And, thanks to Nina Baym's impressive study *Women Writers of the American West, 1833–1927,* we know that Cather has taken her place among some 343 women who published books about the region during this period.[45] In his laudatory review of *O Pioneers!,* Gardner W. Wood announced her triumph: "There have been plenty of realistic studies of the West, but this book . . . is the West in action."[46]

Readers familiar with Frederick Jackson Turner may be thinking of his "Frontier Thesis" at this point. At Chicago's Columbian Exposition in 1893, Turner announced, "The true point of view in the history of this nation is not the Atlantic coast, it is the Great West."[47] To the casual observer, Cather and Turner probably seemed like sympathetic contemporaries. Turner celebrated westward expansion for creating "a composite nationality for the American people."[48] Namby-pamby European niceties had been cast aside to engender a homogenous Western character imbued with resourcefulness and masculinity.

By contrast, when Cather wrote about "the real West," she thought of plurality, of women and immigrants freed, here and there, from certain oppressive conventions, mingling distinct European traits and practices in vibrant spheres of collaboration.[49] Outlining this vision, Rosowski describes an author intent on freeing herself from masculine codes.[50] Building on Rosowski's argument, Stout argues that Cather not only contested "established traditions of representing the West" but actually helped to found "an alternative western tradition, a tradition of women's own" aimed at "gender liberation."[51]

I think we gain a sharper picture of *how* Cather's experimentation led to this alternative West by locating it within the territorial imagination. In the chapters that follow, I want to mark the places where feisty, yet venerable impulses from territorial days inspired and informed Cather's gambits, which were always pushing back at the masculine visions of male writers such as Brett Harte, Hamlin Garland, William Allen White, and Owen Wister. When the latter author announced the arrival of the modern Western in 1902 with *The Virginian,* Cather immediately recognized a coherent and powerful recasting of territorial impulses and materials. In the fiction that followed, the author was always competing for control of these elements. As John Swift remarks, Cather recognized "that she herself might also be a sort of cowboy writer."[52] Having charted this alternative vision, Rosowski is surely right to argue that Cather's *My Ántonia* triumphs by establishing "its independence from the Western."[53]

Over the years, Cather did her best to manage her relationship with the West, both publicly and privately. Early in her career, she offered myth. In what may be the first portrait of the emerging celebrity, Jeanette Barbour recounts the youth of a successful "woman editor" in the March 28, 1897, edition of the *Pittsburg Press:*

> She went west with her family to Red Cloud, Nebraska, a small ranch town. When she was a girl of fifteen her father foreclosed a mortgage on the only newspaper in the town, and as he was not a newspaper man, he left the paper in charge of his daughter until he could get someone else to conduct it. (*WCP,* 2)

In this well-crafted story, the junior Horace Greeley simply goes west and inherits a newspaper. When *The Troll Garden* appeared in 1905, the reviewer in *The Bookman* explained that in Nebraska Cather "lived for a while a healthful, quite unliterary life, spending most of her time in the open on horseback" (*WCP,* 5). A gentle unliterary creature of the grasslands, Cather needed no roof to shield her from the elements.

This myth took its final form in the story Cather told Latrobe Carroll in a 1921 interview: "On the Nebraska prairie some years ago, a little girl rode about on her pony, among settlements of Scandinavians and Bohemians, listening to their conversation, fascinated by their personalities. She was Willa Sibert Cather, who, as a woman, was to give in her novels the story of their struggle with the soil" (*WCP,* 19). In Carroll's retelling, Cather's relationship with the West was spare and fateful, the road to success inevitable.

Cather knew otherwise. She knew that her relationship with "the real West" was complicated, and she knew she would never try to explain all of the complexities to her reading public, many of whom would never comprehend the prairie world she wrote about. So, over the course of her career, she developed a number of conventional ways of talking about her origins to people who did not appreciate the Great Plains. Her often-quoted interview from 1913 in the *Philadelphia Record* stands as a perfect example. "How," the interviewer inquires, "did you come to write about that flat part of the prairie west, Miss Cather, which not many people find interesting?" Cather responded by mapping the world of *O Pioneers!,* which had just appeared. She explained that although she did not see the country at the very beginning of settlement, "it was still wild enough and bleak enough when we got there. My grandfather's homestead was about eighteen miles from Red Cloud—a little town on the Burlington, named after the old Indian chief" (*WCP,* 9). Cather was clearly implying that a "wild" prairie is fascinating, even if it seems flat to someone who does not know it. More important, she was insisting that the Nebraska of her fiction was more than prairie. It was also Red Cloud, the prairie town that served to orient her recollections. In other words, Cather's Nebraska was both *territory* (an old Anglo-Norman word for the land surrounding a town or manor) and *town* (an older word for land enclosed for habitation). When she mapped and remapped Nebraska in her fiction, Red Cloud was always the compass rose.

Nevertheless, the West remained a problem for Cather. In the aforementioned interview from 1913, she confessed her love for "the woods and hills and meadows" of Virginia, but she recalled being "jerked away from all these and thrown out into a country as bare as a piece of sheet iron" (*WCP,* 10). Cather did not simply "go west"; she had been "jerked" and "thrown." The oppositional terms are clear in this impassioned declaration, and the prairie, with all its treeless beauty, comes up lacking. Pressing on in what would be a rare mood of disclosure, she admitted, "I thought I should go under." This is how she described her arrival in Nebraska in the wake of writing *O Pioneers!*.

At first glance, she seems to be contradicting the novel's glowing descriptions of the prairie, but on closer inspection it becomes clear that her confession in the interview is all about her first days in the new land. As James Woodress explains, "The year and a half that they spent on the farm in Webster, County, Nebraska, was made up of happy months for Willa despite the culture shock."[54] For Cather, the difference between her first days on the prairie and her months on the farm was a crucial distinction that she had been exploring for years in her short fiction. Just after the publication of *The Troll Garden* in 1905, Cather wrote to Witter Bynner at *McClure's:* "Things are a good deal better out there now, you understand, but, whenever I go back, I see the old tragedies that I knew so intimately in the background" (*SLWC,* 88). This is certainly not the story we read in *The Bookman.* By this time in her career, as we shall see in chapter 3, Cather had good reason to be careful with her public descriptions of Nebraska, whether in newspapers or short stories. How could she explain to the people back home that the Nebraska of the past always haunted the Nebraska of the present?

An even more pressing problem for Cather (another one she did not discuss with interviewers) was that the Great Plains could still unsettle her. In a candid letter to Sergeant dated April 20, 1912, Cather confessed, "I used always to be sure that I'd never get out, that I would die in a cornfield. Now I know I will get out again, but I still get attacks of fright. I wish I didn't. I somehow feel that [if] one were really a fit person to write about a country they wouldn't feel that" (*SLWC,* 150). Even as she was writing about the country she loved in *O Pioneers!,* her discomfort with the region made her feel inadequate.

Inevitably, Cather was more troubled by these feelings because she was always returning to Nebraska to face them. As long as her parents were alive, she tried to go back to Red Cloud for visits, usually during the summer or at Christmas. Red Cloud, in the words of Woodress, "drew her like a magnet."[55] After her parents moved from her childhood home on Cedar Street to a much grander house on Seward Street in 1903, Cather spent the next twenty-eight years returning to a place that did not quite jibe with her memories. Nevertheless, she continued to have memorable visits. Woodress singles out 1922 when "she went home for Christmas to help her parents celebrate their fiftieth wedding anniversary, which was a joyous occasion. All the children were there. Then after Christmas she and her parents joined the Episcopal Church together."[56] It was a rare and memorable event, but Cather realized that she was always a kind of time traveler during her visits, popping back and forth between memories and present circumstances. Her short stories and poems transform these "looping journeys," exploring the feelings of delight and displacement with growing sophistication.[57]

The fact is, Cather often found it difficult to be herself and feel at home with her family. She seems to have loved her father simply and dearly, but she had a complicated relationship with her mother. She often enjoyed spending time with her siblings and, in later years, she took particular delight in the company of her nieces and nephews who seem to have felt the same way about her. Helen Cather Southwick remembers spending "many happy days there [at the house on Seward Street], especially when Aunt Willa was visiting."[58] Southwick goes on to recall afternoon teas on the front porch and trips to the soda fountain for cherry phosphates. During her stays, Cather would go for drives in the country, taking time to catch up with family and friends.

None of these activities guaranteed a successful visit. In a touching letter to her brother Douglass on July 8, 1916, Cather remembered difficult times during the previous summer visit: "I won't sit around and weep. I can't be hurt again as badly as I was last summer. After this I'll be more philosophical; I won't expect too much, and I mean to enjoy any goodwill or friendship I get from any of my family" (*SLWC*, 225). As the years went on, Cather's recollections of her home country must have been colored by this "philosophical" attitude, which sounds more like stoicism than epicurean pleasure.

In any event, Cather seems to have persevered in her wise approach to family life, taking the ups and downs in stride even though the larger community of Red Cloud presented other challenges. In 1927, while visiting her hometown for Christmas, Cather sat down for tea with fellow Red Cloudian Jo Frisbie. Their conversation appeared in the pages of Julius Temple House's *Present-Day American Literature* the following year. Frisbie opens the article by assuring her readers that "Red Cloud is proud of her" (*WCP*, 104).

Although the rest of the article is meant to unfold as a tribute to the hometown celebrity, Cather could hardly have been cheered by the effort. Frisbie reports: "One year when she was spending the holidays at Red Cloud she went in to Cotting's Drugstore. A farmer was buying a book for a Christmas present. Miss Cather noticed that he had decided on *One of Ours*. With her customary thoughtfulness, although she did not know the man, she approached him and said: 'Would you like to have me autograph it for you?' He looked a bit puzzled and, seeing that he did not know her, replied haughtily: 'No I don't want nobody writin' in my books.' " Frisbie seems to want to illustrate the author's kindness with a humorous anecdote, but the effect is rather different. It sounds more like comeuppance. The famous author is not entirely famous in Red Cloud, where her graciousness is simply scorned.

Cather probably felt a queasy sense of déjà vu. As a youth in Red Cloud, her neighbors had not always acknowledged her talents. Some envied her; others were confounded by her habits. Like some of her most famous characters, she longed for a larger stage and a more appreciative audience. At times, the unsatisfying response could be attributed to simple envy. On other occasions, as in the anecdote above, it was something more profound, something like a fundamental disconnect between different cultures. As if making this point, Frisbie concludes her article with a little epiphany: "As I was walking home that evening it suddenly occurred to me that during the whole afternoon no mention had been made of any of Willa Cather's books, or of herself as a literary lady" (*WCP,* 107). All of Cather's real accomplishments in the world had been relegated to the sideboard, alongside the hand-painted creamer and sugar bowl, in the dining room on Seward Street.

Is it any wonder that Cather's relationship with her hometown was doomed to ambiguity? Red Cloud was always "home" for Cather, but it was also the source of a distinctly modern brand of homesickness. She could live a good life in New York, London, and Paris, but a sense of longing and displacement haunted her days. In the 1921 *Omaha Bee* interview, Cather described Nebraska as "the happiness and the curse of my life" (*WCP,* 32). She went on to describe her time in Paris the previous autumn when "she would sit by the Seine and feel weepy and homesick for the Republican valley. 'I always come back to Nebraska,' she concluded" (*WCP,* 32).

Or so she said. Looking toward the end of the author's life, Woodress offers an eloquent summing up: "Among the several dichotomies in her life, this is one. Throughout her life she was drawn back to the hills and mountains despite her acquired affection for the prairie. When she discovered Jaffrey, New Hampshire, in 1916, she immediately fell in love with the area and returned year after year for a month or more; and when she died, she was not buried in the family plot at Red Cloud with her parents, but on a hillside at Jaffrey, where one could look up and see 'a familiar mountain' (Monadnock) against the sky" (*WCLL,* 37). Thousands of visitors arrive every year from around the world in order to explore what has come to be known as Catherland. They tour Red Cloud and drive around the countryside, lingering in what is now known as The National Willa Cather Center, searching high and low for glimpses of the author they admire. But the old irony persists. Cather's remains are not in Nebraska. She was too Western for that. As Wallace Stegner reminds us, it is a fact that "few Westerners die where they were born, that most live out their lives as a series of uprootings."[59]

More than a decade ago, I was one of those pilgrims. I marveled at the way the prairie really rolled up and down, greener and sweeter than I had imagined. The red brick streets promised a kind of enchantment. So, I signed up for the tours, drove into the country, scrambling in and out of the cellar that I knew from reading *My Ántonia,* visited Cather's childhood home, gawking at her attic bedroom with its famous wallpaper that I knew from reading *The Song of the Lark.* Walking into the auditorium of the Red Cloud Opera House, I shivered at the notion of Cather standing on the same stage delivering her high school commencement address. I was hooked.[60]

These days, I return for the Willa Cather Foundation's annual spring conference, where people come from all over the world to talk about everything from literature and World War I to kolaches and opera. I saunter out over the Willa Cather Memorial Prairie and poke around in the archives. Anyone who wants to understand the seductiveness of studying Cather's fiction through archival research should read music critic Alex Ross's description of finding himself caught up in the mystery of Cather's piano teacher Albert Schindelmeisser.[61]

But one of my favorite things to do is to walk the streets of Red Cloud around twilight, when something like living memory seems to hover in the shadows. I like to stand in front of the Cathers' first home on Cedar Street, looking over toward the home of the Miner family (referred to by many as "the Harling House"). With a rustle of wind, I can almost see Jim Burden in *My Ántonia* bursting through the willow hedge as if witches were after him. Of course, this is fiction, blended with memory, and now my own fancy. How did Cather do it? How, more than a century after the writing, does her work inspire me to this kind of imaginative pilgrimage?

Over the years, a number of answers have been percolating. While walking the country roads that are not the same country roads Cather knew, I began to conjure up the woman on the wheel. I suppose I wanted a beginning. For years, I thought I was writing a simple historical study of "Willa Cather and Nebraska." Eventually, when I realized I was always thinking about imagination and emergence, the book you are reading began to take shape. I hope that even the most seasoned Cather scholars will find fresh insights along the familiar streets and dusty roads.

As a foundation for everything that follows, I explain in chapter 1 how 1880's Nebraska as a whole and the town of Red Cloud in particular were richer and more dynamic than many of Cather's readers have imagined. Growing up in Webster County, Cather was surrounded by people who knew all about the old Kansas-Nebraska Territory, created in 1854, which incorporated parts of present-day Kansas and Colorado. They felt at home in a world imbued with a kind of territorial imagination that manifested itself in a taste for newspapering, town-making, speculation, innovation, and experimentation. In Cather's childhood Red Cloud, the same people who relished territorial campfires installed electric lights—decades before the Rural Electrification Act of 1936. This was the Nebraska that fired Cather's imagination throughout her career.

In subsequent chapters I pay unprecedented attention to Cather's early fiction, violating the wishes of the author, who would have erased most of the stories if she had had the chance. The closer study reveals that the early fiction is better and more heterogeneous than we often admit. Writing at the end of her distinguished career, Slote pointed in this direction, noting that Cather's body of early work, including her journalism and poetry, is "larger than we thought, the design grander, the problems more complex."[62] Rosowski goes further, arguing that "Cather's early fiction tells of seeking ways to save the West from literary speculators—the writers of the Western as America's masculine romance—by shattering their codes and freeing herself from them."[63] Although I doubt that Cather really shattered such codes or ever found complete liberation, I do mean to celebrate and explore her many brilliant attempts to shake things up, resist masculine conventions, expose opportunities, and invent alternative versions of gendered life.

For me, this thrilling experimentation is deeply rooted in Cather's complex relationship to Nebraska. Most of us have been taught that Cather's relationship with Nebraska passed inexorably from a mood of early disdain to the celebration of *O Pioneers!* before concluding with a pessimistic phase later in life.[64] Instead of following this tidy narrative, I have focused on the ways in which Cather's negative responses to the Great Plains in her early fiction, as far back as 1896, are interwoven with (and even enable) moments of recognition, resistance, and innovation. As the young author experimented with elements of her craft that would prove useful over the course of her career, she uncovered nuances in her own feelings. Like a painter in a studio, she was constantly discovering new ways of imagining the West.

Scholars have identified various phases in Cather's long career that help us focus on elements and connections we might otherwise overlook.[65] I think this approach is inevitable and even irresistible, as long as we remember that such constructs are provisional. For instance, scholars have pointed to a long apprenticeship in journalism that began during Cather's university years in Lincoln, but Downs directs our attention to the author's high school contributions to the Red Cloud newspapers. As she puts it, "Cather became a journalist very early indeed."[66] I want to explore this earlier beginning in greater detail. In this longer phase, I find a distinct (and largely neglected) Brownville period that began when Cather and some university friends made a pilgrimage in 1894 to see one of the first territorial towns in the state.[67] During this period, Cather was particularly interested in working out connections between narrative technique and the territorial past.

While writing this book, I have often found it useful to think of Cather as a *decadal artist,* rebooting with remarkable regularity every ten years. Perhaps the rhythm began when she moved to Nebraska in time to celebrate her tenth birthday in 1883? After that, the pattern simply emerged as an organic phenomenon. Cather's first short story appeared in print nine years after her family arrived on the prairie. But her first column for the *Nebraska State Journal* appeared in 1893. She worked for a decade in Pittsburgh. *O Pioneers!* was published in 1913. On May 13, 1923, the Pulitzer Prize was awarded to *One of Ours,* which went through an additional four printings by year's end. In September, *A Lost Lady* was published, marking the end of an extraordinary decade of literary production. Fifty thousand copies of the novel quickly sold. In December 7 of that year, Cather turned fifty. In 1933, Cather won the Prix Femina Americain for *Shadows on the Rock,* but the turning point that year occurred when she sprained her wrist. The injury led to chronic pain that informed the final years of her life. I have no theory for the significance of 1943, and we may not need one. In the end, notions of phases are far more impressionistic than mathematical.

In the same vein, Cather scholars must work hard to make convincing cases for the beginnings and endings we study. While writing this book, I was inclined to begin with the woman on the wheel, but another beginning demands our attention as well. It occurred during the summer of 1887, when the thirteen-year-old Willa Cather decided to invent a town.

Enlisting the aid of her siblings and the Miner children who lived up the street, the future author platted the town of Sandy Point along the fence south of the Cather home on Cedar Street. Packing crates were procured from the Miner Brothers' store. Cather appealed to her father, Charles, for six loads of sand to properly finish the town's Main Street, which ran the length of the Cather property. Willa Cather was mayor and editor of the newspaper.

What inspired the child who wanted to be a doctor to make a town? Bennett suggests that "two events fanned the flame of Willa's dramatic fire. Dr. Gilbert Einstein McKeeby, the Cather family doctor, was elected mayor of Red Cloud and Charles Cather, her father, alderman; and a contract was let for an iron bridge over the Republican River."[68] Bennett is probably right about recent events, but her answer hardly does justice to the implications of the question. Writing of what she calls Cather's "most elaborate childhood scheme," O'Brien suggests that the girl was able "to imagine alternatives to the female role" (*WCEV,* 87). The scholar is surely correct, but she may underestimate Sandy Point's importance.

In this story of youthful townmaking we are very near the original recipe for Cather's creation and career. Although she wanted to be a doctor, Cather already lived for and through her imagination. She recognized, even as a child, that townmaking was an intoxicating enterprise that had much in common with literature. Settings, roles, and conflicts were invented and staged. New dramas ensued. As mayor, she directed the action. As editor, she brought it to life again in prose.

Perhaps even more important for Cather's future career was her youthful recognition that her creativity was stirred by observing real life. Writers and their texts could inspire her as well, but real institutions, projects, sites, events, and personalities functioned like the dynamo on the Republican River that generated power for the town's electric lights: they charged her imagination. Working this process out as she invented Sandy Point, Cather knew it was all make-believe, but she must have recognized that it was so much more.

In fact, Cather was already experimenting with a different process that would produce her great Nebraska fiction. In a 1915 interview for the *Lincoln Daily Star,* the author of *O Pioneers!* explained, "Imagination, which is a quality writers must have, does not mean the ability to weave pretty stories out of nothing. In the right sense, imagination is a response to what is going on—a sensitiveness to which outside things appeal" (*WCP,* 15). When first examined, this definition seems unremarkable. We could say, "The writer is inspired by what she observes." On closer inspection, Cather's idea turns out to be surprisingly supple and fantastically Romantic. The simple "response" is also a sensitivity. The "to which" flips the active element in the sentence so that "outside things" do the engaging. This world of organic and inorganic things animates the would-be artist.

I think Cather was already working out this notion of the imagination in her backyard in 1887. Her townmaking offered a collection of outside things that, once gathered, went on engaging and reengaging the children's imaginations. The whole really was greater than the sum of its parts. Call it emergence. Cather called it Sandy Point.

In any event, it was Cather's first great experiment in imagination, and her "creative process" rewards study. For instance, Cather could have chosen a hundred other cities and towns as her model. The avid reader of Robert Louis Stevenson and Howard Pyle could have conjured a truly exotic locale such as Jerusalem or Paris, a medieval castle or village, but Cather chose Red Cloud as her model. At thirteen, she established a preference that would inform her career from beginning to end.

In Sandy Point, Cather discovered that she liked to work with palimpsests, a term originally applied to a piece of parchment that has been scraped and written over. As Sarah Dillon explains, the fact that the old writing often showed through the new led Thomas De Quincey in the nineteenth century to use the term figuratively to describe "the way in which 'our deepest thoughts and feelings pass to us through perplexed combinations of concrete objects. . . .' The adjective 'involuted' describes the relationship between the texts that inhabit the palimpsest as a result of the process of palimpsesting and subsequent textual reappearance. The palimpsest is an involuted phenomenon where otherwise unrelated texts are involved and entangled, intricately interwoven, interrupting and inhabiting each other. Another word that describes this structure is the neologism 'palimpsestuous.' "[69] There is, it must be said, nothing accidental about this sort of imaginative activity. The artist goes out of her way to erase, knowing full well that what came first will shimmer through the final creation.

In her invention of Sandy Point, Cather realized the pleasures of this process. Standing on Main Street of Sandy Point, the mayor could see the Miner Brothers' store on Red Cloud's main thoroughfare. The suspension of the real and the fictional in a palimpsestuous creation allowed for all sorts of delightful similarities and differences to emerge. Some were ironic, even parodic. Some were illuminating. Some would sound like harmony, others like dissonance. This is how the mature artist would write about Nebraska, renaming and rearranging the prairie world she knew in ways the earliest settlers could have appreciated.

Cather's "scripts" for playtime are also revealing. She could have staged the early buffalo stampede or a Fourth of July parade. She could have come up with a hundred exciting scenes borrowed from her reading, but she thought of *bridge building.* As mayor, she instructed her brothers to construct "a bridge over a ditch on the north side of the Cather yard" (*WWC,* 172–73). When the girl wanted to imagine an adventure, she thought in detail about Red Cloud townmaking, and her invention was inspired by newspaper stories about the construction of a bridge over the Republican River south of town. It is fitting indeed that when Cather sat down to write her first novel, she just happened to focus on a character who built "bridges into the future, over which the feet of every one of us will go."[70]

Certain elements, like the sand in Sandy Point, deserve attention. Many children have probably thought of using crates and boxes to invent playtime habitats, but few have probably paid such close attention to geological ingredients. Several explanations come to mind. The Red Cloud newspapers regularly complained about the state of the town's dusty streets. By "sanding" her main street, Cather was improving on the real. She was also attending to more details than the ordinary child, a penchant that would prove particularly crucial when she began to think like an editor.

Although it is easy to overlook, this kind of attention to detail was also at work in Cather's acquisition of the crates. Their material functionality is obvious, but their symbolic value shines through as well. Because they came from a Red Cloud business, they were imbued with the spirit of real Red Cloud commerce. In other words, Cather's youthful aesthetic depended on a kind of *repurposing.* This is, of course, a different approach than *recycling,* which usually implies the transformation of something discarded into something else. Repurposing preserves the original thing and simply redeploys it. These strategies, as it turns out, would be crucial elements of the mature writer's approach to the West.

In all of these ways, Sandy Point was a laboratory of the imagination, but it may have mattered most to Cather as a place of companionship. For the rest of her life, Cather held on to the experience. In letters to her brothers and friends, she referred to Sandy Point. When times were tough, in the years immediately preceding the publication of *My Ántonia,* she thought of Sandy Point as her beginning. When she wanted to share an intimate sense of adventure with Margie (Miner) Gund in 1908, she sent a postcard from Venice. "At last," the author wrote, "I have found a place that is as handsome as Sandy Point in its best days. It is the first city I've ever found that could touch ours, either in beauty or importance. Still, if I had my choice, I would rather be mayor of Sandy Point than Doge of Venice."[71]

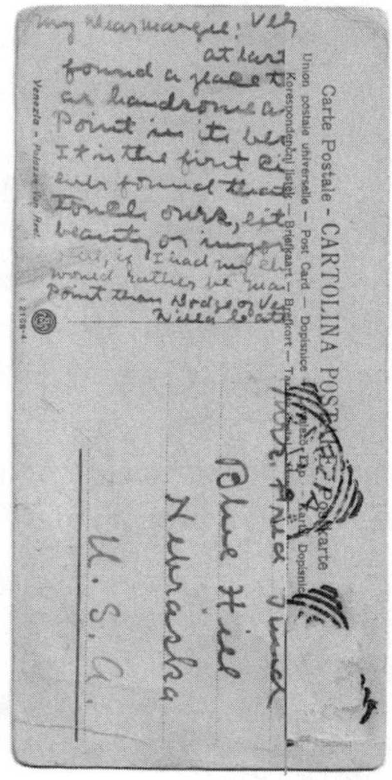

POSTCARD from Cather to Margie (Miner) Gund, 1908. Source: WILLA CATHER PIONEER MEMORIAL COLLECTION. SPECIAL COLLECTIONS & ARCHIVES AT THE NATIONAL WILLA CATHER CENTER IN RED CLOUD, NEBRASKA.

Just how important was Sandy Point to Cather? More than three decades after the work of townmaking, Cather's memory blossomed in the company of Irene (Miner) Weisz during an interview published in the *Omaha Daily News* in 1921. The two friends were recalling their make-believe town when Ms. Weisz declared, "There's no question about it. Willa started her literary career in Stony Point *[sic]*" (*WCP,* 30). The moment is valuable for a number of reasons. Recalling the town by another name, Weisz was clearly speaking from her own firsthand perspective. On the most important point, she spoke with the special authority of an old and dear friend. She knew that Cather's path to becoming a major American novelist began on a sandy street running through the heart of a make-believe town in the middle of Red Cloud, Nebraska. This claim about the evolution of Cather's career has been quoted from time to time, but perhaps never taken seriously.

I suggest that Ms. Weisz's idea should stand front and center in any discussion of Cather and Nebraska for a number of good reasons—not the least of which is that Cather always acknowledged her friend's astute understanding. She explained it in a letter to Weisz on March 12, 1931: "You see you are the only person who reaches back into the very beginning who has kept on being a part of my life" (*SLWC,* 442). We can trust Weisz's interpretation. Willa Cather really could be known as the author from Sandy Point, Nebraska, her first great experiment in life and art.

In one of her most famous pronouncements, Cather's thoughts returned to the idea of the road: "When people ask me if it has been a hard or easy road I always answer with the quotation, 'The end is nothing, the road is all' " (*WCP,* 76). Michelet's words were apt for the woman who once doted on her wheel, but they do not quite capture the true feelings of the inventor of Sandy Point. In the 1931 letter to Weisz, a few lines after the tribute to her friend, Cather confessed her heart's deep desire: "I want somebody from Sandy Point to go along with me to the end."

Notes

1. *WCP,* 76.
2. "To Mrs. Fred Gund," 1908. Special Collections & Archives at the National Willa Cather Center. See also the postcard Cather sent to her brother Roscoe on July 10, [1908], MS 316, Roscoe and Meta Cather Collection, University of Nebraska.
3. *CSF,* 477. These last words come from "Tommy, the Unsentimental" (1896), the early Cather story (filled with biographical details) that inspired this reverie. We know Cather was riding her wheel during the summer of 1895 because she mentions her adventures in a letter to Ellen and Frances Gere on July 30, 1895.
4. Sarah Hallenbeck, *Claiming the Bicycle: Women, Rhetoric, and Technology in Nineteenth-Century America* (Carbondale: Southern Illinois University Press, 2016), xiii, 28–32, and passim, provides a comprehensive analysis of the phenomenon.
5. Frances Willard, *How I Learned to Ride the Bicycle* (New York: Fleming H. Revell, 1895), 24, 47.
6. *CSP,* 90. Cather describes the old farmer in "The Bohemian Girl" (1912).
7. For a discussion of Cather's experience of Bessey's teaching at the university, see Susan J. Rosowski, "Willa Cather's Ecology of Place," *Western American Literature* 30.1 (1995): 37–39.
8. G. H. Lewes, *Problems of Life and Mind* (London: Trübner, 1875), 412.
9. Guy Reynolds, ed. Willa Cather: *Critical Assessments,* vol. 1. (Mountfield: Helm Information, 2003), 4, frames these early commentaries: "Cather's first readers included a network of literary intellectuals whose collective project was the construction of a national literary paradigm. They read her, by turns, as both exemplar of those national characteristics and as an antiphonal voice that opposed the dominant strains of her nation. And these two Cathers—conformist and nonconformist—have been kept in play by critics right down to today." See also Reynolds, *Willa Cather in Context: Progress, Race, and Empire* (New York: St. Martin's Press, 1996), 5–10 and Acocella's excellent account of the early critical response in *Willa Cather and the Politics of Criticism* (Lincoln: University of Nebraska Press, 2000), 18–29.
10. "Short Story: Art and Artifice," *Nation* (September 25, 1920): 352.
11. Carl Van Doren, *Contemporary American Novelists: 1900-1920* (New York: Macmillan, 1922), 116.
12. Whipple, "Willa Cather," *Willa Cather: Critical Assessments,* 188, 192.
13. Ibid., 193.
14. Willa Cather to Louise Pound, October 13, 1897, *SLWC,* 47.
15. Willa Cather to Albert G. Feuillerat, November 6, 1929, *SLWC,* 420.
16. Jo Ann Middleton, *Willa Cather's Modernism: A Study of Style and Technique* (Rutherford: Fairleigh Dickinson University Press and London: Associated University Presses, 1990), 41; Merrill Maguire Skaggs, *After the World Broke in Two: The Later Novels of Willa Cather* (Charlottesville and London: University of Virginia Press, 1990), 2.
17. Daryl W. Palmer, "Recomposing Nineteenth-Century Nebraska: Red Cloud Newspapers and Cather's 'Hired Girls' in *My Ántonia,*" *Willa Cather Newsletter and Review* 55.3 (2012): 2.
18. For a brilliant discussion of these memories, as preserved in the family correspondence, and their impact on Cather's fiction, see Susan J. Rosowski, *Birthing a Nation: Gender, Creativity, and the West in American Literature* (Lincoln: University of Nebraska Press, 1999), 34–57.
19. Elizabeth Shepley Sergeant, *Willa Cather: A Memoir* (1953; Lincoln: University of Nebraska Press, 1963), 107.
20. Henri Bergson, *Creative Evolution,* trans. Arthur Mitchell (1911; Mineola: Dover, 1998), 7.
21. Ibid., 6.
22. Ibid., 5.
23. Tom Quirk, *Bergson and American Culture: The Worlds of Willa Cather and Wallace Stevens* (Chapel Hill: University of North Carolina Press, 1990), 139.

24. For my initial sketch of this theory, see Daryl W. Palmer, "Kansas-Nebraska Acts: Territorial Imagination in 'El Dorado,' *Song of the Lark*, and *The Professor's House*," *Willa Cather Newsletter and Review* 53.2 (2009): 31–35.
25. Rosowski, *Birthing a Nation: Gender*, 32.
26. "The Mighty Craft," *Nebraska State Journal*, March 1, 1896, KA, 417.
27. KA, 3–29; M. Catherine Downs, *Becoming Modern: Willa Cather's Journalism* (Selinsgrove, PA: Susquehanna University Press; London: Associated University Presses, 1999), 28–30 and passim. See also Jean Marie Lutes, *Front Page Girls: Women Journalists in American Culture and Fiction, 1880–1930* (Ithaca and London: Cornell University Press, 2006), 133–45.
28. For perspective on Bennett's career, see Ron Hull, "Mildred Bennett," *The Willa Cather Foundation*, accessed January 31, 2015, www.willacather.org/about-us/mildred-bennett. More famous for his writing about Shakespeare's England, A. L. Rowse, "On the Track of Willa Cather in Nebraska," *Blackwood's Magazine*, 328 (August–September, 1980): 84-92, 164–71, offers a delightful account of paying a visit to Bennett "who has made herself the custodian of Willa's Red Cloud associations. She came to the door, attended by a little French bulldog" (167).
29. Rosowski, *Birthing a Nation*, 1; Janis P. Stout, *Picturing a Different West: Vision, Illustration, and the Tradition of Cather and Austin* (Lubbock: Texas Tech University Press, 2007), xvii–xviii.
30. Elliott West, *The Contested Plains: Indians, Goldseekers, and the Rush to Colorado* (Lawrence: University of Kansas Press, 1998), xv–xxiv.
31. Marilee Lindemann, *Willa Cather and the Queering of America* (New York: Columbia University Press, 1999), 6; Judith Butler, *Bodies That Matter: On the Discursive Limits of "Sex"* (New York and London: Routledge, 1993). See also the analysis of this debate by Jonathan Goldberg, "Willa Cather and Sexuality," *The Cambridge Companion to Willa Cather*, ed. Marilee Lindemann (Cambridge: Cambridge University Press, 2005), 86–88. Joan Acocella offers an adroit analysis of O'Brien's work in *Willa Cather and the Politics of Criticism*, 49–60. Other important studies of Cather's sexuality include Jane Rule, *Lesbian Images* (Garden City: Doubleday, 1975); Eve Kosofsky Sedgwick, "Across Gender, Across Sexuality: Willa Cather and Others," *South Atlantic Quarterly* 88.1 (1989): 53–72; Peter Boag, "Sexuality, Gender, and Identity in Great Plains History and Myth," *Great Plains Quarterly* 18 (1998): 327–40; Goldberg, *Willa Cather and Others* (Durham: Duke University Press, 2001).
32. Ann Romines, "Admiring and Remembering: The Problem of Virginia," *Cather Studies* 5 (2003): 273–90.
33. The relevant passage, *WCW*, 41–42, from "The Novel Démeublé," which Cather wrote for *New Republic* in 1922, is as follows: "Whatever is felt upon the page without being specifically named there—that, one might say, is created. It is the inexplicable presence of the thing not named, of the overtone divined by the ear but not heard by it, the verbal mood, the emotional aura of the fact or the thing or the deed, that gives high quality to the novel or the drama, as well as to poetry itself."
34. Willa Cather, "My First Novels (There Were Two)," *Willa Cather on Writing* (New York: Knopf, 1949), 94.
35. John Swift, "Willa Cather in and out of Zane Grey's West," *Cather Studies* 9 (2011): 3, illustrates this habit of thought by describing Grey and Cather as "midwesterners" who wrote about the West. I describe the contemporary context for Cather's sense of the West in "Willa Cather Here and Now, Out West," *Western American Literature* 52.1 (2017): 95–102.
36. Rosowski, *Birthing a Nation*, 33–34; Stout, *Picturing a Different West*, 6.
37. For example, the June 5, 1887, *Nebraska State Journal* refers to "the usual live western town" (8). See also the *Columbus Journal* (February 13, 1880): 3; the *Lincoln Evening Call* (July 27, 1889): 8; the *Lincoln Journal Star* (June 30, 1893): 7.

38. A glance at the biographical sketches Cather wrote to help promote her publications reveals her constant insistence that she moved from Virginia to, not a farm, but a "ranch." For a discussion of how Cather invented selves through these materials, see David Porter, *On the Divide: The Many Lives of Willa Cather* (Lincoln: University of Nebraska Press, 2008), 3–32.
39. It is a simple fact that just when Cather seemed unequivocal about something, she often shifted her position. Several months after the aforementioned interview, she explained in an interview for *Century Magazine*, *WCP*, 84, "I write only of the Mid-Western American life that I know thoroughly." It was, needless to say, an unusual pronouncement for her.
40. Wallace Stegner, *The American West as Living Space* (Ann Arbor: University of Michigan, 1987), 6, explains, "The West is defined, that is, by inadequate rainfall."
41. Strangely enough, critics often overlook Cather's geography lesson and refer to Nebraska as *Midwestern*. It is a curious fact in literary scholarship that this identification often signals the critic's negative feelings about the state. Hermione Lee, *Willa Cather: Double Lives* (New York: Pantheon Books, 1989), describes her own pilgrimage to Red Cloud as she was writing her book, declaring that Cather grew up in a "little, claustrophobic, provincial town" (3). She sees Cather as part of a group of "American writers growing up in the mid-West in the '80s and '90s" (38). This pattern is also apparent in discussions of the generational movement Van Doren dubbed "the revolt from the village." For example, Edward Bloom and Lillian Bloom, *Willa Cather's Gift of Sympathy* (Carbondale: Southern Illinois University Press, 1964), refer to Cather's roots in the Midwest while denouncing "the moral disintegration and esthetic perversion" of her small towns (3, 58). In one of the definitive discussions of the "revolt," Diane Dufva Quantic, "The Revolt from the Village and Middle Western Fiction, 1870–1915," *The Kansas Quarterly* 5.6 (1973): 7, notes, "these works usually are set in a Middle Western small town for the major part of the action." But Quantic acknowledges what Cather's artists recognize, "that whatever abilities they have are related to their past experiences in the village" (14). Barry Gross, "In Another Country: The Revolt from the Village," *Midamerica* 4.4 (1977), argues that Cather's Nebraskan fiction "deals with the Midwest as frontier" (106).
42. Patricia Nelson Limerick, "The Real West," in *The Real West*, commentary by Patricia Nelson Limerick, intro. Andrew E. Masich (Denver: Civic Center Cultural Complex, 1996), 13; William R. Handley and Nathaniel Lewis, "Introduction," *True West: Authenticity and the American West*, ed. William R. Handley and Nathaniel Lewis (Lincoln: University of Nebraska Press, 2004), 1–17.
43. William R. Handley, "Willa Cather: 'The West Authentic,' the West Divided," *True West: Authenticity and the American West*, ed. William R. Handley and Nathaniel Lewis (Lincoln: University of Nebraska Press, 2004), 90.
44. Rosowski, *Birthing a Nation*, 1.
45. Nina Baym, *Women Writers of the American West, 1833–1927* (Champaign: University of Illinois Press, 2011), 1.
46. Gardner W. Wood, "Books of the Day," *McClure's Magazine* 41 (1913): 199.
47. Frederick Jackson Turner, *The Frontier in American History* (New York: Henry Holt and Company, 1921), 3.
48. Turner, *The Frontier in American History*, 23.
49. Reynolds, *Willa Cather in Context*, 66, 67. See also Reynolds, "The Politics of Cather's Regionalism," 1–19; Bernice Slote, "Willa Cather and Plains Culture," *Vision and Refuge: Essays on the Literature of the Great Plains* (Lincoln: University of Nebraska Press, 1982), 96; Richard C. Harris, "Peck, Turner, and Willa Cather's *O Pioneers!*," *Midwest Review* 7 (1985): 44; Rosowski, *Birthing a Nation*, 60–61; Ann Moseley, "A New World Symphony: Cultural Pluralism in *Song of the Lark* and *My Ántonia*," *Willa Cather Pioneer Memorial Newsletter* 39.1 (1995): 1, 7–12; Jean

C. Griffith, "How the West Was Whitened: 'Racial' Difference on Cather's Prairie," *Western American Literature* 41.4 (2007): 396–97; Renee M. Laegreid, "The Good, The Bad, and the Ignored: Immigrants in Willa Cather's *O Pioneers!*," *Great Plains Quarterly* 27 (2007): 101–15; Tim Prchal, "The Bohemian Paradox: *My Ántonia* and Popular Images of Czech Immigrants," *MELUS* 29.2 (2004): 4; Prchal, "Reimagining the Melting Pot and the Golden Door: National Identity in Gilded Age and Progressive Literature," *MELUS* 32.1 (2007): 29–51. Nobler, in many ways, than Turner's famous "thesis," Cather's vision was not without its limitations. On this point, see Laegreid, "The Good, The Bad," *Great Plains Quarterly*, 102–03 and passim; Griffith, "How the West Was Whitened," 399; Katrina Irving, *Immigrant Mothers: Narratives of Race and Maternity, 1890–1925* (Urbana and Chicago: University of Illinois Press, 2000), 9.

50. Rosowski, *Birthing a Nation*, 59.
51. Stout, *Picturing a Different West*, xviii, 24–25, 179.
52. Swift, "Willa Cather in and out of Zane Grey's West," 3.
53. Rosowski, *Birthing a Nation*, 12.
54. James Woodress, "A Dutiful Daughter: Willa Cather and Her Parents," *Willa Cather: Family, Community, and History*, ed. John J. Murphy (Provo: Brigham Young University Humanities Center, 1999), 22.
55. Woodress, "A Dutiful Daughter," 23.
56. Ibid.
57. Janis P. Stout, *Through the Window and Out the Door: Women's Narratives of Departure, from Austin and Cather to Tyler, Morrison, and Didion* (Tuscaloosa: University of Alabama Press, 1998), 67.
58. Helen Cather Southwick, "Memories of Willa Cather in Red Cloud," *Willa Cather Pioneer Memorial Newsletter* 29.3 (1985): 11.
59. Stegner, *The American West as Living Space*, 23.
60. Readers planning a visit to Red Cloud would do well to explore the Special Collections & Arhives at the National Willa Cather Center website: https://www.willacather.org/. Suzi Yost Schulz's *Walk Red Cloud* is filled with information about the area, past and present, and includes tips for touring: walkredcloud.com/.
61. Alex Ross, "A Walk in Willa Cather's Prairie," *New Yorker* (October 2, 2017): xx.
62. Bernice Slote, "An Exploration of Cather's Early Writing," *Great Plains Quarterly* (1982): 210.
63. Rosowski, *Birthing a Nation*, 64.
64. For examples of this oft-quoted schema, see E. K. Brown, *Willa Cather: A Critical Biography* (1953; New York: Avon, 1980), ix; Bloom and Bloom, *Willa Cather's Gift of Sympathy*, 8; Rosowski, *Voyage Perilous*, 15–18; Cheryll Burgess, "Willa Cather's Homecomings," *Willa Cather: Family, Community, and History*, 55; Robert W. Cherny, "Nebraska, 1883–1925: Cather's Version and History's," *Willa Cather: Family, Community, and History*, 235; Maire Mullins, "'I Bequeath Myself to the Dirt to Grow from the Grass I Love': The Whitman-Cather Connection in *O Pioneers!*," *Tulsa Studies in Women's Literature* 20.1 (Spring, 2001), 124. For challenges to this narrative, see Marilyn Arnold, "Poses of the Mind, Paeans of the Heart: Cather's Letters of Life in the Provinces," *Willa Cather: Family, Community, and History*, ed. John J. Murphy (Provo: Brigham Young University Humanities Center, 1999), 5; Slote, "An Exploration of Cather's Early Writing," 211. More recently, Stout, *Picturing a Different West*, 133, has suggested "The Enchanted Bluff" (1909) as the pivotal piece of fiction.
65. For instance, John J. Murphy, "Nebraska Naturalism in Jamesian Frames," *Great Plains Quarterly* 10.1 (1984): 232, has identified a distinct "anti-Howellsian" phase. Janis P. Stout, *Willa Cather: The Writer and Her World* (Charlottesville: University Press of Virginia, 2000), 89, has observed that we gain a great deal of clarity by recognizing that a little "Troll Garden

phase" occurred in which Cather was imitating Henry James—as long as we remember that this phase did not by any means encompass all of her early fiction. Rosowski, *Birthing a Nation,* 67, has identified a distinct stage in which Cather "moved from male to female protagonist, from conventional man to natural woman." Amy Ahearn, "Full-Blooded Writing and Journalistic Fictions: Naturalism, the Female Artist and Willa Cather's *The Song of the Lark," American Literary Realism* 33.2 (2001): 143–49, has pointed to a taste for naturalism that stretches from the early journalism all the way to *Song of the Lark.*

66. Downs, *Becoming Modern,* 37.
67. My interest in this phase began when I read Downs, *Becoming Modern,* 52–53.
68. *WWC,* 172. Woodress, *WCLL,* 56–57, suggests that the town feud involving Cather's father and Doctor McKeeby was an inspiration, but the feud really heated up in 1888. I discuss this important (and rather mysterious) period of Red Cloud history in Chapter 1.
69. Sarah Dillon, "Reinscribing De Quincey's Palimpsest: The Significance of the Palimpsest in Contemporary Literary and Cultural Studies," *Textual Practice* 19.3 (2005): 245.
70. Willa Cather, *Alexander's Bridge,* ed. Frederick M. Link (Lincoln: University of Nebraska Press, 2007), 17.
71. "To Mrs. Fred Gund," 1908, Special Colections & Archives at the National Wila Cather Center. See also the postcard Cather sent to her brother Roscoe on July 10, [1908], MS 316, Roscoe and Meta Cather Collection, University of Nebraska. I thank Tracy Tucker for directing me to this wonderful artifact.

Chapter 1.

Red Cloud and the "Real West":
Mapping Willa Cather's Territorial Imagination

Farm life in that territory when I knew it fifteen years ago was bad enough, what must it have been before?
—Willa Cather

The West is a young empire of mind, and power, and wealth, and free institutions, rushing up to a giant manhood, with a rapidity and a power never before witnessed below the sun. And if she carries with her the elements of her preservation, the experiment will be glorious.
—Lyman Beecher, *A Plea for the Nation*

A pioneer should have imagination, should be able to enjoy the idea of things more than the things themselves.
—Willa Cather, *O Pioneers!*

In 1923, Willa Cather's cyclical existence was palpable and complicated.[1] On the one hand, she was enjoying unprecedented success. *April Twilights and Other Poems,* an impressive revision and expansion of the 1903 volume, was published by Knopf and dedicated to her father. The author had never been prouder than when she finished *One of Ours,* and the novel was proving quite popular, especially among veterans of World War I. On the other hand, she was unsettled by certain harsh reviews of the book. She had received news of the Pulitzer Prize while in France, unable to write because of neuritis. No one needed to remind her that she was turning fifty. It was in a darkening mood that Cather wrote "Nebraska: The End of the First Cycle." Appearing in the *Nation* on September 5, 1923, the author's only sustained history of Nebraska can be read, at this distance, like an elegy.

It is, in fact, far more valuable as a study of *becoming,* both territorial and authorial. Using the essay as a guide, we will (echoing Huck Finn at the end of the famous novel) *light out* for the Kansas-Nebraska Territory that preceded Cather and attempt to sketch the territorial imagination she acquired from it. We will also need to reconsider Cather's firsthand experience of Nebraska, the heart of the region she called the West and always centered in her hometown of Red Cloud. By delicately (and provisionally) untangling memory and imagination in this analysis, we can begin to identify some of the crucial strategies and techniques that Cather inherited and redeployed in her fiction.

"The state of Nebraska," Cather explained in 1923, "is part of the great plain which stretches west of the Missouri River, gradually rising until it reaches the Rocky Mountains."[2] Sounding like a traditional historian with this opening, she became more personal as she described the climate: "There we have short, bitter winters." On the face of it, Cather was telling Nebraska's story for a national audience, and the state was a "there." But the author also wanted to say something about her place in this history. She wrote as a "we."

Describing Mormon travelers and gold seekers, Cather ever so subtly affirmed, time and again, her place in this history. "When I was a child," she wrote, "I heard ex-Governor Furness relate how he stood with other pioneers in the log cabin where the Morse instrument had been installed."[3] A few paragraphs later, she related, "I have heard the old freighters say. . . ." When she reached the 1880s, she declared, "The county in which I grew up, in the south-central part of the state, was typical."[4] Implicitly, there is no gap between the historian and her subject.

Like Cather's life, the story of Nebraska had unfolded in decadal terms. She explained that the state's "social history falls easily within a period of sixty years, and the first stable settlements of white men were made within the memory of old folk now living."[5] The first settlements were "made," and the makers were still alive. In 1923, at the age of fifty, the first great maker of fiction and poetry set in Nebraska was joining the first makers of Nebraskan settlements in living, breathing memory. More than writing popular history, Cather was commemorating the emergence of both state and artist.

The classical Greeks used a particular word for this sort of making: ποίησις, poiesis. Although the term seems to suggest poetry, the Greeks understood a continuity between all sorts of making. In Plato's *Symposium*, Diotima explains that humans embrace making because they want to transcend the eternal and inevitable cycle of life and death by leaving something of value behind.[6] This, I suggest, is precisely how Cather was thinking of herself as she wrote her history of Nebraska. She saw herself as an aging maker living among older makers. The making—whether of settlements or art—was of a piece, and nothing less than a bold attempt to transcend a "cycle" of settlement and colonization, boom and bust, life and death.

Perhaps it is helpful to recall that the story of territorial making began in 1787 when the Congress of the Confederation passed the Northwest Ordinance, which invented a program of territorial self-government that would lead toward statehood. With a certain bureaucratic economy, the first sentence of the document establishes expectations that would inform territorial thinking for generations to come: "Be it ordained by the United States in Congress assembled, That the said territory, for the purposes of temporary government, be one district, subject, however, to be divided into two districts, as future circumstances may, in the opinion of Congress, make it expedient."[7] Territorial making would always anticipate *unmaking* in a larger *poiesis* governed by expediency and executed through division. A territory would always be a palimpsest, and the territorial imagination would always favor the palimpsestuous. Here, as we shall see over the course of this book, was a formula for territorial expansion that would eventually inform Cather's approach to writing about the West.

Over the decades that followed, people of every stripe—politicians (visionary and mercenary), frontier scouts, fur traders, gold seekers, religious exiles, missionaries, ambitious investors, railroad magnates—mapped, remapped, and renamed the new territory. In the summer of 1803, Lewis and Clark found grapes, plums, and cherries along the present-day Nemaha River. They went on to the present-day Platte River where they met with the Otos and Missourias. This new world was both fecund and populated. In 1805, Zebulon Pike led the first great expedition through the region, and a distinct version of the territorial imagination was sown on the Great Plains. Pike's *Account of Expeditions to the Sources of the Mississippi,* published in 1810, somewhat ambivalently introduced the English-speaking world to a country called "Nebraska" (*GPF,* 27–28).

Two years later, Cather's Divide became part of the Missouri Territory. Eight years later, Congress passed the Missouri Compromise, which attempted to settle the ongoing dispute over whether slavery would be permitted in the new territories by creating a zone of freedom north of the parallel 36°30' north. That summer, Stephen H. Long was making his way along the river we call the Platte. His report, compiled by Edwin James, noted "a manifest resemblance to the deserts of Siberia."[8] Taking this conclusion to heart and committed to expediency, government officials created "permanent Indian boundaries" between the fertile United States and the "desert" west of the Missouri River.

Everything changed when missionaries began arriving in earnest in the 1830s, and "Oregon Fever" blossomed in the following decade as thousands passed along the Platte heading west. West observes, “Between 1841 and 1859, more than 300,000 persons and at least 1.5 million oxen, cattle, horses, and sheep moved up the Platte road.”[9] At the peak of the migration in 1857, at least one hundred travelers a day arrived in Brownville, the territorial town that would play an important part in Cather’s vision of Nebraska.[10]

Over time, motion seemed to become the all-consuming imperative. In an important study of the phenomenon, Joseph Urgo declares that “the overarching myth, the single experience, that defines American culture at its core is migration: unrelenting, incessant, and psychic mobility across spatial, historical, and imaginative planes of existence.”[11] It is of course one of the greatest—if not the greatest—paradoxes in American culture that the same space that inspired motion also enticed the movers to put down roots. The geographer Yi-Fu Tuan explains this seeming contradiction: “Human beings require both space and place. Human lives are a dialectical movement between shelter and venture, attachment and freedom.”[12]

The scale and difficulty of life in the Kansas-Nebraska Territory simply magnified this essential dialectic, the siren call of what Susan Stanford Friedman has called “roots and routes.”[13] As Julie Roy Jeffrey points out, “transiency” was always part of the larger settlement/colonization process.[14] In her own account of the great migration, Cather puts it this way: “The State was highway for dreamers and adventurers; men who were in quest of gold or grace, freedom or romance. With all these people the road led out, but never back again.”[15] Actually, many people did go back, including Cather. A product of this migratory culture, Cather could look back in 1923 at a long life divided and defined (often paradoxically) by deep roots and well-traveled routes.

Not surprisingly, talk of dreams and adventures did not impress the Native Americans whose lands were being stolen. The term “Indian Territory” was “applied, removed, and reapplied, over and over again.”[16] Settlement always involved displacement and appropriation. Black Hawk, the great warrior and leader of the Sauk, gave voice to the injustice: “You have split the country and I don’t like it.”[17] Cather, for her part, seems seldom to have grasped the injustice of territorial expansion. She avoided real stories of appropriation and genocide in her fiction.[18]

Whatever else we make of Cather’s Nebraska, we need to remember this crucial story of its birth. In January of 1854 Iowa senator Augustus C. Dodge offered a bill for the creation of a new territory. No one was happy. So the Committee on Territories, led by Stephen A. Douglas, countered with a bill that divided Dodge’s territory in two. Nebraska would eventually become a

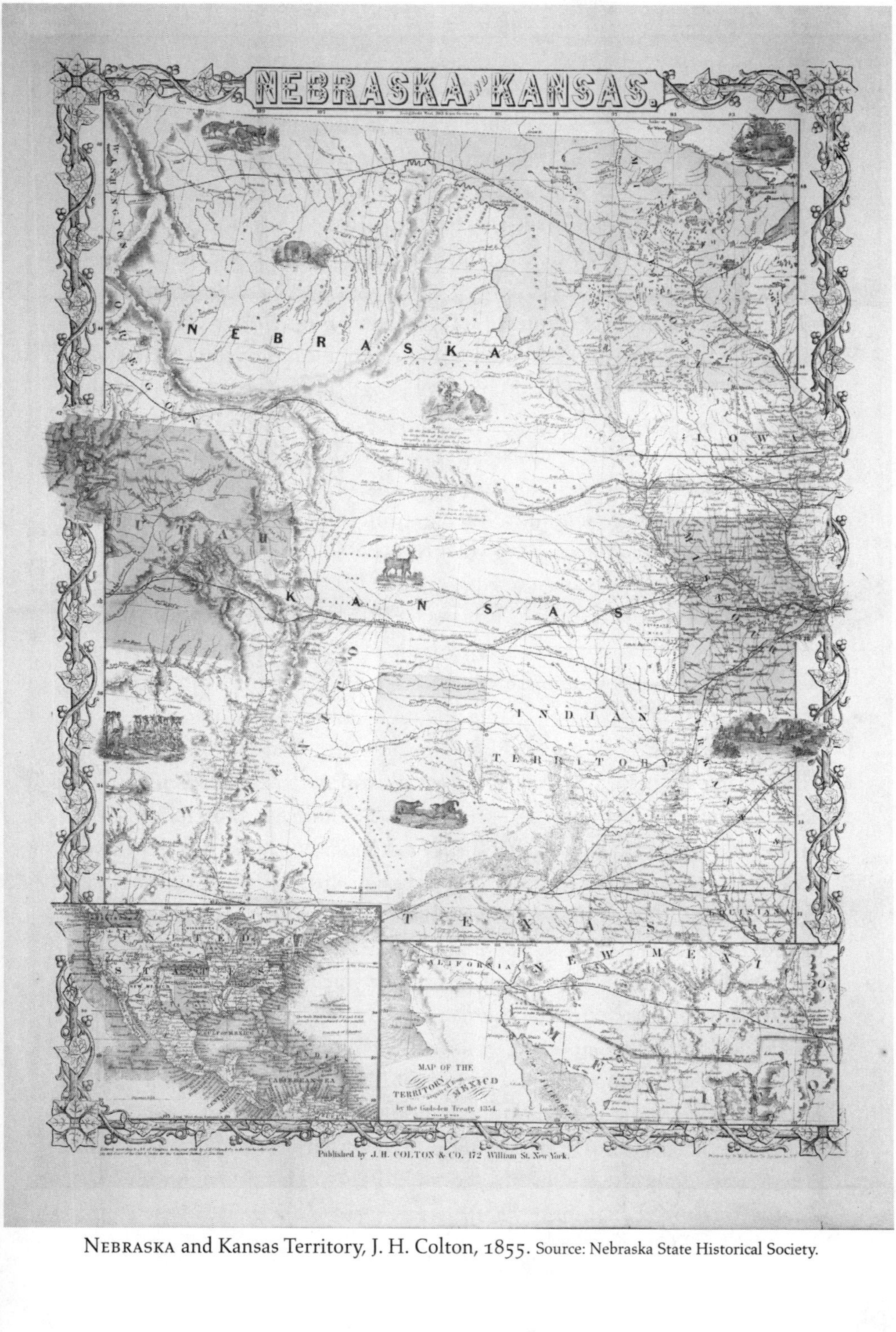

NEBRASKA and Kansas Territory, J. H. Colton, 1855. Source: Nebraska State Historical Society.

Free State while the status of Kansas would be determined by popular sovereignty, or squatters' rights.

On May 30, 1854, President Franklin Pierce signed the Kansas-Nebraska Act, which Roy F. Nichols has called "the most spectacular act in the drama of territorial history."[19] In the moment of its emergence, the territory was divided, doubled, and renamed. For generations to come, the people of the American West would take a simple proposition for granted: "When a human agenda was important enough, the Great Plains could easily be redrawn and renamed."[20] Ultimately, this sense of the region informed the way Cather and the other representatives of Nebraska's "first cycle" thought about the place. As Cather would come to appreciate, Nebraska was all about imaginary lines, and one person's imagination was bound to challenge another person's fact.

Territorial mapmakers certainly embraced this culture. An 1823 map identifies Cather's future homeland as "Indian Territory," with the added tag: "Deep Sandy Alluvion."[21] The map of the United States used in *Mitchell's School and Family Geography* (1852) identifies the region of western Kansas as the "Great American Desert." The J. H. Colton map for 1855 depicts a territory called "Kanzas." What began as a series of finite real-world actions blossomed exponentially in re-presentation and so confirmed what Susan Schulten has called "the malleable nature of geographical knowledge."[22]

At the same time, the maps reveal the aesthetic dimension of the territorial imagination. A. J. Johnson's territorial map *Nebraska and Kansas* suggests the inventiveness (even the whimsy) of the act by dressing Kansas in a gaudy pink that splashes west over Pikes Peak and South Park in present-day Colorado. Sporting a lighter, more roseate hue, Nebraska dominates the document. It controls the plan with golden-haired authority, all the way north to the border marked as "British Possessions." Years later, as she worked toward her own distinctive voice for the prairie, Cather took her place in this tradition by writing like a territorial colorist.

Particularly adept at using colors to highlight territorial revisions, Colton also understood the power of embedded illustrations. In a stunning map for 1854, an Indian hunts a bison in the middle of the golden Nebraska Territory, north of the Platte River. Two deer look out from a grassy ridge above the Smoky Hill Fork on the 103rd meridian in the pink Kansas Territory. "Fremont's Route" runs just below their little island. Although they were hardly innovations in mapmaking, such embellishments exercised a particular power in representations of the prairie. The Colton map focuses on intimate scenes that have the capacity to conjure up feeling. Years later, Cather experimented with this technique as a way of coming to terms with the vast open spaces of the prairie. By the time she wrote *O Pioneers!* she was ready to embed gardens, orchards, and ponds in a novel focused on "the land itself" (21).

At first glance, such imaginative impulses may sound unremarkable. But this prairie *poiesis* really was different. Walter Prescott Webb located the difference at the 98th meridian: "At this fault the ways of life and of living changed. Practically every institution that was carried across it was either broken and remade or else greatly altered."[23] In an extraordinary gesture, the Kansas-Nebraska Act invited settlers into a region of breaking and remaking. Aridity, more than anything else, accounted for these forced adaptations, but the vast open spaces of the region engendered other sorts of changes as well. As Diane Dufva Quantic notes, "On the Great Plains, renaming is a necessary process. Where acts are repeated in the continuing struggle to make the land produce, writers conjure up seemingly endless variations of past experience."[24] In addition to breaking and remaking, I would add *repurposing*. Stegner puts the notion this way: "The West has had a way of warping well-carpentered habits, and raising the grain on exposed dreams."[25]

The West also has a way of transforming the imaginations of people who spend enough time there. In 1823, Vermonter Edwin James described the way the open plains could trick the naked eye.[26] (Nearly a century after James, Cather encapsulated this experience with the prairie mirage of the plow in *My Ántonia.*) In *The Oregon Trail* (1849), Francis Parkman reported: "We all drew rein, and sat joyfully looking down upon the prospect. It was right welcome,—strange, too, and striking to the imagination. . . ."[27] More than anything else, these early writers invite their readers to engage the vast open spaces of the West through the imagination.[28]

It was, to say the least, a challenging invitation. As Thacker explains, George Catlin "solved" the problem of vast landscapes in his paintings by "blocking the horizon with hills or undulations, so the viewer's eye cannot extend farther than the middle distance" (*GPF,* 61). Cather and countless artists after her have followed suit.[29] Elevation was another answer. Thacker points out that when Josiah Gregg and his party ascend "the Round Mound" in *Commerce of the Prairies,* "Gregg uses the view from the summit to unify and encompass the whole of the prairie landscape spread before him" (*GPF,* 45). Approximately four decades after Gregg, Frances Fulton "likened the

ALVAN Fisher's *Pastoral Landscape*, 1854. Source: White House Historical Association (Public Domain).

view from her train one early morning to a picture unrolled from beneath the wheels on a great canvas while we stood still."[30] Motion and an elevated perspective improved everything.[31] Citing the experiences of Adela Orpen on the Kansas prairie, Jeffrey suggests, "Women found the landscape depressing when a flat terrain or confinement in a one-story house or cabin made it impossible to have a panoramic view."[32] Orpen certainly felt this way until her father added an outdoor stairway to the second floor of the house, and the panoramic prairie suddenly seemed "glorious."[33]

For her part, Cather came to appreciate this transformation during the summer of 1893, when she and her brother Roscoe spent their evenings "sitting on top of the fifty foot wind mill tower," feeling that they could see "off the edge of the world."[34] Given the importance of such experiences to the first travelers and settlers of the Great Plains, it seems likely that Cather's windmill climbing played an important part in her emergence as an artist.

Ultimately, it was Walt Whitman who recognized the painterly possibilities inherent in this region of grass and sky. After his visit to the Great Plains in 1879, Whitman reported: "The prairies—as I cross'd them in my journey hither—and these mountains and parks, seem to me to afford new lights and shades. Everywhere the aerial gradations and sky effects inimitable; nowhere else such perspectives, such transparent lilacs and grays. I can conceive of some superior landscape painter, some fine colorist, after sketching awhile out here, discarding all his previous work."[35] Whitman was prescient. A new colorist would indeed emerge, writing in painterly terms about the prairie, repurposing her previous work, eventually paying tribute to Whitman's vision by titling her first Nebraska novel *O Pioneers!*.[36]

Another approach to prairie perception and representation began to take shape when the territorial imagination latched on to the ancient ideals of pastoral. In 1857 Gilpin passionately declared: "These PLAINS are not deserts. . . . They are calcareous, and form the PASTORAL GARDEN of the world."[37] Calling the Great Plains a "garden," Gilpin was invoking an evolving rhetoric that stretched back through Margaret Fuller's description of the "garden" prairies of Wisconsin and Illinois in *Summer on the Lakes* (1844).[38] With allusions to the imaginative universe invented by Hesiod, Theocritus, and Virgil, Gilpin was reframing the Great Plains.

A glance at Alvan Fisher's *Pastoral Landscape* (1854) demonstrates how this strategy could work during the crucial decade of territorial definition and division. In Fisher's peaceful scene, the human figures and their livestock inhabit a warm circle of light protected by trees and mountains. The pastoral scene is emphatically bucolic. Gilpin asks his readers to think of the Great Plains in this way—as safe space in soft light. Nearly sixty years after Gilpin's famous letter, Cather hit upon the idea of combining two stories set in Nebraska as the basis for *O Pioneers!*. She called the form a "two-part pastoral."[39]

Gender, perhaps more than any other factor, informed representations of territorial experience. The land, as Annette Kolodny has shown, was recast as female, mother, and sweetheart.[40] Within this vision, Jeffrey and Rosowski point out that the territory could be described as "birthing" national identity.[41] Expanding on Rosowski's argument, Stout demonstrates that women settlers in general and women artists in particular depicted the Great Plains in various, often conflicting, ways that Cather inherited and often contested.[42]

In daily life, women could step into masculine roles and earn praise for their fortitude, but there were consequences for this kind of adaptation. Jeffrey explains that "a woman could be both masculine and feminine was confusing to any nineteenth-century female reader who had absorbed cultural messages about the differences between men and women. At the very least, it appeared that the frontier could blur distinctions."[43]

In fact, gender could seem downright vertiginous at times. In *A Plea for the West* (1835), Lyman Beecher declared, "The West is a young empire of mind, and power, and wealth, and free institutions, rushing up to a giant manhood, with a rapidity and a power never before witnessed below the sun. And if she carries with her the elements of her preservation, the experiment will be glorious."[44] As Cather would begin to do in her first decade of writing fiction, Beecher celebrates the West as youthful mind and power, female and male, in a grand experiment on the road to emergence. Curiously enough, his contemporary readers seem not to have been startled by his terminology.[45]

On the farm, things were simpler. Labor was increasingly divided according to gendered expectations, while certain larger schemes went forward hand in hand.[46] Perhaps the best example of this second point is the way men and women worked together to transform the prairie into a cultivated landscape. Not unlike the first white artists in the territory, men "blocked" the open vistas with their fields while women made ample gardens that achieved complementary effects.[47] The work was worthy indeed. As Chad Montrie rightly points out, the "large gardens required not only intensive labor but also a considerable amount of accumulated knowledge for planting, cultivating, and harvesting."[48]

Behind all the labor, the perceptions of ordinary women and men overlapped in many ways, and their contributions to the larger territorial imagination were significant.[49] As Sandra L. Myres has pointed out, women and men shared "both realistic and romantic attitudes toward wilderness."[50] Thanks to the research of Jeffrey, we can point to a number of other distinct similarities. Like their male counterparts, some female newcomers saw beauty on the Great Plains. Others saw tedium and even ugliness.[51] Like men, some settlers saw opportunities, while others saw endless frustrations. Like Gilpin, Martha Smith could look at Kansas and see a pastoral garden.[52] Like Catlin, Mary O'Neil surveyed the plains of North Dakota and saw pictures.[53]

Viewed from another angle, the territorial imagination was all about opportunities for ordinary folk to experiment with becoming. A famous ditty from the California Gold Rush captures the excitement:

We have a queer way in the West,
When a fellow his story relates,
Of making this simple request:
Say, what was your name in the States?

Oh, what was your name in the States?
Was it Thomson, or Johnson, or Bates?
Did you murder your wife,
And then flee for your life?
Oh, what was your name in the States?[54]

Cather delighted in such "queer" ways, renaming herself as a youth in Red Cloud and eventually renaming people and places over and over again in her stories. Beginning with "Tommy, the Unsentimental" in 1896, she began to explore this territorial privilege in new ways by experimenting with different names for distinct portions of her own life, past, present, and hypothetical.

Captain Randolph Barnes Marcy can help us understand how such imaginative endeavors could be rooted in such a rough-and-tumble region. In *The Prairie Traveler* (1859), one of the most popular and practical guidebooks for the territorial adventurer, Marcy declares: "The life of the wilderness is an art as well as that of the city or court, and every art subjects the votaries to discipline in preparing them for a successful career in its pursuit."[55] Marcy's vision of art encapsulates the educated sensibility that presided over territorial change on the nineteenth-century prairie. Whether on farms or in seats of government, whether on dusty trails or in pioneer gardens, women and men were using their imaginations to make and remake familiar ways of life.

Cather eventually embraced the spirit of Marcy's notion. When writing about early life on the Great Plains, she always saw herself as both votary and maker, writing about a variety of ambitious makers pursuing their visions. On any number of occasions over the course of her career, she affirmed this vision. In a 1925 interview in *New York World,* she declared, "The one education which amounts to anything is learning to do something well, whether it is to make a bookcase or write a book. If I could get a carpenter to make me some good bookcases I would have as much respect for him as I have for the people whose books I want to put on them. Making something well is the principal end of education" (*WCP,* 80). More imaginatively, Cather viewed her own literary making as an extension of pioneer endeavor. O'Brien explains, "Concerned with the human drive to create culture and civilization by making marks in a new landscape, Cather saw artists and pioneers as dreamers and adventurers on the same highway, driven equally by passion and imagination" (*WCEV,* 74). The territorial imagination was palpable for the author.

Mention Cather in this context and many readers will summon up popular notions of the frontier and homesteading, but in doing so they may miss the more complex author before them. Now, it goes without saying that Cather knew a lot about such things. In 1873, her Uncle George and Aunt Franc moved to Nebraska. Their letters home describe the challenges they faced.[56] More particularly, Cather knew about "the settlers' first work of claiming land—or *preemption,* as it was called in the important land law of 1841."[57] She must have known that women could preempt as long as they were either widows or heads of a household.

But Cather did not write frontier stories of preemption, buffalo, forts, and Indian raids. Although it seems strange, Willa Cather never wrote a story about a woman homesteader. It is a curious irony that the author so often identified with pioneer life paid more focused attention to the First World War as a historical event than she did to the Homestead Act of 1862. Her fiction simply does not fall into the same category as the works of John Ise and O. E. Rölvaag. In the end, it seems reasonable to conclude that Cather preferred to ground her fiction in her own more recent memories. Consequently, her deep sense of continuity with the territorial past lay less in the particular stories of frontier experience and more in the imaginative culture she had inherited from those first efforts.

Ultimately, it was the call of townmaking that really captivated Cather. And, once again, she was following the example set by the territorial folk who preceded her. According to the provisions of the Federal Townsite Act of 1844, speculators bought 320 acres, staked off the townsite, and came up with a name. It was a perfect sort of legerdemain, something akin to theater. Out of nowhere, a group of white people appeared. They stood on a bluff or a riverbank or along a creek. As the tall grass stirred in the wind, the newcomers pounded stakes in the ground. They wrote on scraps of paper. They said powerful words, and suddenly they had enclosed a space, which they promptly named. Past and present were transformed. An idyllic future beckoned. In townmaking, all the disparate strands of territorializing came together in a larger vision of progress. As one early settler put it, describing his feelings before even arriving in the territory, "What magic there was in that word town site!"[58] In this sentiment, the founder of Sandy Point discovered her raison d'être.

Evidence of this purpose is everywhere, in her interviews and letters, in her short fiction and novels. It is there in the opening paragraphs of her essay for the *Nation.* Contemplating how Nebraska's territorial past flowed into the present, she thought in terms of towns. Having sketched the state in broad strokes and described her position in the midst of living memory, she explained: "The earliest of these settlements—Bellevue, Omaha, Brownville, Nebraska City—were founded along the Missouri River, which was at that time a pathway for small steamers. In 1855–60 these four towns were straggling groups of log houses, hidden away along the wooded river banks."[59] Nebraska, before it was a state, was all about its towns. As Quantic explains, "Great Plains society is determined not by the farms that derive their character from the land but by the towns."[60]

It is probably impossible for anyone living today to fathom the allure of all this activity on the territorial prairie. In 1855, the *Kansas Herald* declared that townmaking "has become almost a mania with many speculators in town stock."[61] Two years later, the *Nebraska City News* reported, "New towns are springing into existence so fast that we can hardly chronicle their advents" (Qtd. in Dick, *Sod-house,* 46). The newspapers were not exaggerating. As Kurt E. Kinbacher points out, "Twenty-seven cities were incorporated between March 1855 and January 1857."[62]

Day by day, it was the town newspaper that held everything together in the collective imagination. A new town had to be promoted, and speculators quickly founded a newspaper for that purpose. As Dick explains, "The pioneer newspaper was a pioneer in the true sense of the word. The printing press preceded all other institutions of civilized life."[63] Newspapers, according to Benjamin Pfeiffer, "gave cohesiveness to the early settlements and guided, to a large extent, the political, economic, and social thinking of the pioneer communities."[64] In this spirit, R. W. Furnas, in the first installment of the *Nebraska Advertiser,* published in Brownville on June 7, 1856, forthrightly declared his intention "to advance the already important character of our young and growing town" (3). Like all territorial efforts, the work in this edition of the *Advertiser* began with mapping and division: "Nebraska Territory is divided and known as embracing two geographical Divisions, known as North and South Platte."[65] Aiming for "cohesiveness," the editor envisioned the territory otherwise, dividing the region that had just been divided. Townmaking was always, in other words, an imaginative project of integration and division.

In the Kansas-Nebraska Territory, real towns were made in this way, but they could also be paper fictions. Dick describes how "Crafty speculators founded 'cities' for their own profit without any intention of actually giving value for the money invested by buyers. All that was necessary was to arrange a company under some tree or elsewhere.[66] (This was Cather's process in making Sandy Point.) "It would take little imagination," Dick writes, "to believe that Aladdin himself had been on hand with his wonderful lamp in some places on the prairies during the fifties."[67] Townmaking taught territorial folk a powerful lesson: never underestimate the power of the imagination. Cather learned the lesson well.

So, in the end, what does all this talk of a territorial imagination really mean to our understanding of Willa Cather, her craft, and her fiction? I think we can conclude that by the time Cather graduated from high school in 1890, her consciousness was absolutely imbued with attitudes and aptitudes that had been nurtured by Nebraskans since territorial times. Like Coronado's expeditionaries and the white settlers who came after them, she was uncomfortable with the vast openness of the prairie, but inclined to think of the Great Plains in European terms. Like the creators of the territory, she delighted in renaming and rearranging the region she knew so well. Like the Romantics who informed so much territorial thinking, she believed in the power of the imagination. Like the first territorial newspaper editors, she discovered a special passion for townmaking, especially when she could revisit, through memory and imagination, her hometown of Red Cloud.

Of course, everyone who has studied the life of Cather knows that the town was important to her, but I want to conclude this chapter with a bolder proposition. Borrowing Cather's terminology from her early story "Tommy, the Unsentimental," I suggest that Red Cloud was a "live western town" that served as a kind of laboratory for the precocious girl, who discovered techniques and experimental strategies that eventually helped her become a great American author.

Beginning with Bennett's *World of Willa Cather,* many scholarly works have rehearsed this relationship of author and town, drawing on the author's comments in letters, interviews, and speeches. Yet for all of this attention, a certain skepticism has always arisen when the conversation about Red Cloud turns to Cather's fiction. In 1926, John Chapin Mosher framed his interview by declaring, "Certainly no environment would seem less promising to the literary career than Red Cloud, Nebraska" (*WCP,* 94). When Cather thought of Nebraska, according to Brown, she recalled "the crude village with its hard molds and its rebels."[68] In 1968, Bruce Baker described Cather's departure for college as a chance to get "some relief from the comparative intellectual sterility of Red Cloud and many of its people."[69] Years later, writing of a memorable visit to Red Cloud, Lee confessed: "I couldn't help feeling the extraordinary contrast between the immense landscape and the little, claustrophobic, provincial town."[70] In her study of Great Plains fiction, Quantic concludes, "the small town is hardly adequate socially or culturally."[71] With precision, Joan Acocella finally asks, "Why would so ambitious a novelist as Cather have set most of her novels in the little town of Red Cloud, or versions thereof?" Perhaps, Acocella speculates, the author simply chose to write about what she knew best? Perhaps the "limited cast of characters" and "stark" life "on the plain" suited her classicism?[72]

Such answers quickly inspire a far more challenging question: *How could Cather's deep attachment to a country town produce such great fiction*? Was it, as Whipple suggested, a case of genius triumphing over place? Many scholars seem to have stepped around the question by implicitly making this assumption. But what if Cather's readers have underestimated the liveliness of the country town? What if Red Cloud was more dynamic than we assume, *and* what if Cather's genius just happened to mesh particularly well with that liveliness? Answers emerge when we take a fresh look at the Red Cloud Cather knew in the 1880s, returning to the red brick buildings and railroads, the suicides and ice-cream socials, the friendships and rivalries, that made the youthful Cather plunge through hedges (as Jim Burden does in *My Ántonia*) in search of something she could not (at the time) name but eventually brought to life over and over again in her fiction.

Red Cloud, Nebraska, was founded in 1871. The *Red Cloud Chief*, the town's first newspaper, commenced publication in 1873, the same year that Willa Cather was born. Five years later, the *Argus* began publication. In 1883, the Cather family's arrival in Nebraska just happened to coincide with the arrival of A. C. Hosmer and George Warren, new editors and publishers of the *Chief* and the *Argus,* which happily announced the arrival of the family from Virginia. In the years that followed, Hosmer and Warren had much to say about the Cathers. Willa would even contribute her own prose to the newspapers. Why would an ambitious author be so attached to a country town? One reason is that town, newspaper, and author were contemporaries. They grew up together. In the immediate wake of territorial life, they were collaborators.

The success of this collaboration is evident in the birds-eye view of the town from 1881. A promotional brochure from the early 1890s declares that the town site north of the Republican River "is as beautiful and convenient as nature could make it."[73] This kind of promotional boosting echoes the

BIRD'S-EYE View of Red Cloud (1881). Source: Nebraska State Historical Society.

"booming" of territorial townmakers, but the praise in this case seems just. After a visit to Red Cloud in the 1970s, English scholar A. L. Rowse waxed poetical: "In the clear honeyed light the landscape lay outstretched like the Berkshire downs at home—like and unlike."[74] There is, without a doubt, something remarkably fine about the situation of Cather's little town on the prairie. Slote writes, "The terrain of the Cather region is varied: high, rich land on the Divide; rough clawed-out gullies, draws, and scarred sandhills in other places; pools, ponds, and creeks; high bluffs on the river, lush bottom lands and marshes with wild flowers thick along winding roads."[75] The elevations and the relationship to the river create the kind of panoramic views that white settlers had been seeking since they started arriving on the Great Plains. The five creeks—Farmer's, Indian, Crooked, Elm, and Willow—chisel lines of light and shadow. In the open space of prairie, Red Cloud offers color to sympathetic and imaginative eyes.

It is hardly surprising that a group of settlers led by Silas Garber chose this site for townmaking, and soon there were plenty of stories to tell. A herd of bison stampeded the town's Fourth of July celebrations in 1872.

The Great Easter Storm hit on April 12, 1873. The blizzard lasted two days. Grasshoppers invaded in 1874, and Garber became governor of Nebraska. A March prairie fire in 1875 nearly burned the town to the ground. On January 6, 1876, the *Chief* assured readers that all was well: "The crops in Nebraska this year have been enormous, and the State has been fully restored to the prosperity it enjoyed before the grasshopper scourge" (1). Like their territorial predecessors, Red Cloud newspapers were always ready to interpret the town's stories with enthusiasm.

In the 1880s, these newspapers were weekly operations, and the account of their practices that follows would apply, more or less, to most small-town newspapers all over the country. The editor oversaw every aspect of the product from the newspaper office located in the heart of the community. He purchased national and international news items from a service, and "correspondents" contributed reports from the neighboring towns of Bladen, Blue Hill, Catherton, Cowles, Guide Rock, and Inavale. The editor was always gathering local items, writing many of them himself. This meant that he was always on the move, talking to everyone he met, listening for new stories, inquiring about old stories, checking facts, and even stirring up a bit of controversy when he could. From time to time, he headed out into the county to survey the changing landscape. If the making of Red Cloud was an ongoing process, then it is safe to say that the newspaper editors were at the very heart of the making.

Dozens of diverse stories, some new, some extensions of the old, many echoing each other, were dropped into columns. Week after week, the editors paid serious attention to repetitions and cursory attention to the effect of certain juxtapositions, allowing chance to produce most of the effects, some of them quite startling. Take for instance the March 20, 1885, edition of the *Chief*, which opened with a front page of advertisements and the latest installment of *Dark Days*, the new thriller by English novelist Hugh Conway (Frederick Fargus). Some readers may have plunged into the narrative, but many more probably flipped the page. Some of these subscribers may have paused to read about Austria's conflict with France over custom duties on page two, or to enjoy "The Song of the Snowball" on page three:

> I'm a merry little snowball,
> And I can knock you flat,
> Or take right off your cranium
> Your stylish beaver hat.

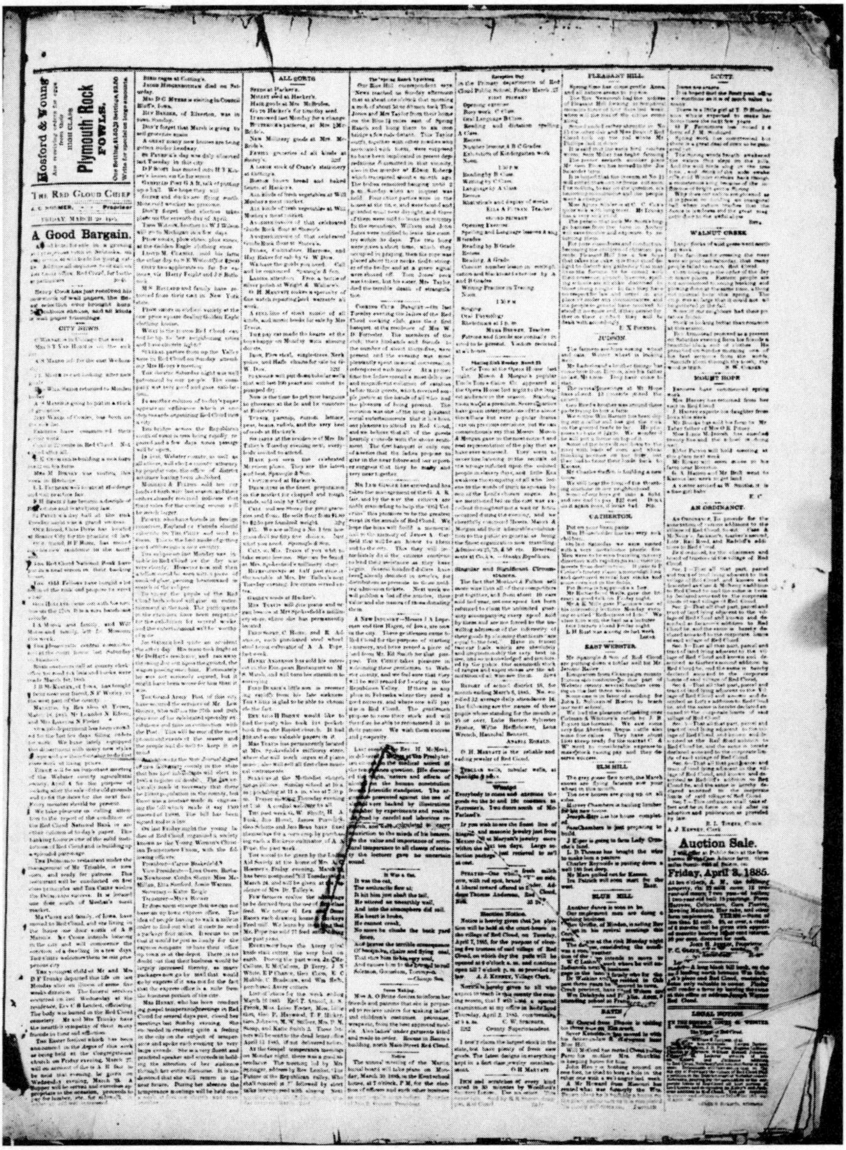

Hosford & Young
Plymouth Rock
FOWLS.

THE RED CLOUD CHIEF

A Good Bargain.

CITY NEWS

ALL SORTS

PLEASANT HILL.

SCOTT.

WALNUT CREEK

JUDSON.

MOUNT HOPE

AN ORDINANCE.

CATHERTON.

EAST WEBSTER.

ELM HILL.

BLUE HILL.

Auction Sale.

Friday, April 3, 1885.

TABLE 1.1. Page 5 of the March 20, 1885, *Red Cloud Chief.* Source: Library of Congress.

Options abound as the reader flips through these pages. But most readers probably navigated directly to page 5, where they found "City News."

			8 Lynching at Spring Ranch	
1 C. Wiener in Chicago	3 Need for electric lights		9 Cooking Club banquet	
	4 Bridge repair proceeding	7 Sociable at Dr. Tulley's		
	5 High school students give entertainment			10 Part of G.P. Cather's timber claim burns in prairie fire
2 Delmonico restaurant opening	6 Complaining about express office			11 Catherton Literary closes

TABLE 1.2. The juxtaposition of articles on page 5 of the March 20, 1885, *Red Cloud Chief.*
Source: Library of Congress.

Arranging a sample of the many items in a table suggests the range of topics being addressed.[76] It also helps us talk in detail about the habits of composition and reading that gave life to the country town newspapers and eventually influenced Cather's fiction. Because the table shows only selected stories, it only begins to capture the busyness of the page. Nevertheless, a number of essential features of the medium are clear. Quantity mattered. More news items meant that more readers would discover connections to the newspaper (and to the town) as a whole. More items also created a simple visual effect, suggesting the rhythm of a live Western town. As a feat of data collection carried out largely by one hardworking editor, the work is impressive. He must certainly be forgiven if he happens to be identified on the page as "A. C. Hosmer—Propieor."

The point is not that there is something unprecedented in this example of newspaper composition from Red Cloud. The reason to study these practices in detail is that Cather seems to have absorbed and eventually transformed elements of this newspapering craft. For instance, this page of "City News" achieves real liveliness by juxtaposing a variety of different story genres. There are Red Cloud stories, country stories, and stories from other towns. Red Cloud stories include items about government business, merchant happenings, construction projects, and so on. The Delmonico restaurant has opened. The repair of the bridge is moving forward. Hosmer praises, complains, and occasionally condemns. Red Cloud needs electric lights. The express office is inconvenient. Stories of violence, like the lynching near Spring Hill, take center stage, while little anecdotes of everyday life and brief announcements of births and deaths, weddings and funerals increase the number of readers who find a personal connection in the newspaper each week. A prairie fire damaged G. P. Cather's timber claim. Stories of social life and community organizations such as the Catherton Literary, the Ladies Aid Society, and the Cooking Club register the traditional roles of women in the town. Reviews of entertainments give the editors a chance to display their critical acumen while drumming up support for local venues. Simple observations of seasonal change take their place in the columns. Literary works such as a serialized novel and a poem entitled "It Was a Cat" remind readers that the newspaper is a medium of entertainment, while the ubiquitous advertisements (often posing as stories) help to fund the enterprise.

I do not know how Cather read such pages in her youth, but I can pinpoint places in her fiction that depend on newspaper strategies she encountered in the *Chief* and the *Argus*. *Repetition,* in a variety of forms, animates the page of "City News." The items about the bank and the "sociable" at Dr. Tulley's home create emphasis moving down particular columns. *Snipping* makes such effects possible. The advertisements for the music business of Mrs. Travis and the election stories have clearly been cut up into pieces that can be distributed for a growing, distinctly nonlinear, effect. Musical events dot the "City News" week after week. The repetitions on this page emphasize that they were matters of ongoing concern and debate. The separate pieces supplement each other, implying that life in this Western town is multifaceted and dynamic.

Juxtaposition, better than any other term, names the effect, sometimes intentional, usually accidental. The juxtaposition of the lynching story with news of the Cooking Club banquet provides a perfect illustration. The report explains that "a mob of about 50 or 60 men took Thos Jones and Mrs Taylor from their home on the Blue [River] 1 ½ miles east of Spring Ranch and hung them from an iron bridge a few rods distant." The reader moves from strangulation to "eatables" in the blink of an eye: "On last Tuesday evening the ladies of the Red Cloud cooking club, gave their first banquet at the residence of Mrs. W. D. Forrester. . . . At a proper time the ladies spread a most delicious and magnificent collation of eatables before their guests, which received ample justice at the hands of all who had the pleasure of being present." The editor's intention in juxtaposing the Cooking Club story with this account is much less clear. It may be nothing more than coincidence, but certain striking similarities pop off the page. Like the lynching, the banquet was a communal affair located with precision in Webster County, an event that centered on acts of "justice."

What ordinary readers back in the day made of such effects is here less important than the way the newspaper was modelling practices of juxtaposition that artists and critics would eventually call *Modern.* Cather was no fan of Ezra Pound's poetry, but his "In a Station of the Metro" (1911) may be the quintessential example of the aesthetic she worked to refine:

> The apparition of these faces in the crowd;
> Petals on a wet, black bough.[77]

Platform and petals collide, tied down by an evocative title and a bit of alliteration. The two-line poem demands that we take juxtaposition seriously in art and revel in the possibilities of the minimal artifact. As Middleton has noted, "juxtaposition is critical to all of Cather's mastery of literary technique."[78]

Although Cather did not link it to her early reading of Red Cloud newspapers, she described her version of this aesthetic in the famous interview with Carroll: "Just as if I put here on the table a green vase, and beside it a yellow orange. Now, those two things affect each other. Side by side, they produce a reaction which neither of them will produce alone" (*WCP,* 24). Because scholars continue to live in a world filled with complex theoretical terminology, we can easily overlook the power of Cather's homespun language when it turns theoretical.

Yet it would be a mistake to underestimate Cather's mature notion of *side-by-sidedness.* Whereas *juxtaposition* implies a kind of disembodied contrast, *side-by-side* has more particular and literal implications for an editorial mind considering presentation. It implies a setting down and forth, an arrangement in other words. It implies laterality and verticality, surfaces in juxtaposition. And it certainly describes the "City News" items in the Red Cloud newspapers that Cather grew up reading.

REPUBLICAN Valley, Mouth of Elm Creek. Source: Nebraska State Historical Society.

For the country town editors, juxtapositional effects were often happenstance, but "boosting" was always intentional. In fact, the newspapers of Cather's youth carried out this function with zeal, carefully noting bursts of activity, happily crowing about "the fame of Red Cloud."[79] Like their counterparts in country towns across the Great Plains, Red Cloud editors paid special attention to railroads. By the end of the nineteenth century, no element of townmaking was more pivotal than the coming of the railroad, and town leaders rarely felt they had enough say in matters that could determine the fate of their larger enterprise.

Red Cloud's history of railroading illustrates the point and deserves some study because of the way it eventually mattered to Cather's fiction. Trains began to run through Red Cloud in 1879.[80] In the name of development, the "View on Elm Creek" produced by the Burlington and Missouri railroad follows Gilpin's example from territorial days, employing all the strategies of pastoral to envision a prairie safely defined by trees. The man and woman could be dressed for a stroll around Washington Square in New York as they enjoy the bucolic paradise.

The reality of expansion was rather different. As Bennett explains, "The coming of the railroad had a peculiar effect on the layout of the town. As the only land available for their track lay close to the river, the Burlington constructed the depot a mile from the main part of town" (*WWC*, 108). If territorial life had taught inhabitants anything, it was that maps could always be redrawn. When the Burlington arrived, Red Cloud was divided and doubled. On any number of occasions like the one in Red Cloud, the original town simply failed, but Cather's town endured.[81] "Those who owned property at that end of the village," Bennett writes, "expected a new growth to start around the depot. The railroad put up a large hotel, an eating house and a roundhouse, while property owners laid out their land in lots. However, the movement of the business district south to the depot did not prosper" (*WWC*, 108). It was a genuine triumph because the town actually thrived. As Woodress explains, by 1884 Red Cloud "had a roundhouse and railroad shops and was the center of a rapidly expanding farming community. Eight passenger trains a day passed through the town, going and coming between Kansas City, Chicago, and Denver."[82]

But Red Cloud's railroading prosperity came with a price: the town, at its most prosperous, would always be divided. Seward Street ran the length of the town, connecting the upper and lower parts.[83] The center of town was, more or less, Fourth Avenue and Webster Street. On the northwest corner of these streets, the State Bank Building announced the town's prosperity.[84] The red brick Moon Block, which included the Opera House, was built just north of the bank. Across the street, Cook's Drug Store employed Willa Cather for a time. Just east of Webster on Fourth, the Albright brothers had their jewelry and music store. At the corner of Webster and Third stood the Miner Brothers General Store. The real estate office of Charles Cather was located in an adjacent bay on the second floor of the building. North of this center, Ninth Avenue became the preferred site for building affluent homes. To the south, the appropriately named Division Street separated north and south, the prosperous and the struggling. Like so many lines drawn in territorial times, it was both arbitrary and powerful. The fact that it corresponded to natural elevation changes conferred a kind of inevitability. The trip from the Burlington depot to the center of town was always "up."

Over the years, Cather returned to Red Cloud over and over again by train. When she imagined adventure, she thought of trains. When she wanted to escape, she took a train. When she felt completely overwhelmed in 1912, she "boarded the Burlington and headed west" on the trip to the Southwest that reignited her imagination (*WCLL*, 4). On that trip, she visited her brother Douglass, who worked for the railroad. We have no photograph of Cather racing on her wheel, but we

WILLA Cather riding a railroad handcar.
Source: Archives & Special Collections, University of Nebraska–Lincoln Libraries.

do have a delightful picture of her powering a railroad handcar. The woman on the draisine seems right at home and on her way out West.

Not surprisingly, Cather often looked to country town railroading for her inspiration. Narratives begin with railroad arrivals and a journey up into town, sometimes on a horse-drawn streetcar that resembles the one employed in Red Cloud. Characters face conflicts as they navigate divided topographies that echo their situations. In fact, as Mark A. R. Facknitz observes, "the railroad became a ubiquitous and unobtrusive trope for narrative effects as varied as transfer, estrangement, correspondence, serendipity, and fate in her works."[85]

Cather and her fellow Red Cloudians loved trains, but they loved bricks almost as much. In 1878, the *Chief* was touting the benefits of brick construction.[86] The November 20, 1879, *Chief* reported that William Ludlow had just "burned" 100,000 bricks made out of "native clay" at the local brick factory (4). Such extraordinary production was cause for excitement because it made possible a wave of superior construction that shaped the town's identity for the next century and beyond. It was also significant, in more subtle ways, for privileging the native clay of Nebraska. Rehearsed in the columns of the local newspapers, this link between "native" elements and superior quality contributed to an emerging sense of civic pride.

Red Cloud Streetcar, n.d. Source: Willa Cather Pioneer Memorial Collection. Special Collections & Archives at the National Willa Cather Center in Red Cloud, Nebraska.

In 1883, businessmen began erecting the first commercial brick structures. Building on the growing excitement, the June 14, 1883, *Argus* reported: "Red Cloud is enjoying a genuine boom. Besides the four brick buildings under construction dwelling houses are springing up in all parts of town" (4). The commercial buildings were situated on James Miner's block at Third and Webster and the State Bank block at Fourth and Webster. And a new brick opera house would soon follow.[87]

Cather's readers would do well to remember that the author's formative years in Red Cloud were marked by this wave of townmaking. The August 21, 1885, *Chief* reported, "The Opera House front is now completed, and it, together with the Red Cloud National Bank block are the handsomest buildings in the city. The brick business houses of Red Cloud are indeed a great credit to the Gate City of the Valley" (5). This is a special moment in townmaking, the kind of moment that an adult who valued her childhood would certainly remember. In the extensive commentary devoted to small-town fiction, particularly the scholarship devoted to "the revolt from the village," critics stress the stale monotony of everyday life. But, Red Cloud was a live Western town.

Suffice it to say, it was an age of townmaking that the author never forgot and longed to re-create. Late in her career, as she recalled the friendship of James Miner and William N. Richardson in "Two Friends" (1932),

Cather indulged in familiar pleasures. Just as she does in *The Song of the Lark,* the author begins in a palimpsestuous mood, setting the story "in a little wooden town in a shallow Kansas river valley" (*CSP,* 673). Her narrator recalls, "On my way to and from school, and going on the countless errands that I was sent upon day and night, I always passed Dillon's store. Its long, red brick wall, with no windows except high overhead, ran possibly a hundred feet along the sidewalk of the cross-street. The front door and show windows were on Main Street, and the bank was next door. The board sidewalk along that red brick wall was wider than any other piece of walk in town, smoother, better laid, kept in perfect repair; very good to walk on in a community where most things were flimsy" (*OD,* 164). Woodress comments that Cather "liked the [Miners'] store and the brick wall and the sidewalk because they were solid and well built" (*WCLL,* 52). But this observation hardly does justice to the passage. Cather wants the reader to see the town through her eyes, distanced only slightly by the narrator's eyes. She wants to share the intimate connection between youth and brick. She wants the reader to feel the juxtaposition of brick and board, firm and flimsy, smooth and rough—all centered by "that red brick wall." It is a brilliant painterly effect, an objective correlative for unalterable realities, red bricks from Red Cloud in the 1880s. It is obvious that she cherished these "outside things" and saw them as emblems of a vibrant inner life.

Perhaps the most fantastic bit of townmaking in the 1880s was Red Cloud's plan for electric lights. Nearly fifty years before the Rural Electrification Act, the August 18, 1887, *Argus* was reporting that "the Electric Light Company expects to turn on the lights Monday evening. . . . The immense water wheel was placed in position last week and the dynamo which arrived Wednesday is ready to grind out condensed lightning" (8). Anticipating the age of the dynamo that Henry Adams would famously describe in his *Education* and echoing the rhetoric of Stephen A. Douglas in his territorial speeches, the newspaper invokes a Romantic vision right out of the pages of Mary Shelley's *Frankenstein* as it boasts of Red Cloud's "condensed lightning." Late in her career, Cather returned nostalgically to an electrified townscape, noting, in "Old Mrs. Harris," that "arc lights had been lately installed in Skyline" (*CSP,* 625).

In retrospect, the railroads, bricks, and electric lights epitomized the vitality of Western townmaking for Cather. Against this red brick backdrop, her mind often drifted back to particular elements of everyday life documented by the town's newspapers. A glance at "City News" on any given week turns up a number of events like the aforementioned picnic and the lawn social.

Sprinkled over the page, the stories twinkled like so many party lights strung over country town life. The overall impression was that Red Cloud was a welcoming community. In 1885, many citizens would have agreed with Hosmer when he declared, "Red Cloud is most assuredly a model city."[88]

Hospitality helped to hold all this activity together.[89] Rooted deeply in the territorial imagination, in the early literary societies and prairie dances cherished by the dustiest of villages, the idea made good sense. In Cather's youth, various church and civic groups had these ideas in mind as they hosted events. Men played a part. They belonged to the Garfield Post, no. 80, of the Grand Army of the Republic (GAR), Odd Fellows, Knights of Pythias, and Modern Woodmen. Athletic fellows joined the baseball club, which, as Virgil Albertini points out, had an active following and played their games "a few blocks from Cather's home."[90] Other sporting types joined the lawn tennis club, which welcomed female members such as Cather's cousin Bess Seymour, a prototype for Tillie in *The Song of the Lark*.[91] Then there were the firemen and the so-called "railroad boys," who got together from time to time to host events.

But women made hospitable life in Red Cloud possible. Like their territorial predecessors, these women created and nurtured a variety of social networks. There were the ladies of the Baptist H. M. Society, the Methodist Church, the Congregational Church, and, of course, the Ladies Aid Society. The fact that these societies offered women unprecedented authority and administrative experience would not have been lost on an observant girl like Willa Cather, who watched her mother move in and out of various social circles.

Hosting one event after another, Red Cloud groups often competed for the same portion of the county's three thousand inhabitants. Imaginative organizers contributed to a crazy quilt of occasions that included a rag social, an Easter social, a basket social, a lemon squeeze, a necktie social, a pumpkin pie and doughnut social, a blue tea social, and then a popcorn, apple, and rare painting social, an oriental social, a maple wax social, a fairy social, a skating social, and a Ruth and Rebecca social. Steven Trout points out that many Red Cloudians attended the GAR's "open campfire, an opportunity for non-post members, including women and children, to join veterans amid their Lodge-like meeting hall for an evening of wartime campfire songs, storytelling, and dramatic presentations."[92] Citizens also celebrated Thanksgiving, Christmas, and Easter with elaborate public dinners that raised money for good causes.

It goes without saying that the country town hospitality often centered on food. Oyster events (made possible by railroad cars packed with ice) were particularly popular.[93] The December 6, 1883, *Argus* describes the largess of a typical Thanksgiving affair: "About thirty cans of oysters, and the necessary accompaniments of crackers, pepper-sauce, etc. were consumed, besides immense quantities of bread and butter, baked beans, roasted chickens, pies, cakes, pop corn balls and candy" (3). As Cather made clear many years later in "Old Mrs. Harris," Red Cloudians loved cake. So the February 13, 1885, *Chief* reported: "On Monday evening there will be a grand social ball in honor of Washington's birthday. On this occasion a fine large cake will be given to the most graceful couple in the waltz; another fine cake will also be voted to the most handsome lady in the ball. Everybody is invited" (5). Of course not "everybody" was invited, but the spirit of the invitation rings through.

All this Red Cloud cooking left a powerful impression on Cather. In Cather's mind, cooking was an important art among the many arts she inherited from all the women who cooked before her in Nebraska and Virginia. "The farmer's wife who raises a large family and cooks for them," she explained in a 1921 interview, "contributes more to art than all the culture clubs" (*WCP,* 47). It is no coincidence that Cather's emergence as a major American novelist around 1913 occurs in the pages of "The Bohemian Girl" and *O Pioneers!*—the first two fictional works in which she tells stories of the hospitable cooks she remembered from Nebraska.[94] By the time the author wrote *My Ántonia,* she knew how to center her narratives on what Halverson calls a "sampling of other domestic lives."[95]

Hospitality was central to Red Cloud life, but the newspapers devoted a great deal of attention to other kinds of townmaking as well. Perhaps more than anything else, merchants were viewed as the real dynamo behind Red Cloud's liveliness. On February 15, 1883, the *Argus* preached, "In most towns where trade is dull and times are hard the business men sit down, and Macawber-like, wait for something to turn up. Not so with the business men of Red Cloud" (4). This was an exaggeration, of course, but shoppers had to be impressed by the variety of merchandise available on the streets of Red Cloud. Lingering over the front page of the *Chief* for March 20, 1885, the reader was tempted by R. L. Tinker's proclamation: "Buy your goods at the old reliable Furniture and Undertaking House." Just below, the Nebraska Lumber Co. promised low prices while Henry Cook declared, "Drugs! Drugs!" William Gates touted his meat market, and Fred Birkner proclaimed himself "Merchant Tailor." Perusing the "City News," readers found birdcages and Crane's stationery at Cotting's, seeds at Hacker's, Butterick patterns at Mrs. McBride's, groceries at Mosher's, and clothes for plowing at the Golden Eagle. Sooner or later, nearly everyone shopped the stores owned by Charles Wiener and J. L. Miner.

Cather was particularly fascinated by all the country town commerce. Bennett tells how the future author used to follow Carrie Miner to work at the family store, "asking questions about the people in the community."[96] Many years later, Miner told Bennett that Cather would always ask, "Now Carrie, is that all?"[97] It is no coincidence that mercantile activity was central to Sandy Point or that, when she was old enough, Cather worked at the City Pharmacy. The job helped her acquire books, wallpaper for her room, and good stories.

Ultimately, Cather's intimate experience of mercantile culture also gave her access to shop windows and another version of modern aesthetics. As Juli Highfill explains, "the shop-window encounter became a laboratory for examining a transformed and transformative urban experience."[98] Early on, Cather began trying to capture this laboratory on paper. In the scrapbook she made during her youth in Red Cloud, she pasted—or repurposed—dozens of merchants' advertising cards, toying with the same possibilities of juxtaposition that would fascinate modernist painters and photographers for decades to come. Red Cloud merchants gave her the raw material for the kind of visual experimentation that would eventually inform her fiction.[99]

Boy life, a theme named by Hamlin Garland, fascinated the people of Red Cloud in other ways. A. J. Kenney, founder of the *Argus,* seems to have established boy life as a reportorial convention in Red Cloud. In a September 29, 1881, piece for the *Argus* titled "Bully Boy," he advised, "Some of the great men have been dull boys. Dryden and Swift were dull as boys" (3). On October 20, 1881, he opined: "The natural history of a boy is an interesting study" (4). It was an apt premise for a newspaper that, during Cather's youth in Red Cloud, published one story after another about boys. Alternating between jovial commentary and angry complaint, the editors reported tales of minor dismemberment, arcane discoveries, fishing triumphs, and various criminal pranks.[100] Cather must have had these stories in mind when Jim Burden in *My Ántonia* remembers becoming "another boy" when he moved to Black Hawk (141).

But it should be pointed out that the genre of "boy stories" was more capacious than this and served other, more complex agendas of townmaking. The February 6, 1885, *Chief* reported, "The railroad boys are all kept busy nowadays. Traffic is generally good." *Boy,* it seems, could refer to male children or to young men who did manual labor that was vital to Red Cloud life.[101] It could also refer to the Webster County baseball boys who provided regular entertainment throughout the summer.[102] As Thanksgiving approached in 1889, the

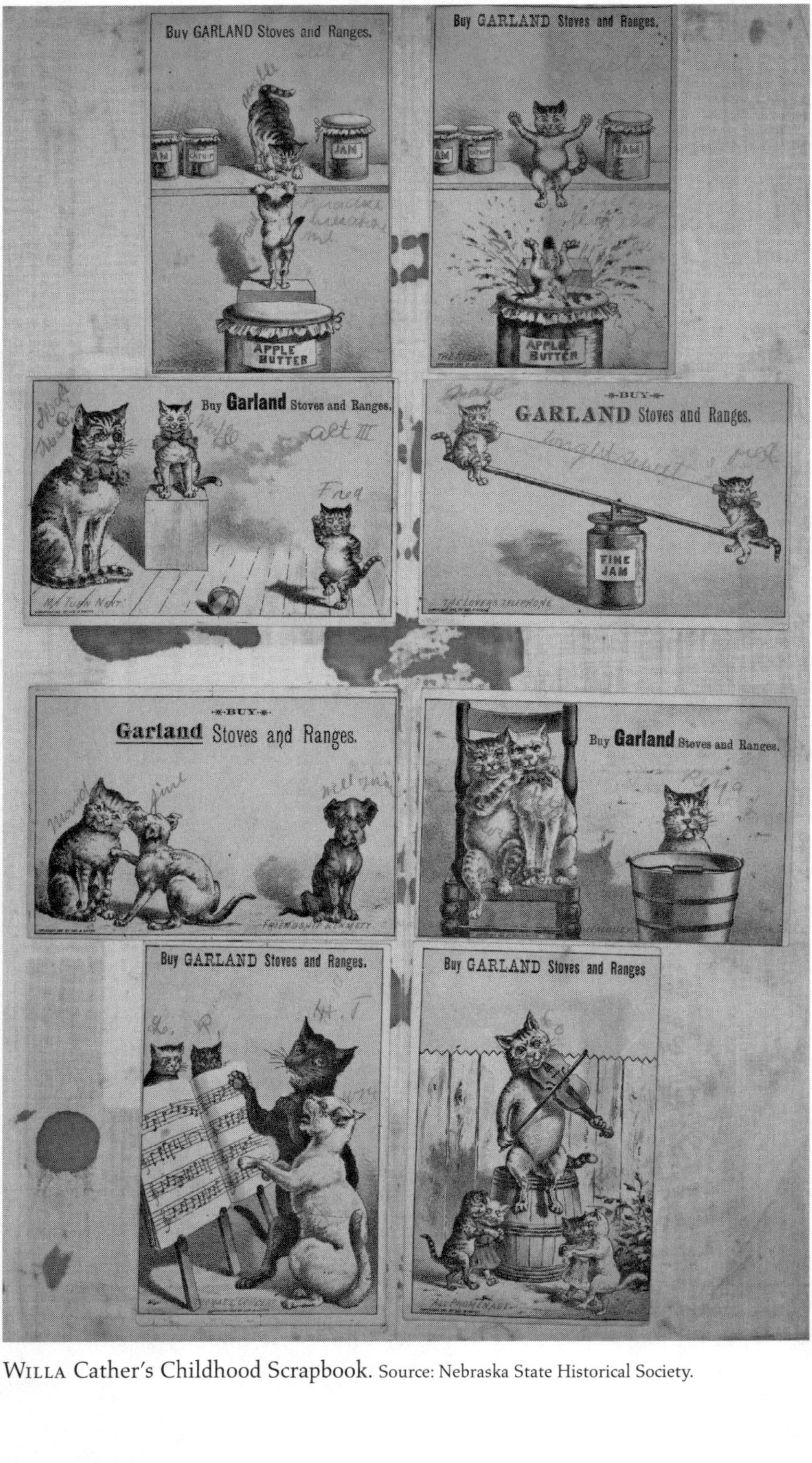

Willa Cather's Childhood Scrapbook. Source: Nebraska State Historical Society.

railroad boys were organizing "a grand ball" for the occasion.[103] The ball turned out to be one of the remarkable spectacles of Cather's youth. Hosmer called it "one of the finest and most social entertainments that has ever taken place in the city."[104] Taken together, these snapshots of "boy life" illustrate how a kind of masculine youth culture mattered to townmaking in Webster County during Cather's youth. The author found such recollections irresistible. She repurposed elements of the railroad boys' ball in "The Bohemian Girl" and paid fond tribute to the big hearts of railroad boys in *The Song of the Lark.*

Amateur and professional performers, more than any other group, added sparkle to life in Red Cloud. Hosmer and Warren certainly did their best to tout recitals, high school concerts, and amateur theatricals. Visiting professionals were announced weeks ahead of time. Positive reviews of their performances in other papers were published. Detailed reviews of Red Cloud performances always followed. The effect of all these juxtaposed stories was obvious: Red Cloud was a live Western town.

In the midst of all this reporting, a few visiting performers stood out. For instance, every reader during the 1880s would have remembered the performances of John William Boone. On October 8, 1886, the *Argus* reported: "Blind Boone the musical prodigy, played to a crowded house Tuesday evening. Those who failed to be present missed a rare musical treat" (8). On January 3, 1889, the newspaper was actively promoting an upcoming concert: "As a musician he is truly a wonder and to miss hearing him will be a matter of regret" (7). For the *Argus,* Boone's appearances were all about wonder and the possibility of regret. A country town newspaper, by definition, had to motivate its readers to come to town, spend money, and widen their horizons. Warren was always thinking in terms of civic opportunities. Set against this backdrop, Jim Burden's memories in *My Ántonia* of Blind d'Arnault become striking.

In the end, people mattered most in the ongoing work of townmaking. Red Cloud newspapers understood this fact. Like novelists, the editors followed a consistent cast of "characters" who played evolving roles in the life of the country town. Years later, Cather often followed the same cast list as she re-platted and re-plotted Red Cloud in fiction.[105] But long before Cather renamed these characters, the newspaper editors had given their hopes and dreams, accomplishments and setbacks, shape in print.

As Christmas drew near in 1885, the *Chief* reported that "Dr. McKeeby's new suite of rooms over the City Pharmacy [where Cather worked], are furnished and arranged in the most elegant and convenient manner possible. The

DR. Gilbert Einstein McKeeby.

SOURCE: Willa Cather Pioneer Memorial Collection. Special Collections & Archives at the National Willa Cather Center in Red Cloud, Nebraska.

Doctor is to be congratulated upon his change of location."[106] An upgraded physician's office was precisely the kind of townmaking that the newspapers prized, especially when it was underwritten by a prominent citizen. In Red Cloud, Dr. McKeeby was citizen, attorney, mayor, newspaperman, friend to Charles and Willa, and the physician who had saved Cather's mother's life. Cather was thinking of McKeeby and his office when she described Dr. Archie reading late into the night in *The Song of the Lark.*

Unquestionably, the story of Red Cloud told in the newspapers was all about certain individuals, revealing a pattern of inclusion and exclusion that always fascinated Cather. Certain individuals, such as Wiener and Miner, led busy lives filled with accomplishments and were recognized for it. Cather reinvented these neighbors in *My Ántonia,* "Old Mrs. Harris," and "Two Friends." Other people made fleeting but memorable appearances in the larger narrative. The May 22, 1885, *Chief* announced a dime social that would include piano selections by Professor Schindelmeisser (5). The music teacher had recently arrived in Red Cloud and gave music lessons to Mary Miner and Cather, among others. In retrospect, we know that his company proved invaluable to Cather, a fact she recalled through the character of Wunsch in *The Song of the Lark.*[107]

Although they inhabited the margins of society, tramps regularly made their way into the columns of city news. On May 1, 1879, the *Chief* reported that a man traveling from Kansas "was assaulted by two German tramps and killed for his money and team" (4). In the January 8, 1885, edition of the *Argus,* across from a lament over the lack of fresh oysters, Warren told the story of the tramp who "fell into the hands of an exasperated mob" (3). That summer, as tramps were passing through town, Hosmer declared that they "should be whooped out of town."[108] On January 29, 1886, below a reminder about Valentine's Day, the *Chief* reported that tramps had broken into the house of A. J. Kenney, the former editor of the *Argus* (7). To editors who filled many a column with stories of euchre tournaments and ice cream socials, tramps were thrilling news. They conjured up a palpable, yet mysterious threat to the community. Instead of sympathy, the editors either preached punishment or indulged in mockery.

Newspapers had less to say about women, a bias that had been passed down from territorial times.[109] When the editors did have something to say about the lives of women, they were often, quite consciously, creating an ideology of womanhood (*WCEV,* 99). A few women owned businesses, and their advertising found its way into the newspapers. But for the most part, women hosted functions, taught school, organized church life, raised money for good causes, and generally maintained the social fabric of the town while tending to what Romines has called "the home plot."[110] From time to time, the newspapers acknowledged women's roles in various organizations. The January 30, 1885, *Chief* described the leadership of the Red Cloud Cooking Club: "The officers are Mrs. W. W. Gardner, president. Mrs. A. H. Brown, vice-president. Mrs. A. I. Funk, secretary, Mrs. Gump, treasurer" (5). On October 9 of the same year, the *Chief* reported: "A very pleasant progressive euchre party was given at the residence of Mr. and Mrs. A. S. Marsh. . . . Mrs. Cather [Willa's mother] received the first prize, and Mrs. Allen the second" (5).

For the most part, these were the kinds of women who were deemed newsworthy in Red Cloud. Other women were largely invisible on the pages of the newspapers. Some were like Lena Lingard and the other "Hired Girls" in *My Ántonia.* Some eventually did enough to challenge traditional notions of decorum and find a place alongside stories of ice-cream socials and picnics. These juxtaposed versions of femininity were illustrated by the *Chief's* "City News" for November 27, 1885, in which readers learned the latest about Red Cloud's most famous madam: "It seems that Fanny Fernleigh, a woman of doubtful reputation who some months ago made herself conspicuous in this city as madam of an infamous bagnio, shot and wounded a man very seriously at Beatrice the other day where she is engaged in running a house of prostitution" (5). In the adjoining column on the left, the *Chief* reported the postponement of the Congregational ladies' dime social because "of the serious illness of Mrs. Aikman." Both stories referred to ongoing narratives, insisting that the reader recognize how the unseemly and seemly coexisted in country town life. A few readers may have had a shock when, distracted by Fanny's doings, their eyes roved upward in the same column to discover that Mrs. Aikman, "who has been suffering from a complication of diseases for several months past, died Wednesday last." Ordinary women disappeared like this from the pages of the local newspapers, while women such as Fanny were denounced and discussed.

European immigrants were a special case in Red Cloud and later in Cather's fiction. The activities and accomplishments of the men were, from time to time, duly noted by the newspapers. The March 7, 1878, *Chief* reported that "Exaver Demers lost his team one night last week at Wheatland" (4). The little story is a nod to life in the settlement of French Canadians located north of Red Cloud. As Kathleen Danker explains, "Between the mid-1870s and mid-1890s, over sixty French Canadian families, primarily from villages around Montreal, emigrated to homesteads in an area of south central Nebraska straddling the county line between northwestern Webster and northeastern Franklin counties, close to the head of the Little Blue River."[111] The families led a rich life indebted to their European heritage, but the newspapers did not attempt to share many of these stories. In regular reports from Wheatland embedded in the "City News," rural life looks just like life in Catherton or Blue Hill—except for some of the names. The same situation applied to other ethnic groups in Webster County, where the "fitness" of various immigrant groups was often questioned.[112]

In her interviews, essays, and fiction, Cather paints a rather different picture. In her oft-quoted interview in 1913, the author explained, "We had very few American neighbors—they were mostly Swedes and Danes, Norwegians and Bohemians" (*WCP,* 10). Later, in her history of Nebraska for the *Nation,* she recalled, "The county in which I grew up, in the south-central part of the State, was typical. On Sunday, we could drive to a Norwegian church and listen to a sermon in that language, or to a Danish or a Swedish church. We could go to the French Catholic settlement in the next county and hear a sermon in French, or into the Bohemian township and hear one in Czech, or we could go to church with some German Lutherans."[113] As Cherny points out, when it came time to quantify this immigrant presence in the general population, Cather reported that it was about 75 percent when it was closer to

45 percent. "Apparently," Cherny suggests, "Cather's deeply held convictions regarding the cultural significance of European immigrants led her to accept erroneous census data."[114] In her history for the *Nation,* Cather explained that Europeans "spread across our bronze prairies like the daubs of color on a painter's palette. They brought with them something that this neutral new world needed even more than the immigrants needed land." Implicitly, as Cather saw it, her emergence as an artist had depended upon her using a palette the newspapers of her youth had ignored.

One reason we can connect Cather's emergence to newspapers in this way is because we know the future author and her family were avid newspaper readers. As Romines points out, in Back Creek, Virginia, the family religiously read the local Winchester newspaper, which they continued to receive in Nebraska.[115] When they opened their newspapers in the 1880s, they often read about themselves. Before the Cather family left Virginia, Red Cloud newspapers dutifully reported grandfather William Cather's travels, Charles's visit to Webster County, the family's plan to move to Nebraska, and Charles's purchase of a new buggy.[116] During their first months out West, they read about the grandparents' trip back to Virginia, move into town, Charles's cattle and hogs, and a successful progressive euchre night at the Cather home.[117] In 1885, Hosmer published an article about Cather family history, heartily endorsing Charles: "C. F. Cather, the new abstract man is thoroughly overhauling the abstract books and records and putting them upon a first class basis. He means business and will soon have the office in good shape. C F is one of the stanch citizens of Webster County and THE CHIEF wishes him success."[118] Following these stories must have been a powerful experience for the girl who would become a fiction writer and embrace side-by-sidedness in her prose.

Things changed in 1887. "The town feud," Bennett explains, "started quietly enough when Mr. Cather was put on a committee to investigate whether or not the county treasurer had been accepting interest on county funds for his own use; but the tension soon flamed into open hostility between those known as the "Big Eight" and the friends of the exploiters of the county treasury" *(WWC,* 24). In broader terms, it was a battle within the Republican Party for control of county funds. The Big Eight included, among others, Charles Cather, McKeeby, Miner, and Wiener. Bennett notes that "every one of these gentlemen appeared later as important characters in Willa Cather stories" (*WWC,* 24).

As compelling as feuds were, the stories about her own accomplishments must have done the most to stir Cather's ambition, introducing the young Willa to her public self. In May of 1885, as *brick mania* reigned, the *Argus* described a Sunday school event at which Cather had "electrified the audience with elocutionary powers" (*WCLL,* 57). That summer, as citizens admired the new façade of the opera house, the *Chief* announced the upcoming Baptist "lawn sociable" where "Miss Willie Cather, the child elocutionist, will give recitations."[119] In an adjoining column, she probably glanced at the notice of a sociable hosted by Mr. and Mrs. Kenney: "The house and grounds will be illuminated, and ice cream, cake, sandwiches and lemonade will be served. Good music by local talent will be one of the features of the evening. All are cordially invited" (5). The effect of the juxtaposition had to be profound. Red Cloud was a vibrant community of food, drink, and entertainment. Against this backdrop, Cather's talent could shine.

Cather seems to have earned her first real fame for these recitations. In 1885, she performed for the Baptist Sunday school at Easter and again for a children's event in June.[120] On September 10 of that year *The Webster County Argus* announced, "A social and OYSTER supper will be given at the residence of Mrs. C. E. Ferguson and Mrs. H. G. Poers, Friday evening. A feature of the evening's entertainment will be recitations by Miss Willie Cather. The proceeds are for the benefit of the Baptist church choir. A. Lauterbach will cook the oysters in his famous style."[121] One day later, the *Chief* proclaimed, "The young elocutionist, Willie Cather, will recite some striking pieces" (5).

It was around this time that the child elocutionist launched another performative venture, signing her name "William" and sporting masculine attire. Should we call it a "masquerade" or "cross-dressing"? O'Brien argues that "in a sense her male impersonation was her first major work of fiction, a text in which she was both author and character" (*WCEV,* 97). Assuming Cather's masquerade/rebellion/impersonation came before her invention of Sandy Point, it probably deserves this rank in her emergence.

Photographs record her efforts over the years. Her hair is "boyish" in one image, and she wears a cap in the style of a Confederate soldier in another. Although these gestures have often been taken as evidence of Cather's emerging gender identification and sexuality, Stout argues that they may have had just as much or more to do with Cather's desire for rebellion and her identification as a New Woman.[122] Describing the "broad context" for Cather's actions that may have included her mother's complicity and the girl's fascination with popular actresses playing male roles, Cynthia Griffin Wolff concludes that Cather's agenda was, at best, "inchoate."[123]

Red Cloud newspapers help us to appreciate how her performances may have been understood by the community. The May 21, 1886, *Chief*

WILLA Cather as the Merchant in *Beauty and the Beast.* Source: Willa Cather Pioneer Memorial Collection. Special Collections & Archives at the National Willa Cather Center in Red Cloud, Nebraska.

reported, "We hear of some more young ladies having an escapade in male attire. We suppose the object is to become familiar with that kind of clothes, the better to enable themselves to wear the family breeches after marriage. That will be all right girls if you happen to hook on the right hair pin" (7). If it predated Cather's own performances, this "review" provides a glimpse of the country town context for some of her actions. If it was directed at her, it would reveal that Cather was not the only girl in Red Cloud experimenting with cross-dressing, which the editor seems more inclined to call a masquerade.

What we know for certain is that Cather earned real praise as an actor on the stage of the Red Cloud Opera House. Reviewing the recent performance of *Beauty and the Beast,* the February 10, 1888, *Chief* declared that Cather "took the part of 'The Merchant' and carried it through with such grace and ease that she called forth the admiration of the entire audience. It was a difficult part well rendered" (1). Of course, Cather was "repurposing" a part already played by Mr. Wiener and Mr. Miner on the streets of Red Cloud. We can only imagine her gratification when she read the review. It is one thing to hear the approval of a live audience, but it is another to have it recorded and confirmed in print. The author is remembering the power of this phenomenon in *The Song of the Lark* when the *Gleam* reviews Lily Fisher's performance (70).

By 1889, Cather had become a seasoned performer and a country town celebrity. In the first edition of the *Argus* that year, she read about herself: "Misses Maud Goble, Willa Cather and Loua Bellows returned Sunday evening from Superior. They report a splendid time and speak very highly of the hospitality of the young people of Superior, their stay having been made a perpetual round of dinner and parties, for which they hope for opportunity to reciprocate in the near future."[124] Cather must have been pleased by the way the editor elaborated on her adventure with uncommon interest, but she could hardly have been surprised. By this point, she had learned to look to Red Cloud newspapers for attention, confirmation, and encouragement.

Charles Cather was seeing things differently. From his vantage point, the newspapers had become weapons in an increasingly hostile struggle that gave him no pleasure. It would be fascinating to pin down every development in the feud with precision, checking story after story from 1887 to 1889, but important editions of the newspapers from this period are mysteriously missing. No one seems to know why. We rely on Bennett to explain that the Big Eight "tried at first to fight their battle through one of the local papers, but when this didn't work, Mr. Cather started editing a paper [the *Republican*] on their behalf" (*WWC,* 24). Although he sided with Big Eight's opposition, Hosmer really thought the whole situation preposterous.[125]

Cather seems never to have talked about the feud in her interviews, but a Pittsburgh reporter in 1897 told the following story: "When she was a girl of fifteen (which probably means 1889, because her birthday was on December 7) her father foreclosed a mortgage on the only newspaper in the town, and as he was not a newspaper man, he left the paper in charge of his daughter until he could get someone else to conduct it. This was not very easily managed, and so for three months little Miss Willa was both editor and business manager of the paper, and what is more, insisted in drawing the salaries for both positions" (*WCP,* 2). Although it is difficult to date the important developments, it seems that the feud began in 1887. The Pittsburgh reporter's story muddies the picture after that. Charles certainly did not foreclose "on the only newspaper in town." Bennett says Charles got someone from Omaha to manage the paper for a time (*WWC,* 24). If the reporter got the age right, then Cather was saying that her father obtained the newspaper either in December of 1888 (after she turned fifteen) or sometime in 1889. But Hosmer's reference to the Big Eight being in the newspaper business occurred in August 1888. As history goes, the picture is fuzzy, but as a snapshot of Cather's country town youth the record is quite useful. At the beginning of 1889, at the age of fifteen,

Cather was smack in the middle of Red Cloud townmaking, perhaps even in the newspaper business herself.

It was about this time that a new opportunity appeared. For some months, the *Chief* and the *Argus* had been running a little column of news from the high school written by a team of two students. Back in October, Cather's neighbor and friend Mary Miner (proprietor of the candy store in Sandy Point) partnered with Charles Garber. The columns were filled with succinctly stated items of news, and a little nod to the season. Miner and Garber opened their effort by reporting the visit of a school board member and then by observing, "The beautiful Indian summer days are here and enjoyed by all."[126] In December, another team of student editors reported the "grand success" of the recent teachers' meeting, which included various exercises: "The recitations by Misses Willa Cather and Trix Mizer were very well rendered. Miss Cather gives fine promise of high elocutionary attainments in the near future."[127] As it turns out, Cather's next attainment was journalistic.

On January 24, 1889, Cather turned to page 8 of the *Argus,* where she found the headline "High School Items" and the column she and her putative partner George Newhouse had written.[128] They declare: "The very pleasant holidays having fled on the wings of time, and school work having been resumed, we have settled down to work in earnest and earnestly hope that at the close of 1889 we may realize the pleasing and profitable result of diligent application to our studies as true students."[129] The editors go on to report "the absence of several large boys last Friday afternoon" thanks to a new skating club. A slightly different version of the same column appeared the next day in the *Chief.*[130] With a touch of the poet's winged metaphor, Cather and her partner had announced themselves as practicing "editors."

Two weeks later, Cather was already transforming the genre. The column was longer than previous iterations. Where previous editors stuck with happenings and the occasional bit of editorial praise for a job well done, Cather launched into professional reflection: "Recesses have been resumed as some pupils prefer relaxation from study, not that their severe application to study necessitates it so much, we presume, as the force of habit calls for it."[131] A literary critic interested in how Cather's journalistic apprenticeship mattered to her fiction can easily identify the seeds of her mature spirit in this item. The parenthetical comment about the degree of "application" begins to create a voice for the newspaper item. It is skeptical, even sarcastic, certainly superior and moralizing as she pauses again with "we presume." The column goes on to report in conventional fashion a number of other activities, but the most compelling detail is the high school reporter's byline: "Willa Cather, Editor." Cather had assumed her role from Sandy Point in the pages of the Red Cloud newspapers. A month later, Cather was on the opera house stage, taking part in the Peak Sisters' "home talent" show, which received a glowing review in the *Chief*.[132]

In her interviews, Cather often talked about the beginning of her career in journalism, usually focusing on her first professional work in Lincoln during college.[133] In 1927, she elaborated on her familiar stories, describing a kind of epiphany in an open letter to the *Journal* on the occasion of the newspaper's sixtieth year of operation: "The first time I was ever confronted by myself in print was one Sunday morning (please don't append an editorial note here, stating just how many years ago it was) when I opened the Sunday *Journal* and saw, stretching out through a column or two, an essay on 'Some Personal Characteristics of Thomas Carlyle,' which Professor Hunt had given you to publish, quite without my knowledge" (*WCP,* 180). Nearly four decades later, Cather explained how the article changed her life: "I thought I would like to study medicine. But what youthful vanity can be unaffected by the sight of itself in print! It had a kind of hypnotic effect" (*WCP,* 180). Although she often denigrated her early journalistic accomplishments, Cather went out of her way on this particular occasion to construct a particular beginning of her professional life in Nebraska. As such stories go, Cather's sounds psychoanalytical as she invents her own latent "mirror stage," dividing herself into writer/performer and reader. For those of us interested in her emergence as an author, the story implies a powerful formulation: the novelist discovered her vocation by *confronting* herself in print in Nebraska. It is a compelling story that has often been repeated, but it is not the only story to be told. Like her two "first" novels, Cather's first confrontation with herself in print had already taken place before the event she claimed, and it happened in the pages of the Red Cloud newspapers. As Downs observes, "Cather became a journalist very early indeed."[134]

With the school year coming to a close in 1889, Cather was in the middle of everything, working for her father's newspaper, now being edited by McKeeby. Animosity was running high, and the *Chief* was ready for a fight. When McKeeby opposed Warren's bid to become postmaster, Hosmer responded with an extended and rather imaginative rant directed at "Doc. McKeeby": "Again with the supreme gall that the 'Artful Dodger' is known to possess, he says that Mr. Warren's opponents are men of far superior ability, That is a direct prevarication on its very face and the slick gentlemen knows it to be so."[135] This is satire in the tradition of Juvenal, not Horace. As he liked to do with stories of importance, Hosmer began anew in an adjoining column in order to intensify his effect: "The dude editor of the Big 8 with his white hat and soft clothes occupies a position that would make a horse laugh himself to death. . . . Vengeance is sweet but awfully expensive some times. Eh, Docky." Hosmer conjured up a bit of territorial humor in this passage when he imagined a horse's skeptical reaction to the doctor's "soft clothes." To heighten the effect, Hosmer indulged in the territorial pleasure of renaming. So McKeeby became the Artful Dodger, dude editor, and Docky. The latter epithet seems to have amused Hosmer mightily because he returned to it over and over again in the months that followed. Eventually, in the columns of the *Chief,* McKeeby evolved into Shylock and Uriah Heep, but the articles often ended with the expected conclusion: "Eh, Docky."

As the dog days approached, Hosmer began to make explicit references to the Cather family in his attacks. In the August 9, 1889, *Chief,* he fumed: "Not a stockholder in it, ever set a type or undertook to edit a paper before, and Mr. Heep has made a miserable failure of the tasks he has undertaken. Not a practical printer or newspaper man in the outfit. The last few issues names *[sic]* the child——.[136] This last was surely a cutting reference to the future winner of the Pulitzer Prize. As autumn progressed, Hosmer began to make explicit references to Charles.[137] On November 1, he elaborated: "Dock McKeeby and Charley Cather who have taken more bonus notes and more usury off the poor people of this county, than any other set of men are now posing as the farmers friends."[138]

What did the young editor make of these attacks? We have no record of her response, but they must have made a considerable impression on her. What we know for sure is that the Red Cloud newspaper editors do not figure in her fiction. Even though Warren and Hosmer published her first journalism, she never mentioned them in interviews. In *The Song of the Lark,* where she writes about "childhood friends" and the "halfway people in this world who help the winners win and the failers fail," she never makes room for a kindly newspaper editor (137). I think we can assume that Cather remembered only too well that the same editor who had praised her talents had relentlessly mocked her friends and family. It was a mercurial power. It made one want to fight, and it made one want to cringe.

In the end, Cather found it all exhilarating. In a letter to Helen Louise Stevens Stowell dated August 28, 1889, she asked: "Do you take the Republican? I wish you did as I am on[e] of the staff reporters and gaurentee *[sic]* it to be the newsiest paper printed in town, you know I have a natural propensity for knowing the business of the town in general. Doctor McKeeby is editor and that insures the intellectual and political items as first class, if you want to know all the social ins & outs, Take the Republican, only $1.00 a year and remember that I am an agent allways ready to recieve subscriptions."[139] The spelling slipped and the sentences ran on, but Cather was clearly delighted by her work. It is telling that she said nothing of the feud, which really brought the whole arrangement into being. She was proud of her role as a "staff reporter." She was also proud of her one credential, her "natural propensity" for townmaking. Last, and not least, she relished being "an agent." Here, at fifteen, Cather anticipated several crucial aspects of her future craft and career. She would follow her natural propensities, write about the business of country towns, and always pay attention to the business of writing.

In countless ways, the townmaking feud informed Cather's psyche, and one is tempted to see its shadow everywhere in her career. Perhaps we see it in her taste for journalistic castigation and controversy? Perhaps we can detect it in the famous author's compulsive desire to manage her public image? We certainly see its influence in Cather's literary townmaking, which centered over and over again on loyalty and betrayal, truth telling and gossip. The recycling must have been particularly satisfying, in part, because she got to publish the last word, over and over again. Hosmer had many names for McKeeby, but we remember Dr. Archie.

What, in the end, are we to make of Red Cloud and Cather's youth there? How did Cather's deep attachment to Red Cloud produce such great fiction? The first question is easy to answer. Townmaking in the Republican Valley in the 1880s was exciting. Trains, bridges, electric lights, and dynamos kept things moving. Bricks meant business, even mania. A spirit of mutuality infused a lively community where many people participated in the daily life of the country town. Towns made town people. The energy of creation was everywhere.

But Red Cloud was not paradise. Rivalries flared. Agendas were crossed. A well-developed sense of propriety put pressure on people who were different. Some were ignored, others excluded. Racism was palpable. Double standards of sexuality and other matters of conduct were tolerated. Many were judged publicly and privately. And much of this activity flowed through the columns of Red Cloud newspapers.

Cather and her family were caught up in this lively web of life the moment they arrived in Nebraska. As the years passed, in one news item after another, they emerged as prominent figures in the unfolding story of Red Cloud. By the time she left the town for college, Cather had ample proof that her deeds would be worth writing about and that she would tell her own version of the story in print.

Red Cloud was also a place of discovery. Before she began to write about and for Red Cloud, she performed as an elocutionist and an actress. In playtime, she discovered that she wanted to be a mayor and an editor. Both at home and in public, she tried out roles and began to embrace the experience of dividedness. The girl who would write for newspapers fell in love with newsprint by seeing her performances recounted in print. There was much at stake for the talented young artist-to-be. O'Brien observes that "during her Red Cloud adolescence, Cather was preoccupied with protecting and discovering what she termed her 'real self'" (*WCEV*, 77). Stout persuasively suggests that the youthful Cather was trying to decide whether she was an "outcast" or a "swashbuckler."[140] As Lee suggests, Cather's experience of the divide between "vivid encounters" and "play-acting" anticipates her lifelong "negotiation" between realism and romance.[141] And here we can surely understand how Red Cloud inspired great fiction. The choices Cather made about her life in Red Cloud were always, in a sense, anticipating choices she would make as she wrote her remarkable novels set in Nebraska.

In fact, the more one knows about Cather's Red Cloud, the easier it is to see how such a relationship was possible. Links between everyday life and high art were everywhere in Cather's hometown. I have taken note of many of them in this chapter, but one remarkable piece of evidence remains. In their account of the high school's Friday afternoon exercises for October 12, 1888, Mary Miner and Charles Garber declare, "We think that these exercises cannot fail to be productive of good results. We do not fail to recognize the fact that all great literary achievements had small beginnings—their distinguished traits developed through effort. Hence, hope of attaining some laudable degree of literary standing as high school pupils will urge us to our work." This is how some of Cather's fellow students described their weekly high school exercises. It sounds a bit like Whitman in the famous poem: "the powerful play goes on, and you may contribute a verse."[142] Did everyone in the school share such sentiments? Certainly not. Is it possible to see how a classmate of Miner's and Garber's in Red Cloud would want to be the first to bring the muse into Nebraska?[143] Of course it is.

Notes

1. For a compelling analysis of this period in Cathers' life, see Skaggs, *After the World Broke in Two,* 1–10.
2. Cather, "End of the First Cycle," *Critical Assessments,* 42–46.
3. Ibid.
4. Cather, "End of the First Cycle," 43–44.
5. Cather, "End of the First Cycle," 41.
6. Plato, *The Symposium, The Collected Dialogues of Plato,* ed. Edith Hamilton and Huntington Cairns (Princeton: Princeton University Press, 1961), 209a.
7. "An Ordinance for the Government of the Territory of the United States Northwest of the River Ohio," www.ourdocuments.gov/doc.php?doc=8&page=transcript, July 14, 2014.
8. Edwin James, *Early Western Travels,* ed. Reuben Gold, vol. 17 (Cleveland: Clark, 1905), 194.
9. West, *The Contested Plains,* 88. For a comprehensive analysis of the process of migration during the period, see John D. Unruh, Jr., *The Plains Across: The Overland Emigrants and the Trans-Missisippi West, 1840–60* (Urbana: University of Illinois Press, 1979).
10. Everett Dick, *Sod-House Frontier: 1854–1890* (1937; Lincoln: University of Nebraska Press, 1979), 5. For a discussion of Cather's discovery of Brownville, see Chapter 2.
11. Joseph Urgo, *Willa Cather and the Myth of American Migration* (Urbana: University of Illinois Press, 1995), 5.
12. Yi-Fu Tuan, *Space and Place: The Perspective of Experience* (Minneapolis: University of Minnesota Press, 1977), 54.
13. The terms are coined by Susan Stanford Friedman, *Mappings: Feminism and the Cultural Geographies of Encounter* (Princeton: Princeton University Press, 1998), 154.
14. Julie Roy Jeffrey, *Frontier Women: 'Civilizing' the West? 1840–1880,* rev. ed. (1979; New York: Hill and Wang, 1998), 101.
15. Cather, "End of the First Cycle," 42.
16. Morgan, *Shovel Full of Stars,* 234, explains how in 1840 a "permanent Indian boundary" was created. The boundary was undone by 1845 when Texas was annexed.
17. Black Hawk, qtd. in Clyde A Milner II, "National Initiatives," *The Oxford History of The American West,* ed. Clyde A. Milner II, Carol A. O'Connor, and Martha A. Sandweiss (New York and Oxford: Oxford University Press, 1994), 176.
18. Mike Fischer, "Pastoralism and its Discontents: Willa Cather and the Burden of Imperialism," *Mosaic* 23.1 (1990): 32–35, 39–41; Melissa Ryan, "The Enclosure of America: Civilization and Confinement in Willa Cather's *O Pioneers!*" *American Literature* 75.2 (2003): 286–96.
19. Roy F. Nichols, "The Territories: Seedbeds of Democracy," *Nebraska History* 35 (1954): 167.
20. Palmer, "Kansas-Nebraska Acts," 32.
21. I discuss these maps in "Kansas-Nebraska Acts," 31–32.
22. Susan Schulten, *The Geographical Imagination in America, 1880–1950* (Chicago: University of Chicago Press, 2001), 3.
23. Walter Prescott Webb, *The Great Plains* (Lincoln: University of Nebraska Press, 1931), 8.
24. Diane Dufva Quantic, *The Nature of the Place: A Study of Great Plains Fiction* (Lincoln: University of Nebraska Press, 1995), xvi.
25. Stegner, *The American West as Living Space,* 3.
26. Edwin James, *Account of an Expedition from Pittsburgh to the Rocky Mountains, The Tallgrass Prairie Reader,* ed. John T. Price (Iowa City: University of Iowa Press, 2014), 16. As Thacker points out, "James is the first commentator to analyze the manner by which unfamiliar animals or objects are apprehended on the prairie" (*GPF,* 39).
27. Francis Parkman, *The Oregon Trail,* ed. William Ellery Leonard (Boston: Ginn and Company, 1910), 56. My summary of Gregg and Parkman's significance is indebted to Thacker, *GPF,* 43–46,

81–88. Stegner, *The American West as Living Space,* 3, observes that the American West "has been as notable for mirages as for the realization of dreams."

28. In his edition of *The Oregon Trail,* William Ellery Leonard concludes: "Thus in Parkman the writer we see, as in Parkman the man, again two qualities of chief note: that of the imagination and that of truth" (xvi).
29. For an excellent and compact history of such painterly innovations, see Stout, *Picturing a Different West,* xviii, 10–22.
30. Julie Roy Jeffrey, "'There Is Some Splendid Scenery': Women's Responses to the Great Plains Landscape," *Great Plains Quarterly* 8 (1988): 70.
31. Stout, *Picturing a Different West,* 10, explains how painters took advantage of this phenomenon.
32. Jeffrey, "There is Some Splendid Scenery," 71.
33. Qtd. in and discussed by Jeffrey, "There Is Some Splendid Scenery," 71.
34. "To Mariel Gere," August 1, 1893, *SLWC,* 20.
35. Walt Whitman, "Art Features," *Specimen Days, Prose Works 1892,* vol. 1, ed. Floyd Stovall (New York: New York University Press, 1963), 214.
36. For a discussion of Whitman's importance to Cather's growth as a writer, see Mullins, "I Bequeath Myself,"123–36.
37. William Gilpin, *The Central Gold Region* (Philadelphia: Sower, Barnes, and Co., 1860), 120; qtd. in Roy E. Gridley, "Some Versions of the Primitive and the Pastoral on the Great Plains of America," *Survivals of Pastoral,* ed. Richard F. Hardin (Lawrence: University of Kansas Publications, 1979) 62.
38. Henry Nash Smith, *Virgin Land: The American West as Symbol and Myth* (Cambridge: Harvard University Press, 1950), 123–32, 174–83, provides a standard introduction to the evolving rhetoric and discusses the transformation of that rhetoric on Great Plains. See also Roderick Nash, *Wilderness and the American Mind* (New Haven: Yale University Press, 1967), 1–17; Quantic, *The Nature of the Place,* 30–31. For an important discussion of the way Fuller shaped this vision, see Annette Kolodny, *The Land before Her: Fantasy and Experience of the American Frontiers, 1630–1860* (Chapel Hill and London: University of North Carolina Press, 1984), 112–17. Fuller's anatomy of the prairie is relevant in rhetorical terms for the present study, but her experience of space and grasslands is of a different order. Thacker, *GPF,* 78, n. 36, points out that Fuller's "prairie is better watered and more lush than the landscape farther west, the plains area in American usage."
39. For a discussion of this moment, see chapter 4.
40. Annette Kolodny's *The Lay of the Land* (Chapel Hill: University of North Carolina Press, 1975), 4, 72.
41. Rosowski, *Birthing a Nation,* 1–3; Jeffrey, *Frontier Women,* 27.
42. Patricia Trenton, "Preface and Acknowledgements," *Independent Spirits: Women Painters of the American West, 1890–1945* (Los Angeles: Autry Museum of Western Heritage and Berkeley: University of California Press, 1995), x; Stout, *Picturing a Different West,* xviii, 25–30.
43. Jeffrey, *Frontier Women,* 27–28.
44. Lyman Beecher, *A Plea for the Nation* (Cincinnati: Truman and Smith, 1835), 12.
45. John Mason Peck, in *A New Guide for Emigrants to the West* (Boston: Gould, Kendall and Lincoln, 1836), vi, quotes the passage without remark.
46. For more on the paradigm of the farm family on the Great Plains, see John Mack Faragher, *Women and Men on the Overland Trail* (New Haven and London: Yale University Press, 1979), 40–65, 179–87; Sandra L. Myres, *Westering Women and the Frontier Experience, 1800–1915,* (Albuquerque: University of New Mexico Press, 1982), 141–66; Glenda Riley, *The Female Frontier: A Comparative View of Women on the Prairie and the Plains* (Lawrence: University Press of Kansas, 1988), 76–101.
47. Jeffrey, "There Is Some Splendid Scenery," 72.
48. Chad Montrie, "'Men Alone Cannot Settle a Country': Domesticating Nature in the Kansas-Nebraska Grasslands," *Great Plains Quarterly* 25.4 (2005): 251.
49. Faragher, *Women and Men on the Overland Trail,* 12; Thacker, *GPF,* 48; Myres, *Westering Women and the Frontier Experience, 1800* 98–139.

50. Myres, *Westering Women and the Frontier Experience,* 36; Craig Miner, *West of Wichita: Settling the High Plains of Kansas 1865–1890* (Lawrence: University Press of Kansas, 1986), 145–59.
51. Jeffrey, "There Is Some Splendid Scenery": 70–73; Montrie, "Men Alone Cannot Settle a Country," 247–49.
52. For a discussion of Smith, see Jeffrey, "There Is Some Splendid Scenery," 72–3.
53. Jeffrey, "There is Some Splendid Scenery," 71, 72.
54. Carl Sandburg collected the tune in *The American Song Bag* (New York: Harcourt, Brace, and Company, 1927), 106.
55. Randolph Barnes Marcy, *The Prairie Traveler, Kansas Collection Books,* http://www.kancoll.org/books/marcy/index.html, February 3, 2013.
56. For a discussion of these letters, see Jeffrey, *Frontier Women,* 27; Rosowski, *Birthing a Nation,* 40–57.
57. Dick, *Sod-House Frontier,* 19–20. For a colorful description of preemption by a foreign observer, see T. H. Gladstone, *The Englishman in Kansas or Squatter Life and Border Warfare* (1857; Lincoln: University of Nebraska Press, 1971), 149.
58. John A. MacMurphy, "Part of the Making of a Great State," *Here You Have My Story: Eyewitness Accounts of the Nineteenth-Century Central Plains,* ed. Richard E. Jensen (Lincoln: University of Nebraska Press, 2009), 234.
59. Cather, "End of the First Cycle," 41.
60. Quantic, *The Nature of the Place,* 18.
61. Qtd. in Dick, *Sod-House Frontier,* 41.
62. Kurt E. Kinbacher, "Imagining Place: Nebraska Territory, 1854–1867," *Regionalism and the Humanities,* ed. Timothy R. Mahoney and Wendy J. Katz (Lincoln: University of Nebraska Press, 2008), 261.
63. Dick, *Sod-House Frontier,* 417.
64. Benjamin Pfeiffer, "The Role of Joseph E. Johnson and His Pioneer Newspapers in the Development of Territorial Nebraska," *Nebraska History* 40.2 (1956): 120.
65. Ibid.
66. Dick, *Sod-House Frontier,* 48.
67. Ibid., 45.
68. Brown, *Willa Cather,* ix.
69. Bruce Baker, "Nebraska Regionalism in Selected Works of Willa Cather," *Western American Literature* 3.1 (1968): 19.
70. Lee, Willa Cather: *Double Lives,* 3.
71. Quantic, *The Nature of the Place,* 19.
72. Acocella, *Willa Cather and the Politics of Criticism,* 77.
73. *Red Cloud, Webster Co. Nebraska: The Gate City of the Republican Valley* (Red Cloud: Argus Steam Press, c. 1890).
74. Rowse, "On the Track of Willa Cather in Nebraska," *Blackwood's,* 166.
75. Bernice Slote, "Willa Cather as a Regional Writer," *Kansas Quarterly* 2.2 (1970): 8.
76. The discussion that follows borrows from and elaborates on Palmer, "Recomposing Nineteenth-Century Nebraska," 2–9.
77. For an extended discussion of this poem in the context of modernism, see Pericles Lewis, *Cambridge Introduction to Modernism* (Cambridge: Cambridge University Press, 2007), 84–85.
78. Middleton, *Willa Cather's Modernism,* 48.
79. *Chief* (April 3, 1885): 5.
80. "Lands of the Burlington and Missouri River Rail Road" (1879). "View of Elm Creek in Webster County, Nebraska," detail from a Burlington and Missouri Railroad map (1880).
81. See John C. Hudson, *Plains Country Towns* (Minneapolis: University of Minneapolis Press, 1986), 1–7.

82. *WCLL*, 44. See also "Webster County and Red Cloud," *Chief* (April 18, 1884): 1; "The B. & M. Time Card," *Chief* (October 3, 1884): 5.
83. This survey can be re-created today with the "Town Tour" map from the National Willa Cather Center.
84. The June 21, 1883, *Argus* reported, "Traveling men say the new State Bank building is the handsomest and best structure in western Nebraska" (4).
85. Mark A. R. Facknitz, "Changing Trains: Metaphors of Transfer in Willa Cather," *Cather Studies: Willa Cather and Modern Cultures* 9 (2011), 70.
86. *Chief* (November 20, 1879): 4.
87. *Chief* (October 19, 1883): 4; *Chief* (November 30, 1883): 1; *Argus* (November 29, 1883): 3.
88. *Chief* (August 21, 1885): 5.
89. For more on this subject, see Daryl W. Palmer, "'The Bohemian Girl,' 'Old Mrs. Harris,' and the Hospitalities of Red Cloud," *Willa Cather Newsletter and Review* 54.2 (2010): 48–51.
90. Virgil Albertini, "Willa Cather and Baseball: Some Personal and Literary Connections," *The Platte Valley Review* 17.2 (1989): 17.
91. *Chief* (April 9, 1886): 7.
92. Steven Trout, "From 'The Namesake' to 'One of Ours': Willa Cather on War," *American Literary Realism* 37.2 (2005): 125.
93. *Argus* (December 15, 1881): 4. C. Robert Haywood, *Victorian West: Class and Culture in Kansas Cattle Towns* (Lawrence: University Press of Kansas, 1991), 188, comments, "No other delicacy tantalized the frontier palate quite like fresh, or at least unspoiled, oysters."
94. For a delightful discussion of the kitchens in Cather's fiction, see Roger L. and Linda K. Welsch, *Cather's Kitchens: Foodways in Literature and Life* (Lincoln: University of Nebraska Press, 1987), 9–36. Given Cather's delight in food and appreciation of fine cooking, it is curious that she never chose to write a story about the Red Cloud Cooking Club, whose story unfolds in the pages of the newspapers. See, for instance, the *Chief* (January 30, 1885): 3.
95. Halverson, *Playing House in the American West,* 143.
96. Mildred R. Bennett, "The Childhood Worlds of Willa Cather," *Great Plains Quarterly* 10.1 (1982): 207.
97. Mildred R. Bennett, archival notes, Special Collections & Archives at the National Willa Cather Center, Red Cloud, NE.
98. Juli Highfill, *Modernism and Its Merchandise: The Spanish Avant-Garde and Material Culture, 1920–1930* (University Park: Pennsylvania State University Press, 2014), 58.
99. For more on Cather's scrapbook, see Jennifer L. Bradley, "A Glimpse inside Childhood: Willa Cather's Childhood Scrapbook," *Willa Cather Pioneer Newsletter and Review* 46.2 (2002): 32–34.
100. See, for example, *Argus* (August 30, 1883): 4; *Chief* (June 12, 1885): 5; *Chief* (July 17, 1885): 5; *Argus* (August 12): 8.
101. On December 22, 1881, the *Argus* announced a shooting tournament: "Fun for the Boys" (4).
102. *Argus* (September 1, 1881): 4; *Argus* (August 3, 1882): 4.
103. *Chief* (November 15, 1889): 5.
104. *Chief* (December 6, 1889): 4.
105. The curious reader of Cather need only overlay the charming map of 1880s Red Cloud with the contemporary walking tour map provided by the Special Colections & Archives at the National Willa Cather Center in order to locate these "characters" then and now.
106. *Chief* (December 18, 1885): 5.
107. For more on Albert Schindelmeisser, see John March and Marilyn Arnold, with Debra Lynn Thornton, *A Reader's Companion to the Fiction of Willa Cather* (Westport, CT: Greenwood, 1993), 838; Ross, "A Walk in Willa Cather's Prairie," *New Yorker,* xx.
108. *Chief* (August 31, 1885): 5.

109. Jeffrey, *Frontier Women,* 107.
110. Ann Romines, *The Home Plot: Women, Writing, and Domestic Ritual* (Amherst: University of Massachusetts Press, 1992), 17.
111. Kathleen Danker, "The Influence of Willa Cather's French Canadian Neighbors in Nebraska in *Death Comes for the Archbishop* and *Shadows on the Rock,*" *Great Plains Quarterly* 20 (2000): 36. See also Laegreid, "The Good, The Bad," 106–07.
112. Griffith, "How the West Was Whitened: 'Racial' Difference on Cather's Prairie," 394.
113. Cather, "The End of the First Cycle," 43–44.
114. Cherny, "Nebraska, 1883–1925, 234.
115. Ann Romines, "Historical Essay," *Sapphira and the Slave Girl,* ed. Charles W. Mignon, Kari A. Ronning, and Frederick M. Link (Lincoln: University of Nebraska Press, 2009), 326.
116. *Argus* (March 6, 1879): 1; *Chief* (July 6, 1882): 4; *Argus* (July 26, 1883): 4.
117. *Argus* (November 1, 1883): 3; *Argus* (November 8, 1883): 3; *Argus* (January 22, 1884): 4; *Argus* (25 March 1886): 8.
118. *Chief* (May 8, 1885): 5.
119. *Chief* (July 24, 1885): 5.
120. Bennett, archival notes, Special Collections & Archives at the National Willa Cather Center, Red Cloud, NE; *WCLL,* 57.
121. *Webster County Argus* (September 10, 1883): 3–5.
122. Stout, *Willa Cather: The Writer and Her World,* 16, 19. See also, among many possible sources, *WCLL,* 55–56; Patrick Shaw, *Willa Cather and the Art of Conflict: Re-Visioning Her Creative Imagination* (Troy: Whitston, 1992), 6.
123. Cynthia Griffin Wolff, "Dressing for the Part: [What's] the Matter with Clothes," *Willa Cather's Southern Connections: New Essays on Cather and the South,* ed. Ann Romines (Charlottesville and London: University Press of Virginia, 2000), 212.
124. *Argus* (January 3, 1889): 7.
125. *Chief* (August 10, 1888): 1.
126. *Chief* (October 12, 1888): 4.
127. *Chief* (December 14, 1888): 4.
128. Newhouse received second billing on the column, but I think we can assume that the girl who served as both mayor and newspaper editor of Sandy Point was probably in charge of the prose.
129. *Argus* (January 24, 1889): 8.
130. *Chief* (January 25, 1889): 4.
131. *Chief* (February 8, 1889): 5. Compare the column in the *Argus* (February 7, 1889): 8.
132. *Chief* (March 8, 1889): 5.
133. "Willa Cather Talks of Work," *Philadelphia Record* (August 10, 1913), *WCP,* 7; "The Vision of a Successful Writer," *Lincoln Daily Star* (October 24, 1915), *WCP,* 12.
134. Downs, *Becoming Modern,* 37.
135. *Chief* (July 12, 1889): 4.
136. *Chief* (August 9, 1889): 5.
137. *Chief* (August 23, 1889): 4; *Chief* (November 1, 1889): 4.
138. *Chief* (November 1, 1889): 8.
139. Willa Cather to Helen Louise Stevens Stowell, August 28, 1889, *SLWC,* 11.
140. Stout, *Willa Cather: The Writer and Her World,* 15.
141. Lee, *Willa Cather: Double Lives,* 37.
142. Walt Whitman, "O Me! O Life!," *The Complete Poems,* ed. Francis Murphy (1975; London: Penguin, 2004), 298.
143. I refer, of course, to Jim Burden's reading in *My Ántonia,* 256.

Chapter 2.

Writing the West Otherwise:
The Short Stories of the First Decade, 1892-1902

To people who live by imagination at all, that is the only life that goes deep enough to leave memories. We were artists in those days, creating for the day only; making epics sung once and then forgotten, building empires that set with the sun.
—Douglass in "The Treasure of Far Island"

Starting with her first published story "Peter" in 1892 and with vignettes she wrote for the *Nebraska State Journal* in 1893, Cather's earliest stories and poems mark a winding road that led her from Red Cloud to Lincoln, back to Red Cloud, and on to a new life in Pittsburgh, where she saw the publication of "The Treasure of Far Island" in 1902. It was a decade of opportunity, energy, excitement, and accomplishment. As O'Brien rightly observes, "the first stories are important biographical and literary documents: in their aesthetic deficiencies are hidden the sexual and creative conflicts Cather would resolve before becoming the author of *O Pioneers!* and *My Ántonia* (*WCEV*, 196). Read side-by-side, the author's letters and stories reveal a complex pattern of experimentation with life and craft.

Because Cather wrote all the stories while she was busy producing journalism, we can hear her young public voice ruminating along the way. Slote points out that "as early as 1896 Willa Cather had written nearly a half million words of criticism, self-analysis, and explorations into the principles of art and the work of the artist" (*KA*, 4). The aging author would have been delighted if all of these words had vanished along with her early stories. Indeed, she went out of her way to repress them, but the body of work demands to be studied with renewed attention by anyone interested in Cather's growth as an artist.[1] Slote concludes, "Except for the letters of Keats, I know of no comparable body of personal writing that shows so much of the creative process itself, or enables us to see it working out in the created thing" (*KA*, 5).

In this chapter, I want to focus on the six stories that most clearly reveal key evolutions in the author's creative process: "On the Divide," "Tommy, the Unsentimental," "The Way of the World," "Eric Hermannson's Soul," "El Dorado," and "The Treasure of Far Island." As Rosowski observes, "Cather's early stories tell of finding her way toward her version of the West."[2] But it may be more accurate to suggest that the author was discovering *versions* of her West, some more radical than others. Indeed, these stories reveal a writer trying to assay conventions of realism and romance, while actively speculating about craft and career, gender and modern identity, life back East and out West. The earliest stories matter for all these reasons, but they also invite the kind of close reading that we tend to reserve for the later fiction. Arnold suggested as much some time ago: "Cather proved herself an artist long before *O Pioneers!* appeared in 1913. Some of her very earliest stories have the earmarks of genius, and a good many of them before *O Pioneers!* are superb."[3]

On June 6, 1890, the public schools of Red Cloud celebrated their annual commencement exercises at the Red Cloud Opera House. Surrounded on her graduation day by the red bricks that epitomized Red Cloud prosperity, Cather was finally speaking not as a mere performer, but as an authority looking into the future. She had a great deal to say. "All human history," she declared, "is a record of an emigration, an exodus from barbarism to civilization . . ." (*WCP*, 141). Although her topic was "Superstition versus Investigation," Cather's first sentence seems rooted in her experience of Nebraska, and even more deeply in the territorial past that continued to inform the present. Everything that Cather cared about had a migratory current behind it. People and ideas emerged out of translation, out of motion from site to site. New ideas, like new people, were transplants that could be nurtured by investigation and imagination. Cather was framing her own emergence and claiming her own momentum.

In September, she went to Lincoln where she began preparatory work at the University of Nebraska. In loving detail, Slote has described how the Easterners who founded the city "moved in, took out their white kid gloves, subscribed to *Century*, shipped in oysters frozen in blocks of ice, and tried to keep life very much as it had been in Ohio, New York, Illinois, or Virginia" (*KA*, 7). There were libraries and social clubs, professional theatrical performances and concerts, fine hotels and restaurants. But the crown jewel was the university, "a little Renaissance world" as Slote calls it (*KA*, 9).

Cather thrived. During her first year in Lincoln, one of her professors submitted her essay on Thomas Carlyle to the *Nebraska State Journal,* which published it on March 1, 1891. The *Hesperian,* the university literary magazine, published the essay on the same day. Soon Cather was writing for—and eventually editing—the magazine, whose masthead announced, "W. Cather—Managing Editor" (qtd. in *KA,* 11). As the years passed, she wrote more short stories and contributed columns to the local newspapers. She acted in plays, went to the theater to see touring companies, and attended concerts. In 1895 she got her first taste of Impressionist painting when she attended the Haydon Art Club Exhibit.[4]

All the while, Cather did her best to cultivate an active social life. She enjoyed the company of Tom Wing, cousin of Edith Lewis, Cather's future partner. Although the younger Lewis and Cather seem not to have met until 1903, Melissa J. Homestead and Anne L. Kaufman have described the ways in which their family and social networks overlapped.[5] In Lincoln, Cather also delighted in the company of the Westermann family, who many years later served as prototypes for the Erlich family in *One of Ours.* She became friends with Dorothy Canfield and her family. Dorothy's father was chancellor of the university. Mariel Gere and her family became lifelong friends. Mariel's father, Charles, was editor and publisher of the *Nebraska State Journal.* Gere and his managing editor, Will Owen Jones, became trusted mentors.

And Cather met Louise Pound. The daughter of one of the founding families of the city, Pound was smart, trendy, and popular. An accomplished athlete and pianist, she was the embodiment of the "New Woman" who could retain her feminine beauty while firing a Springfield rifle. The friendship deepened, but eventually failed as Cather struggled to work out the terms of same-sex intimacy. In a passionate letter on June 15, 1892, Cather complained to Pound: "It is manifestly unfair that 'feminine friendships' should be unnatural" (*SLWC,* 17). As the friendship was deteriorating, Cather published a lampoon of Pound's brother Roscoe in the *Hesperian* and so ruined her relationship with the family.

Through it all, Cather was writing. In her freshman year, she took a course taught by Herbert Bates, who asked his students to write a series of "themes." Cather wrote her first short story about Nebraska, and her professor liked the work so much that he submitted it to the *Mahogany Tree*, a Boston magazine. "Peter" appeared in May 1892, and Cather was suddenly a published author. "Peter" is the story of a Bohemian musician who has been broken by the trials of homesteading. "This is a piece of narrative," Woodress writes, "that any college freshman could be proud of" (*WCLL,* 77). It is certainly economical and powerful. If we want to understand how Nebraska mattered to Cather, this first story is an essential part of the puzzle.

In a number of ways, some more obvious than others, this little story presaged all the fiction that followed. It is obvious, for instance, that Cather discovered in her main character four figures with life-long interest for her: the immigrant, the settler, the musician, and the suicide. In so doing, she began to work out her own relationship to realism, a relationship rooted, as Downs observes, in newspapering, but also in personal memory.[6] It is no coincidence, for example, that the author happened to write her first published story about a Bohemian suicide.[7] In Cather's youth, the Red Cloud newspapers had, with some regularity, linked Bohemians to passion, drunkenness, and suicide. This matrix of collective memory was punctuated by Cather's own charged recollection of arriving in Webster County and hearing stories of how Francis Sadilek, the prototype for Mr. Shimerda in *My Ántonia,* had recently killed himself. In recasting these memories, Cather began to focus on the initial settlement period, creating a version of "Nebraska" rooted in the territorial imagination.

Inspired by her success, Cather wrote more stories, but the appearance of her own column in the state's leading newspaper must have confirmed a new version of her ambitious self.[8] The first installment of Cather's regular column "One Way of Putting It" appeared on November 5, 1893, in the *Journal,* a month or so before the author's twentieth birthday. In a series of seven vignettes, the writer moves from a minister preaching a sermon in a church to a chaplain saying goodbye to prison inmates. A woman watches a couple and their child at a concert. An old German fiddler finishes playing for a dance. The column concludes with three scenes around a Salvation Army tent. Initially, the little pieces seem spare and unremarkable, but they deserve more attention.

On closer examination, we find an aspiring author experimenting with her form in ways that would matter to her craft as fiction writer. Stout explains, "Here we see her groping for material for the paying work she now had an opportunity to do and trying out her hand at elements of fiction writing: anecdote, visual scene, cameo characterization, dialogue."[9] Juxtapositional effects emerge. The churchgoers listening to the minister's sermon have something in common with the inmates listening to the chaplain. The people in each vignette watch each other, and the writer examines the watching, allowing us to mark what the spectators do and do not see, and so on. In this way, each of the elements is carefully pressed into service by an authoritative voice that

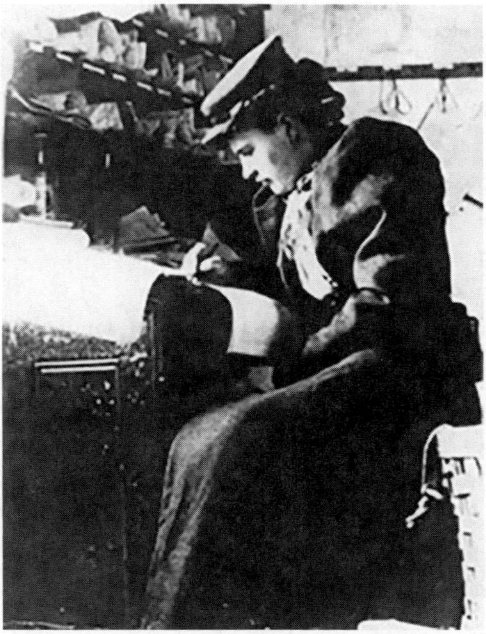

WILLA Cather at the *Nebraska State Journal,* c. 1893–95. Source: Willa Cather Foundation Special Collections & Archives at the National Willa Cather Center in Red Cloud, Nebraska.

owes something to the moralizing voice of her Red Cloud high school columns as it takes advantage of the newspaper's side-by-sidedness.

With this first installment of "One Way of Putting It," Cather was looking forward to more mature fiction, but she was also glancing back with deep feeling (as she would do throughout her life) to Red Cloud. The precise moment occurs in the description of the Salvation Army woman singing "Rock of Ages." "It is hard," Cather writes, "to hear that song with indifference, for most of us have heard it sung over the coffins of those we loved best." Cather was thinking of the funerals she had attended that year. Her grandmother Rachel (the inspiration for the title character in "Old Mrs. Harris") died in June. William Ducker, who had coached her in the classics and shared his laboratory, died in August; and Fannie Wiener (the inspiration for Mrs. Rosen in "Old Mrs. Harris") died in September.[10] Even as the teenager was boldly launching her career as a professional journalist away from home in the bustling world of Lincoln, her heart was haunted by those she had loved and lost in Red Cloud.

Because the youthful Cather never stopped thinking about the people and habits of life in a live Western town, it is hardly surprising that she would want to spend part of her summer vacation visiting one of the original territorial towns in Nebraska. In 1894 Cather, her brother Roscoe, and friends Mariel Gere and Grace Broady headed east for Brownville, on the banks of the Missouri River about eighty miles south of Omaha. The young people arrived in town on one of the hottest days Nebraskans had ever seen. It could have been a miserable experience, but it turned out to be one of the truly memorable moments of Cather's college days.

When she got home, she could hardly stop writing. The result was "her first long feature story, more than three thousand words, which the *Journal* published the next month" (*WCLL,* 97). Brownville residents were infuriated by the story. Cather was thrilled. In a letter written later that summer to Broady, she concluded: "After this I will get all I can out of a town on my first visit."[11] Referring to their trip as an "expedition," Cather demanded: "Did'nt *[sic]* we have lots of fun down there though?" The delighted tourist also reported that she and Roscoe had been playing cards with "the memorable Brownville deck."

Cather went on to get all she could out of her expedition, adapting and repurposing pieces of what she called her "Brownville tale" in later work.[12] She nods to Brownville's history in *The Song of the Lark,* and she was still thinking of the feature when she wrote her history of Nebraska for the *Nation.* In a 1945 letter to Mariel Gere, Cather remembered the trip. Something had happened to the college student when she visited Brownville, "the sleepy little town on the Missouri where the beginnings of Nebraska history were made" (*WP,* 104). Exploring the territorial map of Nebraska, Cather felt that she had discovered "the beginnings" of her West.

For the young reporter, it was a story of fact and fiction, solo effort and old-fashioned collaboration. She mused, "It is as though there had once been a high tide of prosperity there, and when it went out it had left for its watermarks rows of ruined houses and stranded homes" (104). With an imaginative flick of her pen, Cather personified the river: "The old river, rich with disappointment and chagrin, has tried to commit suicide by burrowing and burying itself in the sand" (106). Turning to the Episcopal church, she declared: "The ruin and neglect of the place is pitiful" (107). An illustration in the newspaper seemed to document the description, but the photograph had been taken by Gere, after Cather got her friends to rip out pews and pile them in front of the church. As she told Broady, "those prayer benches we wickedly piled up in the aisle showed up in great shape."[13] Many years later, in a letter to Mildred Bennett, Mariel Gere remembered being "somewhat shocked" by Cather's staging.[14] The former mayor of Sandy Point had orchestrated a collaborative "expedition" of repurposing, unmaking the town in order to ornament a story that would pass for simple reporting. Journalism and fiction had begun to merge for the author, who was, as Downs suggests, "inventing realism."[15]

Like most of her fiction set in Nebraska, this early piece of journalism was also about past and present on the Great Plains. "It is almost unheard of," Cather began her feature, "to find a town in Nebraska that has a past; it is sometimes rather difficult to find one that has a present, though all of them have, or think they have, a future. A country cares very little about its early history and traditions until it has had a great many trials and disappointments, until the first feverish impetus of its growth has been checked and it settles down" (103). The author is characteristically sardonic in this opening, but she is also visionary. In the decades that followed, she would make it a point never to take the past, present, and future of Nebraska towns for granted. Her fiction would highlight the mutability—the radical fragility—of past, present, and future in what she called "the real West," and *Nebraska* would name a particular sort of metaphysical conundrum in that region.

When Cather graduated from the university in 1895, she was superbly educated in idiosyncratic ways that can hardly be reckoned. Slote concludes, "In the end, Willa Cather's formal education does not explain how she happened to know what she did" (*KA,* 37). I have no better explanation, but *emergence* certainly names the phenomenon.

In 1895, Cather was also an established and respected journalist with "no regular job" (*WCLL,* 103). During the summer, she was shuttling back and forth between Lincoln and Red Cloud, visiting friends, angling for serious employment, writing, and riding her wheel.[16] A headline in the May 31 *Lincoln Evening Call* could have been written for the new graduate: "The New Woman Riding into Freedom on the Bicycle" (3). In striking ways that Stout has identified, Cather's emergence coincided with the emergence of the New Woman in American society.[17]

Here narratives of Cather's life after college tend to move swiftly toward her years in Pittsburgh, but this little period is more complicated and revealing than the author's biographers have suggested. The standard version remarks Cather's temporary success at the *Courier* in Lincoln. As Stout explains, "From August through November 1895 she worked as associate editor of the *Courier*. . . ."[18]

In fact, it was something of a coup. Cather was joining two relatively young, yet experienced and idealistic newspaper professionals. W. Morton Smith was in his mid-twenties and had a penchant for politics and controversy. Sarah Harris was thirty-five, gifted, passionate, and respected.[19] Announcing Cather's arrival on August 3, 1895, the *Courier* declared: "Miss Cather's reputation extends beyond Nebraska. She is thoroughly original and always entertaining. Her writing has a piquant literary flavor, and her services are a valuable acquisition to any paper" (1). Far from being at sixes and sevens, the new college graduate had found both respect and employment. The state took notice. An article in the *Beatrice Express,* reprinted in the *Chief* on August 16, reported Cather's position, suggesting that she had invested in the newspaper, praising her abilities, but noting (with what turned out to be foreshadowing) that "She is rather too much given to indiscriminate roasting" (5). Later that fall, Elia W. Peattie described Cather as "a young woman with a genius for literary expression" (qtd. in *KA,* 26). The former editor of the Sandy Point newspaper, "High School Items" column, Red Cloud *Republican,* and the University of Nebraska *Hesperian* was an editor once more.

Cather had much to be happy about and clearly launched herself into the work, which lasted until sometime in December, when she left the newspaper. Slote puzzles over "the reason for her leaving—money, politics, personalities—or whatever tension might have existed at the time" (*KA,* 25). Over the years, scholars have simply remarked the perplexing event.[20] Stout perceptively adds that Cather felt "banished from civilization."[21] In fact, the author had good reason for such feelings, better than we have imagined.

Lewis provides the framework for understanding when she remarks, "In the *Courier* she [Cather] carried on fierce political campaigns, for which she wrote the editorials" (*WCL,* xxvi). When Cather joined the newspaper in her editorial capacity, the Capital National Bank scandal had been raging for months. Stories of embezzlement and fraud by the bank's chief officers, C. W. Mosher and R. C. Outcalt, had filled column after column in the city's newspapers.[22] The trial of Outcalt in federal court was garnering particular scrutiny that autumn, and on November 30 the *Courier* had had enough. In an editorial piece called "Plain Truth on Local Topics," the newspaper complained, "In Lincoln and Nebraska corruption in its many forms has become so common that its existence seldom excites comment any more. We are so used to being defrauded and sold out and flim-flammed and walked on that we take all this in our daily portion as we take our Pear's soap" (8). With no regard for the newspaper's vulnerability, the writer or writers proceeded to accuse the presiding judge of jury-rigging and conspiracy. On December 13, 1895, the *Lincoln Herald* reported the outcome: "Col. W. Morton Smith has been fined $50 and fifteen days in jail by the federal court at Omaha, for the naughty things he said about the Outcalt case in his valuable paper. Miss Sarah Harris one of the editors was subpoenaed as a witness and Miss Willa Cather the third and best looking of the trio, quietly resigned her position and left the city" (1). In this way, Cather saw her new professional life in Nebraska crumble almost as soon as it had begun.

As a footnote in the story of Cather's emergence, the *Courier* episode is illuminating in a number of ways. It invites us, for instance, to consider the New Woman's evolving modes of self-presentation and recognition in light of the *Herald* comment about her being the "best looking." The episode also recalls the bitter political feuding that Cather observed in Red Cloud while working on the *Republican* alongside her father and Dr. McKeeby. It would seem that Cather's early life was touched by corruption in more ways than we have reckoned. Finally, Cather's near obsession with "roasting" must be remarked. As the editor of "High School Items," she had used her columns to chastise boys for skipping class and preach about the value of recess. At the *Hesperian,* she had (among other enterprises) attacked ladies' literary clubs, her Shakespeare professor, the dilapidated condition of Brownville, and Louise Pound's brother Roscoe, thus ruining her friendship with his family.

Perhaps most important of all, the *Courier* episode reminds us that although the author had been learning, changing, and growing for years, she was in 1895—and would always be—quintessentially Willa Cather, editor and comrade. From Sandy Point to Lincoln to Pittsburgh to New York, Cather would call herself "editor." Cather would seek out partners who were willing to collaborate in all sorts of ways in her imaginative experiments.

If we want to appreciate her disillusionment during the winter of 1895–1896, we need to remember that the new college graduate had no way of knowing where this indefatigable self—committed to art, castigation, and forward motion—would go. As the weeks wore on, she managed to find time for dances and visits with friends, but was often miserable. As the new year began, Cather was writing from Red Cloud, which she identified as "Siberia" at the top of her page, sounding a bit Chekhovian as she contemplated suicide in the "provinces," asking Mariel Gere for a favor: "Sarah Harris has a little book of mine, 'Sapho', by Alphonse Daudet. . . . Now considering the existing relations it would be snippy of me to write and demand it from Sarah."[23]

Cather went on writing for Harris, and they remained friends. Indeed, years later, Cather met her partner Edith Lewis while visiting Harris in Lincoln (*WCL,* xxv). A few weeks after Cather wrote her letter from "Siberia," Harris was presiding over a meeting of the Nebraska State Press Association when Cather read a short paper entitled "How to Make a Newspaper Interesting." The former editor of the *Courier* was adamant: "A neutral newspaper is an abomination. The newspaper should be personal" (qtd. in *KA,* 27). At the beginning of 1896, the words were particularly true for Cather, "the existing relations" sad indeed.

It was in this January mood that Cather saw her story "On the Divide" appear in *Overland Monthly.* As Woodress points out, it was "the first time she had appeared in a magazine of national prominence" (*WCLL,* 106). She should have been delighted, but her letters tell us nothing. Perhaps she was so intent on getting a good job that another publication seemed unworthy of celebration. Perhaps because Bates had helped to shape the story, her pleasure in it was undermined.

In any event, Cather's hand is still evident in this wintry work, and it merits a closer look because of the way the author begins to experiment with her Western setting. A third-person narrator tells the tale of lonely Canute Canuteson, who frightened his neighbors and drank too much. The narrator personifies a stream that lacked "ambition," adding that were it not "for the few stunted cottonwoods and elms that grew along its banks, Canute would have shot himself years ago" (*CSP,* 8). In Cather's developing vision of Nebraska, as we know from her writing about Brownville, rivers and creeks are animate, and just as depressed as the people who settle near them. In case we miss the point, a little later in the story, the narrator adds: "Insanity and suicide are very common things on the Divide" (10). Cather was convinced of this notion in the 1890s, and it was still haunting her more than two decades later when she wrote *My Ántonia.*

The narrator goes on to tell how Canute's life changed when Ole Yensen, wife Mary, and daughter Lena moved onto the Divide, how Canute began drinking with Ole and soon fell, in his brooding way, in love with Lena. Then one bitterly cold winter night, Canute abducts Lena, coercing her to accept him. A serious disciple of romance and ready to embrace what John Murphy has called the "anti-Howellsian" spirit of the decade, the youthful author could have entitled the story "Canute and Lena," but her title invokes the Divide that will inform so much of her subsequent fiction.[24] Cather was embracing the tension between romance and realism.

Innovation followed. Her first sentence maps the landscape around Canute's shanty with a touch of color: "North, east, south, stretched the level Nebraska plain of long rust-red grass that undulated constantly in the wind"

(8). A larger territorial perspective materializes when the narrator explains, "Those scorching dusty winds that blow up over the bluffs from Kansas seem to dry up the blood in men's veins as they do the sap in the corn leaves" (10–11). As Rosowski has pointed out, Cather's prose hints at an incipient ecological perspective based on "direct observation" as the narrator captures "the drama in the vegetation."[25] In the midst of this "unremittingly grim" landscape painting, the narrator describes an alternative (*GPF,* 148). We learn that Mary Lee "went to town" and came home "to startle Lena with stories of ten cent theaters, firemen's dances, and all the other esthetic delights of metropolitan life" (13). In this story, Cather discovered another important divide that would eventually transform her fiction. In her mind, Nebraska would always be divided into farms and towns, the latter standing as an attractive alternative to the former.

Finding the right voice for this sort of storytelling was more difficult. Writing about the prevalence of suicides on the Divide, she declares: "It causes no great sensation there when a Dane is found swinging to his own windmill tower" (11). This is the hyperbolic and sardonic voice of Cather's letters from "the provinces," the voice Cather used when she was, in Arnold's apt phrase, "playing the village wit" for her friends up in Lincoln.[26] Writing in this vein to Mariel Gere during the hot summer of 1894, she reported, "We have had a little rain here and are hoping for more. Of course I want it to rain but I am rather disappointed in loseing *[sic]* such a good crop of suicides as dry weather would certainly have brought."[27] In "On the Divide," this voice is not out of place, but it could never serve for the substantial fiction Cather would one day create.

The young author needed a way of looking backward while speaking with an engaging voice in the present. She needed irony without sarcasm, gravitas without pomposity. So the narrator begins a section with "One spring . . ." and the following section with "Next spring . . . (13). Perhaps she could write about Nebraska as a chronicler of long-past deeds, leaping from season to season? It was a venerable and viable approach that would serve her well when she wrote *O Pioneers!.*

In this story, she also begins to explore the generational frames that would make it possible to write that first prairie novel: "It may be that the next generation on the Divide will be very happy, but the present one came too late in life" (11). A casual reader could easily be confused by the narrator's reference to "the present one." But Cather is clear that Canute does not represent the present generation in 1896; he represents the present generation in the story of early settlement.

Nevertheless, the mood of Cather's story has been influenced by the recent hardships of the early 1890s (*WCEV,* 207). The drought had begun in 1890 as Cather left for Lincoln, the summers growing increasingly hot until they turned into the inferno of 1894. Crops had failed. Soon, farmers and banks had followed suit.[28] As this recent period of hardship merged with a vision of early settlement in Cather's imagination, the author was coming to recognize that past and present were unstable entities in Nebraskan life.

Because many of her subsequent works of fiction depend on this vision, they can confuse readers who want to understand her work as "documenting" a single period of struggle in a homogenous place called "Nebraska." But time and again, as Reynolds has pointed out, Cather looks backward in order to speak to and about the present.[29] Eudora Welty put it this way: "Willa Cather brought past and present into juxtaposition to the most powerful effect. And the landscape itself must have shown her this juxtaposition."[30] Contrary to the traditional narrative about Cather needing years to come to terms with the Great Plains, the author seems to have been making discoveries like this from the moment she began writing serious fiction.

With the same innate confidence, Cather makes gender central to the story. Focusing on the limits of what women and men can do on the Great Plains, she describes Canute as a "big man" who can homestead on his own, drink a lot, contemplate suicide, and subdue a kicking stallion with his bare hands. Although he cannot communicate his feelings, he can abduct the woman he wants. Lena, by contrast, is a "pretty daughter, [who] was not afraid of man nor devils" (13). Lena, the narrator confides, has "little pride beyond that of vanity" (19). She can tease Canute, go to work in town, and kick when abducted. Her vanity touched by Canute's attention, Lena can accept the man as her partner. She opens the cabin door to find Canute frozen and sobbing in the snow.

At the story's end, romance claims a temporary victory over realism, but Cather's innovations are more important. Describing Canute's abduction of Lena, she hit upon a stunning motif when the farmer "lifted the girl in his arms" (17). In this moment of lifting, Cather discovered an image of masculine power that would be central to Alexandra Bergson's imaginative life in *O Pioneers!*. Whether she recognized its importance right away is anyone's guess, but she clearly wanted to heighten its effect.

In doing so, she hit upon another innovation. "So it was," the narrator explains, "that Canute took her to his home, even as his bearded barbarian ancestors took the fair frivolous women of the South in their hairy arms and bore them down to their war ships" (*CSP,* 17). With this simple gesture, Cather realized that a story of life in Nebraska could gain resonance through allusions to the Old World.[31] She went on to spend the rest of the decade experimenting with this technique. As Reynolds explains, "Cather turned an apprentice writer's tic—the need to seem *au fait,* conversant with culture (resulting in a gauche display of cultural reference)—into a strength."[32] Over the years, she came to realize that her ability to write important literary works about Nebraska depended on this combination of vision and craft.[33]

In all these ways, "On the Divide" was a remarkable step in Cather's career, but the author was feeling stuck—emotionally and professionally. In a March 12, 1896, letter to Mariel Gere, she complains: "You are about the worst person about writing letters I know, here I am in bitter exile. . . . Occasionally to vary the monotony I try my hand at cooking, and when the weather is decent I ride my bicycle."[34] She needed a miracle, and late that spring she got one when James Axtell, a Pittsburgh publisher with Lincoln connections, offered her a job editing a new magazine called *Home Monthly.*[35] Cather accepted the offer.

When Cather first left Nebraska for Pennsylvania, it must have seemed as though she was burning her bridges behind her, but her return to the wheel probably felt inevitable. On August 4, 1896, she wrote to Mariel Gere about a feud with her university classmate Tom Wing, Bohemianism, the hard work, her self-doubt, and her conviction that "there is no God but one God and Art is his revealer" (*SLWC,* 39). In this mood, she went on to confide: "The only form of excitement I indulge in is raceing *[sic]* with the electric [street] cars on my bicycle. I may get killed at that, but certainly nothing more" (*SLWC,* 39). The woman on the wheel was on the verge of something.

Later that fall, she set out on a cycling trip through the Shenandoah Valley that allowed her to explore what would become an abiding disposition. As Woodress explains, commenting on this cycling adventure, "Among the several polarities that pulled at Cather all her life was the attraction of the eastern mountains against the tug of the prairie of her adopted state" (*WCLL,* 112). Cather the cyclist was beginning to wheel imaginatively between Red Cloud and Pittsburgh, between the East and the West.

In the summer of 1896, with a publication deadline at *Home Monthly* approaching, she began a cycling story for her magazine. J. M. Barrie's new novel *Sentimental Tommy,* the story of young man unwilling to grow up, written by the creator of Peter Pan,[36] gave her a push and the author pedaled back over an imaginative bridge between Pennsylvania and Nebraska as she wrote "Tommy, the Unsentimental." Although she could have signed the story with a pen name, as she would often do in the months to come, she signed this contribution with her own name, claiming every bit of the unconventionality as her own.[37]

"Tommy" is an important, yet underappreciated story that has engendered a variety of interpretations. Labeling the story "slight," Rosowski frames the conversation by focusing on the work's delightful and rebellious version of gender and sexuality.[38] Acknowledging those impulses, I would argue that no story until "The Bohemian Girl" is more pivotal in Cather's career. Viewing Nebraska from a new perspective, Cather discovered how to recast recent memories, her hometown, and the gendered conventions she used to resist. The story could certainly be used to support Stout's contention that Cather's fiction ultimately offers "an inclusively androgynous vision in which women and men alike were freed of prescriptive and rigidly conventional gender roles."[39]

Tommy is a strong-willed woman of business who has, according to the narrator, a "peculiar" relationship with Jay Harper (474). The heroine knows "plenty of active young business men and sturdy ranchers, such as one meets about live western towns, and took no particular interest in them" (474). This is an experimental opening in all sorts of ways. In her domestic magazine, Cather is presenting a heroine who is interested in neither domesticity nor male courtship. Viewing Red Cloud with fresh eyes from her new position in Pittsburgh, Cather creates Southdown as one of these "live western towns" where gendered conventions can be negotiated. It is a fascinating paradox that Cather's time "back East" in Pittsburgh inspired her to begin recasting her hometown in the West.

The story's opening paragraphs reveal just how experimental Cather was willing to be in her new domestic publication. Instead of the kind of geographical scene-setting she had been using in her early stories set in Nebraska, the author drops the reader into the middle of a conversation as Tommy and Miss Jessica discuss Harper. Most readers are probably still trying to determine who is talking about whom when the narrator declares, "Needless to say, Tommy was not a boy, although her keen gray eyes and wide forehead were scarcely girlish, and she had the lank figure of an active half grown lad" (473). The "needless to say" is utterly disingenuous.[40] No reader would have suspected that Tommy is female. In fact, Cather has eased the reader into a fictional world where gender and identity are fluid and obliquely erotic.

Recognizing her *Home Monthly* readers might be startled by the effect, she indulges in a long paragraph that links gender to geography, explaining how *Theodosia* became *Tommy.* To the now unsettled reader more likely to identify with Eastern versions of the feminine, Cather's narrator explains that things are different out West: "That blunt sort of familiarity is not unfrequent in the West, and is meant well enough. People rather expect some business ability in a girl there, and they respect it immensely" (473). With this single gesture to region and commerce, Cather rationalizes every unconventional turn that follows, even as she celebrates an openness in the West that her own experience did not always confirm.

Woodress is not wrong to suggest that "Tommy" is an "autobiographical story" that illustrates aspects of Cather's life in Red Cloud,[41] but it is perhaps more accurate to say that the story offers a palimpsestuous vision of her recent life in Red Cloud layered with experiences and ideas from Lincoln and Pittsburgh. In this involuted (to apply De Quincey's terminology) fiction, Tommy is, quite obviously, a palimpsest of the author and Louise Pound, Cather's accomplished friend and college crush.[42] It was an extraordinary moment of experimentation for the young author as she discovered the pleasures of seeing herself and the world through another's eyes. Years later, in 1913, Cather would describe the thrill of seeming to inhabit "another person's skin" (*WCP,* 10).

Inspired to shift her focus from early pioneer struggles on the prairie to contemporary life in Red Cloud, Cather followed this palimpsestuous impulse in her first foray into townmaking. The narrator explains that Harper's father set him up in a bank in the little town of "Red Willow, some twenty-five miles north, upon the Divide" (475). In Nebraska, the county of Red Willow, with McCook as its county seat, lies about one hundred miles west of Red Cloud. Twenty-five miles north of Red Cloud is Blue Hill, a community always conscious of its colorful name, home of the Blue Hill Blues baseball team.[43] Cather's transformation is playful indeed, and worthy of Colton's territorial mapmaking, as Blue turns to Red and Hill becomes Willow.

In this mood, Cather recalled, for the first time in her fiction, the Big Eight, a group of friends that included her father, McKeeby, Miner, and Wiener. Not unlike Cather, Tommy's "best friends were her father's old business friends, elderly men who had seen a good deal of the world, and who were very proud and fond of Tommy" (474). More surprisingly, the narrator goes on to explain, "She was just one of them; she played whist and billiards with them, and made their cocktails for them, not scorning to take one herself, occasionally" (474). Writing from personal experience, Cather is making a case for a young woman's freedom to enjoy billiards, cocktails, and male friendship. In the description of friends conjured up from Red Cloud memories, Cather was already beginning to sketch her vision of Red Cloud for *The Song of the Lark.*

Dancing was also on her mind as she created the layers of this fictional world. The February 21, 1896, *Chief* helps us reconstruct some of Cather's recent memories with its report that Margie and Mary Miner (Cather's childhood comrades in Sandy Point), along with other "ladies of Red Cloud," had organized the Leap Year Ball held on February 14. Doctor McKeeby's name appears at the top of the list of "Messrs and Mesdames," Cather's name at the top of the list of "Misses." The *Chief* paints a romantic picture: "While the Red Cloud orchestra played strains of sweet music, nimble feet and light hearts kept perfect time" (5). We have no letter to confirm it, but readers of *The Song of the Lark* may want to imagine Cather and the "elderly" McKeeby dancing together on Valentine's Day.

Another dance that spring seems to have inspired key elements of "Tommy." In a letter to Mariel Gere back on the second of May, Cather reported driving "overland twenty miles to Blue Hill with [her brother] Douglass to a dance. It sounds giddy, but I went because the kid was wild to go" (*SLWC,* 28). At the dance, she just happened to meet "old Fred Gund, once a co-editor of the Hesperian with me. He was a cigarette smoking sport of the Sawyer gang then, but now he is a sane manly business fellow and cashier of the Blue Hill bank. He was awfully nice and devoted himself to me the whole evening and it was good to see him and talk over old times" (*SLWC,* 28). Cather went on to report that she had danced all thirty-five dances that night. One wonders whether she ever enjoyed a comparable evening of "manly" attention and extreme exertion. It was, in short, a remarkably good time that seems to have fueled a bit of daydreaming and soul-searching about a banker in Red Willow as she wrote her new story. Four years later, on the day after Christmas, Fred married Margie Miner. In a number of subtle ways, "Tommy" seems to recast and explore past, present, and future.

The author was also recalling and imagining the difference leaving home had made and would make to her perceptions of the West. Tommy has gone east for a year of college, where she followed her own course of study (like Cather) and distinguished herself in athletics as Pound had done in Lincoln.[44] The narrator tells us, "Her evident joy on getting back to Southdown was appreciated by everyone" (475). We know that leaving home helped Cather appreciate the place and its people, but the author may have been fantasizing a bit here about the community's appreciation

EVELYN Brodstone, Margie Miner, and Willa Cather, c. 1890.
Source: Archives & Special Collections, University of Nebraska–Lincoln Libraries.

for the young woman's change. Tommy elaborates, "It's all very fine down East there, and the hills are great, but one gets mighty homesick for this sky, the old intense blue of it, you know. Down there the skies are all pale and smoky. And this wind, this hateful, dear, old everlasting wind that comes down like the sweep of cavalry and is never tamed or broken. O Joe, I used to get hungry for this wind!" (475–76). With her reference to "the hills," Tommy could easily be speaking of Cather's Pittsburgh. What seems certain is that Cather, writing from Pittsburgh, is being proleptic, already imagining a homecoming in which she will share her new vision with "everyone" and be appreciated for it. The author of "On the Divide" was ready to praise the sky and the wind of the American West.

Tommy has returned home with her friend Miss Jessica, who quickly catches the eye of Harper. (A reader intent on picturing Tommy and Jessica might consider a photograph from around 1890 of Evelyn Brodstone, Margie Miner, the future Mrs. Gund, and Cather.) Instead of exploring the romantic and rather autobiographical triangle, Cather introduces a sudden calamity. Tommy gets a telegram from Harper, pleading with her to help him save his failing bank. The clock ticking, Tommy must figure out a way to get funds to Harper in time. The New Woman's good humor shines through as Tommy declares, "There is nothing left but to wheel for it" (477). In a single dramatic detail, Cather was compressing her final summer days out West and her thrilling rides through Pittsburgh streets. She may have been inspired by a (perhaps apocryphal) story about Pound.[45]

Some of Cather's readers will always identify with her delight in cycling, but more than a few of the story's first readers were probably expecting a popular story of romantic courtship while entertaining doubts about the young woman's well-being and decorum.[46] When Cather arrived in Pittsburgh that summer of 1896, the city's newspapers were offering a steady stream of articles discussing women and bicycles, raising all sorts of questions about proper clothing, posture, dangerous riding practices, courtship, etc.[47] As Jennifer Bradley points out, Cather participated in the conversation by publishing nine articles about cycling during her tenure at the *Home Monthly*, covering such concerns as damaged digestion, improved complexion, safe riding techniques, and the danger (for women) of unintended arousal.[48]

In this context, Tommy's bank-saving ride is, as Virgil Albertini points out, "heroic."[49] The narrator explains, "The road from Southdown to Red Willow is not by any means a favorite bicycle road; it is rough, hilly and climbs from the river bottoms up to the big Divide by a steady up grade, running white and hot through the scorched corn fields and grazing lands" (477). If we recall the Safety Bicycle that Tommy uses to complete this ride of twenty-five miles in less than seventy-five minutes, the feat seems truly daunting. Jessica, for her part, fails.

Tommy sums up the situation: "Poor Jess. . . . Well, your kind have the best of it generally, but in little affairs of this sort my kind come out rather strongly. We're rather better at them than at dancing. It's only fair, one side shouldn't have all' " (478). Cather's heroine seems to be making a case for a distinct identity with the phrase "my kind." In so doing, she constructs a telling opposition between bicycle riding and dancing that echoes the author's recent past, dancing the night away at the Leap Year Ball in Red Cloud and in Blue Hill with Fred Gund, the bachelor banker. Perhaps the author was saying goodbye to this memory of heterosexual dalliance.

Analyzing Jessica, who may owe something to Margie Miner, Tommy helps us understand this line of thought in literary terms: "I think the lack of romance in the escapade did her up about as much as anything; she is essentially romantic. If we had been on fiery steeds bespattered with foam I think she would have made it, but a wheel hurt her dignity" (479). Jessica would be at home in the framework of a Howard Pyle novel, but categories of *romance, romantic,* and *realistic* are too rigid for Tommy. Debra Seivert explains that "Cather subtly infuses romance with realism," allowing her "readers to experience the wonder and adventure of a romantic tale while concurrently maintaining a firm footing in reality."[50] I would agree, but also emphasize that Cather is boldly experimenting with notions of gender, identity, and sexuality.

Readers familiar with cycling fiction, expecting a story of successful courtship, must have been amazed when Tommy urges Jay to marry Jessica. The heroine tries to help the poor fellow understand: "we have been playing a nice little game, and now it's time to quit. One must grow up sometime" (479). In this experimental ending, the strong heroine's decision to give up the man is rooted in her maturity. For the young author, it was a declaration of and rationale for liberty; and it was a revelation that palimpsestic fiction could allow her to explore options for living otherwise and truly become Bergson's *artisan, creating herself continually.*[51]

Although it has received little attention, Cather's evolving relationship to Nebraska in "Tommy" deserves scrutiny in this context. In this story, the prairie is "softened" and relegated to the background as the "live western town" takes center stage.[52] Like a territorial mapmaker, Cather embeds this gentler prairie in a larger zone she calls "the West," a region that can be appreciated in all sorts of ways by the main character—especially after she has lived back East. With this palimpsestuous version of Red Cloud, Cather set out on a road that would run through *The Song of the Lark* and *My Ántonia* and on to MacAlpin, Nebraska, in "The Best Years" (1945), the last story Cather ever wrote.[53] Surrounded by metropolitan life in Pittsburgh, the young author was suddenly able to write about Nebraska with a bright spirit that complicates easy generalizations about how she had to grow out of her distaste for Nebraska.

In many ways, the emergence of talented people is an art in itself. Some people, like Cather, seem to have an instinctual sense of the elements necessary for success. As she settled in Pittsburgh, she returned to a version of life that she worked out first in Red Cloud and later in Lincoln. She was writing fiction, journalism, and letters, joining organizations, attending and reviewing concerts and theater, and riding her wheel. Stout sketches Cather's mindset at the time: "The stories she was writing during the years when she earned her living primarily as a journalist, then as a schoolteacher, and finally as a magazine editor are characterized by multiple sets of unresolved dualities: between male and female, between Nebraska and the East, between the world of art and the world of ordinary human relationships and endeavors, between art as escape and art as immersion in familiar reality."[54] A serious look at "Tommy" invites us to add to this list of dualities. Cather's Nebraska was both prairie and town. The former was populated by farmers and ranchers, the latter by would-be metropolitans who attend events at the Opera House. To make matters more complicated, Cather's Nebraska was a place in the past, a harsh world inhabited by struggling homesteaders often stuck in rigid conventions of gender. But Nebraska was also a place in the present, a vibrant world of convention breaking, boom, bust, banking, and bicycles. Nebraska, like the larger West, could always be written otherwise.

Meanwhile, Cather had a magazine to fill, and her mind returned to Brownville. "A Resurrection" appeared in the April 1897 edition of *Home Monthly.* It is a largely neglected work that Arnold describes as "a sentimental love story."[55] But I think it shows how Cather was using fiction to probe her own most pressing anxieties over intimacy, sentimentality, realism, and romance.

In "A Resurrection," Cather tells the story of a relationship lost and reborn. Years before the beginning of the story, Martin Dempster left Marjorie Pierson to run off and marry Aimée de Mar. A son was born and Aimée was soon spending all of Martin's money, on clothes and "second-rate theatre, ordering ices brought to her between the acts" (*CSF,* 432). When Aimée was found dead in the river, Martin asked Marjorie and her mother to take care of his son. As the story begins, Martin has been living in shame for years, operating the old ferry in Brownville. In what would be a rare gesture toward the eastern border of the old Kansas-Nebraska Territory for the author who preferred to look toward Denver, Cather imagines Martin returning from a trip to Kansas City with a job offer and plans for a new life.

Home Monthly readers were no doubt hooked by the romance formulas in play, but they may have been more fascinated by the narrator's ruminations about women. Noting that "Miss Margie was no longer a girl," the narrator explains that most of Margie's contemporaries had married, implying that the heroine really is "an old maid" (426). Expanding the reflection, the narrator declares: "When a woman retains much of her beauty and youthful vigor, the world, even the petty provincial world, feels a delicacy about applying to her that condemning title that when once adopted is so irrevocable" (426). The prose becomes tendentious here and may suggest the awkwardness of the woman's position.

Warming to this analysis of gender, the narrator observes that Margie's eyes "were serious and frank like a man's" (426). At this point, the paragraph takes off with a passion that exceeds the context of the story: "She was one of those women one sometimes sees, designed by nature in her more artistic moments, especially fashioned for all the fullness of life; for large experiences and the great world where a commanding personality is felt and valued, but condemned by circumstances to poverty, obscurity and all manner of pettiness. There are plenty of such women, who were made to ride in carriages and wear jewels and grace first nights at the opera" (426). Inspired by her own furious meditations on gender roles and their limitations, Cather—perhaps quite consciously—falls back on the newspapering strategies she learned in Red Cloud and Lincoln. Just as she did in the inaugural installment of "One Way of Putting It," the author inserts a vignette, a cameo characterization of Margie, along with an extended bit of moralizing on the vicissitudes of gender. In an instant, the short story form has evolved in ways that will matter to the author's later experiments in modernist juxtaposition.

Recognizing her opportunity, Cather turned to recycling and repurposing. When Martin fails to propose marriage to Margie, he goes to the river: "For the river means everything to Brownville folk; it has been at once their making and their undoing" (429). Cather inserts another vignette in the flow of her short story: "Brownville was not always the sleepy, deserted town that it is today" (429). In the *Journal,* she had written, "The town calls to mind that scathing epigram which Heine applied to de Musset, 'A young man with a brilliant past' " (*WP Vol.1,* 109). In the aforementioned paragraph from the short story, Cather offers this repurposed version: "No, the town has had a history, a brief, sad little history which recalls the scathing epigram that Herr Heine once applied to M. Alfred de Musset" (429). Like the reference to Heine, passage after passage in this little section has been snipped and adjusted, including her now characteristic treatment of the river as pathologically human. Quoting the *Journal* feature, she writes, ". . . Overcome by shame and remorse, it had been trying to commit suicide by burying itself in the sand" (430). The young editor was employing a pragmatic tactic for filling pages, but she may have already decided that the process of juxtaposing quoted material transformed both old and new. In any event, Cather's agenda is clear and powerful. In four long paragraphs, she revels in the history of territorial townmaking and the practice of newspapering.

Cather had found solid employment and a modicum of celebrity in Pittsburgh. On March 28, 1897, the *Pittsburg Press* published a tribute to "Pittsburg's Pioneers in Woman's Progress," which featured a caricature of a "Woman Editor" named Willa Cather, "a thoroughly up-to-date woman . . ." (11). In many ways, Cather's dreams had come true. She was a recognized editor, New Woman, and—in her own right—a pioneer.

Less than two months later, the magazine was sold, and Cather resigned. Returning to Red Cloud, she commenced a summer ritual that she would follow quite faithfully for more than three decades. She probably began writing "The Way of the World" at this point. Structurally, the story is quite conventional as the third-person narrator describes the rise and fall of Speckle

Burnham's backyard "town." Although she is fascinated by Cather's revisions of gender in the West, Rosowski calls the story "slight."[56]

I see the work as another landmark in Cather's life and craft for a number of reasons. Conjuring up the author's cherished memories of Sandy Point, this is the first short story that explores, from an adult perspective, the Red Cloud childhood that Cather would write about for decades to come. Echoing the palimpsestic experiments of "Tommy," Cather takes a leap forward by creating for the first time a male protagonist who is also, in certain ways, herself. This is also the story in which she begins to dabble in metafiction, using fiction to explore the making of fiction by creating a palimpsest of Red Cloud, Sandy Point, and Speckleville. The stakes were high, and she knew it.

Perhaps for this reason, she begins with her own verse, gingerly hinting at the story's complexity:

O! the world was full of the summer time,
    And the year was always June,
When we two played together
    In the days that were done too soon. (395)

The lines epitomize the sweet nostalgia of simple nineteenth-century lyrics, the kind of verse that might have been included in the *Advertiser* and the *Huntsman's Echo,* the *Argus,* and the *Chief,* just across the page from stories of booming development and boy life.

In the second stanza, Cather foregrounds gender, childhood, memory, and imagination in the realm that C. Robert Haywood has dubbed the "Victorian West."[57] The speaker remembers: "When you were the king of the cornlands / And I was a queen with you." In this region of gingerbread front porches and grasslands, piano lessons and literary societies, youthful role playing echoes Old World fancies. The final stanza offers a mythical version of the imaginative realm while putting pressure on the way we approach the story that follows:

When I could believe in the fairies still,
    And our elf in the cottonwood tree,
And the pot of gold at the rainbow's end
    And you could believe in me.

In the Victorian West, Cather can envision the "elf in the cottonwood tree," a combination unheard of in the land of Barrie and Tennyson. Of course such extraordinary pairings are possible only under special conditions: everything teeters on shared belief. The female speaker used to be able to believe in a magical world. The male speaker used to believe in her. Knowing something about Sandy Point, a reader would naturally assume that the story will be autobiographical and center on an imaginative female protagonist who inspires this belief.

Cather had other ideas. The protagonist in charge of townmaking and fancy is the boy Speckle. As we know, this kind of switching became a defining gesture in Cather's later fiction, most dramatically in *My Ántonia.* What should we make of it in this early story? Is Cather attempting a disguise or is she, in some sense, cross-dressing?[58] Perhaps she is seeking an even more complex effect, inviting her readers to explore feelings of gender fluidity. I suspect, with the story's emphasis on the way intimacy depends on shared fancy, she may be implying that masculine and feminine are nothing more or less than matters of belief.

As territorial folks recognized, the same might be said about townmaking and the craft of fiction. In prose that might have described Cather's childhood creation, the narrator explains: "In Speckle Burnham's back yard were half-a-dozen store boxes of large dimensions, placed evenly in a row against the side of the barn, and there was Speckle's empire. It had long been a cherished project of the boys on Speckle's street to collect their scattered lemonade stands and sidewalk booths and organize a community; but without Speckle's wonderful executive ability the thing would never have been possible" (395). Here are the repurposed merchant crates that Cather and her friends remembered, along with some of the mercantile enterprises. Here, too, is editorial comment on the ways of childhood: imagination without direction goes nowhere. Townmaking, even by children, requires "executive ability." The former newspaper editor and mayor of Sandy Point, having just struggled to assert her authority over *Home Monthly,* must have relished making the point—but felt she had to make the story about a boy.

In the paragraphs that follow, Cather is in no rush to engage her plot. She takes time to lovingly depict a childhood version of merchant life. We glimpse, perhaps, her view of her own backyard at 241 North Cedar Street in Red Cloud: "In the first place, Speckle had the most disreputable back yard in the community" (396). As hints in the various comments about Sandy Point imply, Speckleville was not "a transient town, such as boys often found in the morning and destroy in the evening" (396). The detail is important to the author because it suggests both more ambition and a different sort of imaginative enterprise.

The children create a virtual universe that unfolds over and over again while the citizens play defined roles. "No boy," the narrator explains, "was allowed to change his business or his place of business without due permission from the assembled council of Speckleville" (396).

With the kind of attention to detail that looks like memory, Cather's narrator goes on to describe each boy's part. Jimmy Templeton keeps the grocery store, selling cinnamon barks and soda crackers. Cather was so fond of the family name that she returned to it in "Old Mrs. Harris." Tommy Sanders runs the hardware store, which he stocks with bows and arrows and other boyhood weapons of choice. Shorty Thompson keeps a pool room, and Dick Hutchinson runs a museum, featuring his "fearless" snake demonstrations. Finally, Reinholt Birkner, the son of the town undertaker, makes "little tombstones and neat caskets for the boys' deceased woodpeckers and prairie dogs" (396). Versions of this latter character, modeled on Cather's childhood friend Rhine Birkner (1878–1946), appear in "The Treasure of Far Island" and *A Lost Lady.* In fact, Speckle joins Reinholt in the former work as Cather's writing process continued to echo and transform the virtual universe of Sandy Point.

Speckle, as Cather was in Sandy Point, is at the center of all townmaking, and Cather's autobiographical indulgence is revealing because of what it says about imagination and creativity and the beginning of her life as an artist. The narrator explains that "he had a right to be autocratic, for it was Speckle's fecund fancy more than his back yard that was the real site of that town, and his imagination was the coin current of the realm" (397). It hardly needs to be remarked, at this juncture, that Speckle has much in common with the first white settlers of Nebraska. At the same time, the author's use of the older term "fancy" suggests that Speckle is a compatriot of the Romantics. Sounding a bit like Samuel Taylor Coleridge, the narrator observes, "For Speckle, by a species of innocent hypnotism, colored the mental visions of his fellow townsmen until his fancies seemed weighty realities to them" (397). Thanks to their leader, the residents of Speckleville share the kind of magical belief alluded to in the opening poem.

Gender complicates imagination and craft in Speckleville. The narrator tells how the town thrived until *one day* . . . "Mary Eliza Jenkins had peered at them through the morning-glory vines on her back porch and had envied these six male beings their happiness" (397). David and Bathsheba. Acteon and Diana. Peeping Tom and Lady Godiva. The Old World liked to tell stories about male voyeurs and the harsh consequences of their actions. In this opening complication, Cather reverses the gender roles and introduces a theme of voyeurism that would fascinate her throughout her career.[59] With the intrusion of "Peering Mary" in this backyard paradise, Cather begins to blend past and present, her childhood memories and her professional doubts, exploring questions of gender and creativity she could not resolve in journalism. When the other boys make it clear that they do not want any girls in their town, Speckle finds himself "wondering whether Mary Eliza could meet the large demands on the imagination requisite to citizenship in Speckleville. He was not wholly certain as to the enduring qualities of feminine imagination, but he did not know exactly how to express his doubts, so he remained silent" (399). In this passage, the author has imposed her ruminating spirit on the mind of her youthful avatar, recalling the columnist who declared, "I have not much faith in women in fiction." It is as if Cather were trying to travel back in time to her own primal scene of imaginative triumph in search of answers.

Platting and plotting come easily, but distinctions between boy and girl are fraught. Recalling how Mary Eliza "deposed Speckle" (400), the narrator explains, "For all boys will admit that there are some girls who would make the best boys in the world—if they were not girls" (401). Cather may have been convinced at this juncture that the imagination she admired most was masculine. Boy life seemed to explain the origins of this capacity, and Cather probably chafed at the fact that she could not claim her "boyhood" with the confidence of her heroine Tommy. Trying to reconcile her notions of imagination, creation, and career with her culture's assumptions about gender, Cather remained uneasy and perhaps a bit misogynistic.[60]

Of course, the old territorial folk knew only too well that townmaking in the West was always a fraught business. So, it seems fitting that the story's finale comes straight from what Cather called Nebraska's "first cycle": "Under Speckle's very eyes his town vanished as many another western town has done since then" (404). In her beloved feature on Brownville a few years earlier, Cather had written, "It is almost unheard of to find a town in Nebraska that has a past" (103). Speckle's town fits this description, but Cather's cherished archetype of Sandy Point does not. In writing this story, she gave her seemingly vanished creation a past, present, and future.

Cather was ready to move forward with a career that would inevitably flower east of the Mississippi. On September 7, she wrote to Jones to report that the *Pittsburgh Leader* had offered her a job and she would soon be heading back to Pittsburgh. Cather confessed,

> I almost hate to go just now. Have been writing stories and getting on at it better than I have ever been able to do before. But I don't dare let this chance slip. Somehow though I can do better work in stories down

> here than anywhere. I do the society act too much in Pittsburgh. They don't often "take a stranger in" down there and I am as vain as all the rest of my sex and can't do the hermit act one bit. But dear me there is next summer and a lot of summers ahead (*SLWC,* 45).

In this remarkable piece of self-analysis, Cather puts many aspects of her emergence into perspective. She clearly had real artistic ambition in 1897, but professional journalism with a more stable income and a certain amount of prestige called to her just as strongly. In ways that would persist throughout her career, Cather already associated the writing of fiction with summer and travel. Her sense of her career already seemed to stretch out across "a lot of summers," distinct little phases of creativity and respite over a long life. Finally, Nebraska was much more than a focus for her writing in 1897. It was the ideal place for writing.

Back in Pittsburgh, she became the new day telegraph editor, taking cables from foreign correspondents and turning them into articles for the newspaper (*WCLL,* 131). In an October 13, 1897, letter to Louise Pound, she called her new position "an experiment" (*SLWC,* 47). The work was intense, and her year was remarkable. She met the young composer Ethelbert Nevin, and a serious relationship developed, even though Nevin was married (*WCLL,* 131–33). In August 1898 she went home to Red Cloud, where she soaked up family life. Among other activities, she and Roscoe set off on a shooting trip to the Big Horn Mountains of Wyoming, an important early trip that inspired her interest in the West beyond Nebraska.

Cather was, in many ways, beginning a new period of experimentation, casting about for the next important work and more ambitiously for her real purpose as a writer. In letters to her friends back in Nebraska she complained of loneliness. Then one unforgettable evening, Cather met Isabelle McClung, and the two quickly became inseparable. Lewis writes that McClung's "friendship with Willa Cather gave her life the direction and absorbing interest it had lacked" (*WCL,* 53). From this moment on, Cather's life had an emotional center, but she was still quite unclear about how her professional life should unfold. Perhaps because it increased her self-confidence, her relationship with McClung emboldened Cather to experiment more freely in the coming months.

In this frame of mind, she wrote a bad play entitled "The Westbound Train," but she also wrote "Eric Hermannson's Soul," the story of a happy fiddle-playing Norwegian who joins a grim group of fundamentalist Christians known as the Free Gospellers. Eric gives up his fiddle and his happiness until he meets

Margaret Elliot, a beautiful, passionate, and sophisticated young woman from back East who has come out West with her brother Wyllis for an adventure.

The story was published in *Cosmopolitan,* and Bennett calls it "her first important one" (*WWC,* 198). Woodress believes that it "marks a clear advance in her narrative skill" (*WCLL,* 145). It also marks a kind of experimental fruition in the young author's career. Arnold calls it "a significant piece of work" and "an important forerunner of Cather's prairie novels."[61] David Stouck points to the distinctive way that "mythic allusions are apotheosized in the Nebraska landscape."[62] Cather may have fumbled about with drama that summer, but she was more than ready to recast the short story form in the service of romance, realism, and Nebraska. In so doing, she began to write convincingly about the West through Old World frames, deftly invoking music and painting in ways that would become central to her mature fiction.

Drawing upon her journalistic experience, Cather divided "Eric Hermannson's Soul" into three sections. The first section offers an elaborated vignette of Eric's conversion, the second a sketch of brother and sister that unfolds into an equine adventure, and the third an aperçu of a country dance that unwinds as romance. The result has something in common with both "Tommy" and "A Resurrection," but it points more convincingly than the previous stories toward structural innovations down the road.

In a number of telling ways, the opening section of "Eric" hearkens—both in theme and form—back to the first installment of "One Way of Putting It" in the *Journal.* Like several of the characters in the newspaper column, Eric loves music and performance. Like the violin player in the column and Peter in Cather's first story, Eric's love of life is symbolized by his violin and embodied in his fiddle playing.[63] Like the people in the various audiences in the first installment of "One Way of Putting It," the Gospellers crowd together, intensifying the occasion of the performance. Just as she did in that first newspaper column, Cather analyzes religious experience, freely moralizing about its motivations and effects. But this is no newspaper column. The author expands her paragraphs, flashing back to Eric's flirtation with Lena Hanson in order to give the character greater depth. The section ends dramatically with Eric smashing his violin.

However we choose to value this effort at storytelling, our estimation must increase when we view this section in the context of Cather's career and craft. Newspapering had by this point freed her to sketch a milieu, embed incidents, and be satisfied with the result as a separate and rather static artifact. At the point where simple codes of realism would encourage a closely connected expansion of Eric's story through plotting, Cather was more than willing to shift abruptly to another vignette. As it eventually would do in her greatest novels, juxtaposition stands in for action.

The reader of "Eric Hermannson's Soul" in the pages of *Cosmopolitan* probably did not feel this effect in the first paragraph of the second section as Cather gestures toward romance: "For more than two years Eric Hermannson kept the austere faith to which he had sworn himself, kept it until a girl from the East came to spend a week on the Nebraska Divide" (362). Cather even adds a bit of generic framing to explain her shift. Margaret Elliot, the narrator explains, "had no business to be in the West at all; but ah! across what leagues of land and sea, by what improbable chances, do the unrelenting gods bring to us our fate!" (362). For centuries, writers of romances have been liberated by "improbable chances" in the worlds they describe. The appearance of a dragon, for instance, can free the author to do all sorts of things with the plot. Cather is claiming exactly this kind of license when she introduces Margaret, making the great territorial expanse the foundation for a distinctly Western version of the old literary form.

Then, just as she has negotiated a smooth generic transition between segments, Cather shifts in the next paragraph to sibling vignettes: "It was in a year of financial depression that Wyllis Elliot came to Nebraska to buy cheap land and revisit the country where he had spent a year of his youth. When he had graduated from Harvard it was still customary for moneyed gentlemen to send their scapegrace sons to rough it on ranches in the wilds of Nebraska or Dakota" (363). This is the classic story of the young Easterner abroad in the West, perhaps nodding back to Theodore Roosevelt's *Winning of the West* and to Roosevelt's brother Elliot, but with no obvious connection to Eric Hermannson's story of conversion.[64] The vignette leads into a portrait of the young man's sister, and Cather seizes on the opportunity to write once more about female types: "It comes to all women of her type—that desire to taste the unknown which allures and terrifies, to run one's whole soul's length out to the wind—just once" (363). As O'Brien has so astutely noticed, the young author liked to use "the brother-sister relationship to question the culture's polarization of 'masculine' and 'feminine' " (*WCEV*, 262). Structurally, this kind of questioning and moralizing only heightens the sense of the segmented story.

At this juncture, Cather might have moved on toward another portrait, but she was intent on writing the West otherwise. In an extended conversation between Margaret and Wyllis, we see Nebraska in new ways as they sit "on the wide piazza of the ranchhouse, staring out into the afternoon sunlight and protesting against the gusts of hot wind" (364). Returning to the vista she had first described in "On the Divide" and echoing the first white settlers' desire for panoramas, Cather attempts something different here. Anyone familiar with the early story would expect to read about endless prairie, dashed hopes, and suicide. But this is not the early settlement period. This ranch has a *piazza*.

Viewed from the perspective of these young, well-educated Easterners, Nebraska and Nebraskans look different. Wyllis explains, "This wind is the real thing; you don't strike it anywhere else. You remember we had a touch of it in Algiers and I told you it came from Kansas. It's the keynote of this country" (364). Viewed through the worldly eyes of Wyllis, the wind is territorial, rising up from Kansas. Instead of provoking despair, this wind inspires admiration, inviting exotic comparisons and inspiring wonder. Edward and Lillian Bloom have recognized that Cather needed to discover and refine this perspectival approach in order to write well about Nebraska, pointing to "The Enchanted Bluff" (1909) as an "early" example.[65] But it should be pointed out that Cather's discovery was rooted in the Red Cloud newspaper accounts of birds and blizzards, wind and sand, she read during her youth, and her experimentation with it was already evident in this story from 1900.

In this territorial frame, the author returns to her cherished theme of suicide on the prairie, but she takes up the idea through music. Margaret recalls hearing about the suicide of Eric's cousin. Then she recalls how she sang *Cavalleria Rusticana* for Eric: "It's queer to sing familiar things here at the world's end' " (365). She goes on to explain that the performance actually "gave him [Eric] speech, he became alive' " (366). Eric may inhabit a "cultural desert," but a rare traveler from the East can make a withered life blossom because the beauties of the Old World continue to resonate even at "the world's end."

Having grown up in Red Cloud, where musical education and performance were valued, Cather was recognizing that this gesture toward an opera by Mascagni was in the right key. She knew that Nebraskans like herself were quite capable of making such connections and feeling them deeply. But the presence of cultured Easterners in her story gave her a rationale for including this material. It looks less like affectation and more like studied realism. The insight into her craft was clear: music could serve as a bridge between the world and the parish, between the Old World and the New, between the East and the West. The author had only to exploit it.

At this point, the vignette and the dialogue could stand as a complete section in the story, but Cather experiments. She shifts to another scene, elegantly expanding her story's arc. Eric escorts Margaret on an evening ride "through the most attractive part of the Divide country" (368). The presence of the two young people on horses transforms the territory for the narrator, and the equine effect should not be underestimated. We need to remember that one of Cather's most cherished memories of her first months on the prairie (central to her public myth of growing up on a ranch in the West) was riding her pony Dude over the Divide. In this passage, as Cather imagines a scene of both sentiment and action, she is recollecting these fine memories of Nebraska, marking the recollection, time and again, by referring to Margaret's "pony."

In this romantic setting, Margaret wants to gallop. They set off, and Cather attempts (to borrow her phrasing for the technique) *to get into the skin* of the young man as he watches Margaret ride (*WCP,* 10). After suggesting how men of letters would describe the young woman, the narrator turns to Eric: "To him this beauty was something more than color and line; it was a flash of white light, in which one cannot distinguish color because all colors are there. To him it was a complete revelation, an embodiment of those dreams of impossible loveliness that linger by a young man's pillow on midsummer nights" (370). Scholars call this technique, of suddenly seeing through a character's eyes, focalization, but the terminology only begins to mark the depth of the seeing. Here, in one of her best early stories set in Nebraska, Cather is attempting what she would do with genuine brilliance in a mature work such as *One of Ours:* the author is giving language to a person of great sensitivity who would never have the words to share his discriminating perceptions.[66]

Not content with this stunning effect, Cather sets her sights on real action. Perhaps she was haunted by the words of her 1895 *Courier* diatribe: "When a woman writes a story of adventure, a stout sea tale, a manly battle yarn, anything without wine, women and love, then I will begin to hope for something great from them, not before" (277). In the summer of 1899, Cather was ready to better the "stout sea tale" with Western adventure, while refusing to abandon her interest in "women and love." Suddenly engulfed in a herd of wild horses, Margaret's pony goes mad. In an echo of Canute's famous struggle in "On the Divide," man battles horse, and man prevails. Eric declares, "I am not a coward; I was afraid because I love you more than Christ who died for me, more than I am afraid of hell, or hope for heaven" (372). The man has found words through action. It is a common enough turn of events in fiction, but it was not Cather's instinctive mode of writing. She had to learn how to do it in her own way, and this story shows her making progress.

In a masterful and rather operatic touch, Cather brings her story together with a dance and a windmill. Again, the author begins with a vignette, and even allows herself (what she once called) a "purple passage": "To-night there was hot liquor in the glass and hot blood in the heart; to-night they danced" (375). Eric is unafraid and Margaret passionately confused. So the two young people leave the dance and climb the windmill. Readers familiar with European romance will be surprised by this turn of events, but the narrator explains that she is simply describing life out West: "Since the older folk had begun dancing, the young Norwegians had been slipping out in couples to climb the windmill tower into the cooler atmosphere, as is their custom" (375). Romantic windmill climbing is a prairie custom, and it certainly makes sense as a final act in the story.

Of course Cather is also writing about emergence on the Great Plains. The narrator offers an interpretation: "The woman, on a windmill tower at the world's end with a giant barbarian, heard that cry tonight, and she was afraid! Ah! the terror and the delight of that moment when first we fear ourselves! Until then we have not lived" (377). It is a moment of psychological insight worthy of Henry James. And even in Nebraska, stamped as "the world's end," they have begun to live. The next morning, Margaret leaves, and Eric is unrepentant before the leader of the Gospellers.

The story succeeds on its own, but it becomes even more fascinating when we see the author's hand rearranging her memories of Nebraska. Six years earlier, she and her brother Roscoe had been climbing the windmill on her Uncle George and Aunt Franc's farm. In a letter to Mariel Gere on August 1, 1893, Cather reported, "It was great on calm evenings. We could see for miles and miles, see 'right off the edge of the world' as Ross said" (*SLWC,* 20). It is suddenly easy to see how Cather's brother shifts back and forth as a model for Wyllis *and* Eric in this story. Like Wyllis and Margaret, Roscoe and Cather were travel companions, having taken the hunting trip to Wyoming in 1898. Like Eric and Margaret, Roscoe and Cather indulged in windmill climbing, but Cather's accretive imagination is even more fluid. After reading her letter to Gere, we know where Margaret's sense of Nebraska as the "edge of the world" comes from. Her seemingly feminine and decidedly Eastern sensibility that helps to engender an aura of romance over Nebraska owes something to the language of Cather's brother Roscoe.

Now, if we really want to grasp Cather's vertiginous sense of gendered adventure in this story, we need to notice the bit of Cather in each of her main characters. At this point in her career, having lived and traveled east of the Mississippi, she felt she saw Nebraska through the eyes of Wyllis.[67] At the same time, she understood Eric's interior life because she knew what it was like to have feelings for art and people that would not be understood. Finally, like Margaret, she knew what it meant to seek adventure in the West as a woman—and she really did long for the "one thing," the one moment.

In April 1900, when "Eric Hermannson's Soul" appeared in *Cosmopolitan,* it must have been a heady experience. Woodress, noting that Cather was clearly "getting tired of daily journalism," suggests that the appearance of the story gave her courage to quit her job at the *Leader* (*WCLL,* 144). Another person might have settled down to produce new versions of the successful story, but not Cather. A distinct and restless phase of her career was commencing.

At some point during this period, she wrote "El Dorado: A Kansas Recessional," which eventually appeared in the *New England Magazine* in June. "El Dorado" tells the story of Virginian Josiah Bywaters' final days in the Kansas town of El Dorado. It is a story of early settlement like "Peter" and "On the Divide," a narrative focus quite distinct from the settings of "Tommy" and "Eric Hermannson's Soul." This story recalls how the unscrupulous Apollo Gump conned investors in the town, including Bywaters. On the day of the story, Gump returns in the midst of a terrible thunderstorm to reclaim the money he has buried on the prairie. Lightning flashes through the pouring rain. The conman digs—until he is bitten by a rattlesnake. The next morning, Bywaters finds the dead man and the money. The Virginian sets fire to his store and rides away.

Although Cather did not, in later years, want scholars to study the story, "El Dorado" rewards examination because of the way the author engages the territorial imagination. As Thacker points out, the author is clearly struggling "to come to terms with the prairie, to pioneer the prairie through her art" (*GPF,* 148). In previous stories, she happily renamed Red Cloud, while faithfully invoking the Divide and Nebraska by name. In "On the Divide," she nodded to the territorial vision by noting (as Red Cloud newspaper editors liked to do) that the parching wind came up from Kansas. These moves were all "Kansas-Nebraska acts," literary gestures that echoed territorial habits.

Cather sets her story in the Solomon Valley of Kansas, a region that looks very much like Webster County. In fact, Red Cloud sits at 98°31'22"W, while the western source of the Solomon River in Kansas lies at 98°26'0"W. Yet Cather's narrator is adamant that this story is about Kansas: "People who have been so unfortunate as to have traveled in western Kansas will remember the Solomon Valley for its unique and peculiar desolation" (*CSF,* 293). In case we miss the point, the author refers to Kansas sixteen times, and her sense of purpose is clear: "But he [Bywaters] had come West, worse than that, he had come to western Kansas, even to the Solomon Valley, and he must abide the consequences" (295).

Like their counterparts in Brownville, Kansans were not pleased by Cather's depiction of their world. Vehemently denying the portrayal, a writer for the Kansas City *Journal* lamented that the female author "according to the chivalrous code of western Kansas, cannot be killed or scalped."[68] Perhaps it goes without saying that a streak of invidiousness runs through the territorial imagination.

Students of Cather's early Nebraska stories will recognize familiar strategies. The narrator describes the Solomon River: "Never having been a notably ambitious stream, in time it grew tired of giving its strength to moisten barren fields and corn that never matured" (293). As she does in her stories of Brownville, Cather anthropomorphizes the river, which flows through a desolate landscape that looks a lot like the topography of "On the Divide": "The flat plains rolled to the unbroken horizon vacant and void, forever reaching in empty yearning toward something they never attained" (294).

Up to this point in her career, Cather had little to say about agriculture. Now, she takes a long look at the miserable corn, which she frames with Old World ornamentation: "Nature always dispenses with superfluous appendages; and what use had Solomon Valley corn for tassels? Ears were only a tradition there, fabulous fruits like the golden apples of Hesperides; and many a brawny Hercules had died in his own sweat trying to obtain them" (294). Kansas may be the grimmest of Great Plains settings, but it is ennobled by the same classical frame of reference that applies to Nebraska. Infused with the spirit of the ancient world, the corn joins the river in expressing its pain: "Sometimes, in the dusk of night . . . the dry little corn leaves whispered to each other that once, long ago, real yellow ears grew in the Solomon Valley" (294). Agriculture meets gothic in a moment that suggests the hand of a young writer experimenting with literary registers.

Cather may have found models of this reverie in the pages of Red Cloud newspapers. The September 29, 1881, *Argus* included a poem called "The Corn and the Lilies" that opens, "Said the Corn to the Lilies . . ." (2). In the summer of 1893, banks were failing and the drought was growing worse. On June 9, the *Golden Belt*, a recent addition to the newspapering world of Webster County, reported the failure of the Kansas Grain Company (1). Then, on July 28, in addition to reviewing the recent Blind Boone concert, the *Belt* included this report from nearby Cowles: "Give me water or I die says the corn in this locality" (4). Whether Cather read these words or not is less important than the recognition that this Kansas-Nebraska "belt" was imbued with its own imaginative approach to storytelling. In Webster County, talkative vegetation really did define a locality.

It is in this context that we meet Bywaters and Gump in cameo vignettes. The narrator tells us that there is something respectable in the appearance of the Virginian: "His appearance was not that of the average citizen of western Kansas" (294). Describing Bywaters's situation, the narrator explains, "The tide of emigration had gone out and had left him high and dry, stranded on a Kansas bluff" (295). Gump, who introduced himself "as Mr. Apollo Gump of Kansas" (296), is a version of those unscrupulous territorial townmakers who conjured up metropolitan fictions all over the Kansas-Nebraska Territory, bilking good people out of their money.

The author who would one day write her own history of Nebraska for the *Nation* positions her protagonist so he can meditate on the future of prairie settlement. She gets inside his skin, and what she finds there is not a rational appraisal of Great Plains homesteading but the embittered thoughts of a damaged venturer: "he wondered whether some day the whole grand delusion would not . . . vanish utterly and completely, as a bubble that bursts, as a dream that is done" (303). It is a bitter passage that captures the feelings of many failed dreamers. The rumination concludes with an emphatic statement of territorial blame: "He hated western Kansas" (303). In Cather's Kansas, emotions (unlike rivers) run deep. Loneliness, hatred, and despondency pervade the region.

This is how Cather divides the old Kansas-Nebraska Territory in "El Dorado." What would appear largely homogenous to most observers, the writer separates into a *here* and an *elsewhere* called *Kansas.* The valley becomes a vessel for negativity otherwise associated with the territory as a whole. She creates a perfect vignette to make the point. When a creaking wagon pulls up to the store, Bywaters listens to an ailing mother trying to get her family back to Missouri: "We moved there ten years ago, when the country was lookin' mighty green and purty. It's all done burnt up long ago. It's that dry we couldn't raise any garden stuff there these three years" (305). In this anecdote, Kansas is a brown "there" where nothing will grow. Like a territorial mapmaker, Cather was in charge of coloring this map. Ultimately, "Kansas" becomes recessional, a mythical realm where people yield to prairie hardships. In this fantastic territory, rivers meditate, corn whispers, and uncertainty looms like a funnel cloud. In such a region, one might think of geography as "an implacable and malevolent fate."[69] Perhaps a landscape becomes less threatening when we can divide it on our own terms?

At the end of the story, Bywaters burns his store and rides away, "never once casting back a look at the last smoking ruin of El Dorado" (310). It is an operatic ending, a fantasy of Western escape, that must have delighted the author. Cather may have repudiated the story later, but at the time she enjoyed it. Writing to George Seibel in July of that year, she reported: "I had a story in the June 'New England Magazine' that I would like you to read if you have time. My mother has basely filched all my copies and sent them to deaf great-aunts etc, but perhaps you'll have time to look it up at the Library some day."[70]

In February of 1901, Cather's mind turned to education. A month later, she moved in with the McClung family back in Pittsburgh and began teaching at Central High School. Cather clearly loved her life with Isabelle, but love did not diminish the workload. She was soon complaining to Canfield: "The first month of teaching is at an end and I have about decided to let some one else take up the good work for the rest of the year. I want to go home to Red Cloud and work for awhile."[71] Cather's professional life was in flux. She was capable of writing good things and weak things, and it was not always clear that she knew the difference.

Through it all, one notion always returned: "I want to go home to Red Cloud." When school was over, she did indeed go home, where she confided to George Seibel: "I arrived home two weeks ago very much worn out by the years hard work, and am not feeling much rested yet. I am twenty pounds thinner than when you saw me last. I dont object to that but I do object to the good for nothing feeling that comes with it."[72] Cather was exhausted, but she was home again, where she wanted to be.

The feeling became more complex one Friday night in August when Cather went down to the depot to join the friends of Amos Cowden waiting for the arrival of his body on the night express. With alacrity, the August 2 *Chief* (appearing in the afternoon) reported his death that morning from a mysterious illness and announced his return that night. Cather was moved. Like Cather, Cowden had seen his activities described in the pages of the local papers for years. The August 4, 1893, *Chief* had let everyone know that "Amos Cowden returned Tuesday from his trip abroad with the phonograph" (5). The July 26, 1895, *Chief* had reported his wheeling up to Blue Hill to watch a baseball game with friends (5). Describing Cowden's sudden death from a mysterious illness, the *Chief* declared: "Amos had a host of friends in this city who will be sorry to hear of his death" (5).

It required no great leap of imagination for Cather to see her own life summed up in one of the *Chief*'s columns. As Bennett reports, Cather "heard comments to the effect that the boy 'didn't amount to much anyway' and that 'he was a cigarette fiend' " (*WWC*, 198). She must have imagined the kinds of things the editors would say about her. The effect of the little drama on Cather was electric. Like the visit to Brownville, it was the kind of experience that she would go on to recycle and repurpose in her writing for years to come.

As she did after the trip to Brownville, Cather realized that she had to capture the experience right away. She wrote "The Night Express" and "The Treasure of Far Island." It is not clear which work came first, but what seems evident is that Cather needed to write both verse and prose in order to come to terms with her experience. Published the following summer in *Youth's Companion* and the *Nebraska State Journal*, "The Night Express" begins with a striking sketch of the Great Plains that looks nothing like the barren world depicted in "On the Divide" and "El Dorado":

> From out of the mist-clad meadows, along the river shore,
> The night express-train whistles with eye of fire before.
> A trail of smoke behind her enclouds the rising moon
> That gilds the sighing poplars and floods the wide lagoon.
> Through yellow fields of harvest and waving fields of corn
> The night express-train rumbles with whistle low and lorn. (*WCAT*, 94)

The lines stretch out as though the poet can hardly begin to do justice to the lush landscape. Enjambed lines suggest the vibrancy of the scene with the moon shining on the poplars and the train passing the corn. This poet is neither revolting from the village nor struggling to come to terms with her home country. This is a poet who claims membership in the boy life of this Western town: "With restless heart of boyhood we watched that headlight when / The whistle seemed to call us to dare the world of men."

At this point, Cather could have written a proper elegy for the young man she calls a "comrade," but she is less interested in Cowden than she is in her own reaction to the drama: "Ah! let my fight be fiercer, the little time before / They bring me still and weary along the river shore." The writer might have given this declaration to a character in a story, but the poem lets her claim the fiercer fight for herself. Rattled by the sad return of Cowden's corpse, sounding like Ulysses in Tennyson's famous poem, she indulges in a bit of heroic bravado.

She also indulges in a bit of fantasy, a poetry of *what if* that presages some of her most important works on the road to *My Ántonia.* Line by line, she imagines how it will be "when I come home to rest me in the ground that nurtured me." In this vision, after a fiercer fight, "youths will watch with burning to seek the world of men." Although the ungendered "youths" and "the world of men" may imply her ongoing struggle with gender, her life will have mattered because it will inspire. And her remains will rest in the Red Cloud cemetery not so far from Cowden's grave.

Lyric poetry can be so satisfying because it makes these compact consolations possible. They serve the present moment, even if they do not really predict the future. Cather, of course, was not buried in the Red Cloud cemetery, an irony that haunts her own vision of her relationship to Nebraska. But it should be pointed out that in 1901, confronted in dramatic fashion with her own mortality on the platform of the Red Cloud depot, she was moved to celebrate the magical beauty of Webster County, imagine her own body resting "in the ground that nurtured me," and ruminate in ways that pointed to "The Sculptor's Funeral."

It was in this summer humor that she also wrote "The Treasure of Far Island," a remarkable story that appeared in *New England Magazine* the following autumn, a little more than ten years after the publication of "Peter" in *The Mahogany Tree.* Woodress describes the story as "mawkish and uncontrolled" (*WCLL,* 156), but Stouck rightly calls it "an essential story in the Cather canon, for it embodies in both emotion and dramatic incident the substance of the author's imaginative life which gave shape to the major novels."[73] Ultimately, "The Treasure of Far Island" ends this chapter because, while looking forward, it also represents the author's heartfelt attempt to look back over her life and recollect her evolution as a young artist. It is as though the woman on the wheel, more than a decade before the publication of *O Pioneers!,* were trying to say in fictional form, *this is how I became who I am in Nebraska, and this is how I return.*

"The Treasure of Far Island" returns to Douglass Burnham, Speckle from "The Way of the World," and an obvious avatar of Cather. Burnham, a successful playwright living in New York City, is going home to Empire City, a country town that looks very much like Red Cloud. Like "The Way of the World," the story sounds precisely autobiographical, until the narrator explains that twelve years have passed since our hero has last seen the town. Burnham is a famous and successful author. Once again, Cather is working with autobiographical materials while indulging in a bit of *what if.* I suppose one could call it "authorial reinvention," a little genre of fiction writing that was fast becoming one of the author's favorite options.

What if Willa Cather had already become famous? What if she had stayed away until she had become a triumphant success? Her fantasy in the story is that the writer returns to a hero's welcome and quickly rekindles his relationship with Margie Van Dyck. They revisit Far Island, which (as Bennett pointed out some time ago) is really a faithful description of the island where Cather and other Red Cloud children played near the mouth of Indian Creek on the Republican River (*WWC,* 43). At the end of the tale they are still on the island—old friends in love and oblivious to the world around them.

In counterpoint to "The Night Express," Douglass (named for one of Cather's brothers) is very much alive, scooting boyishly around a railroad car in order to see his home country as the train approaches the station. One little scene follows another, like so many intimate scenes on a colorful map of the old territory. The motion of the train focalizes the panorama, echoing early settler accounts, as Burnham's car swings "into the Republican Valley from the uplands" (*CSF,* 266). The narrator easily slips into Burnam's senses: "As the train rumbled over a trestle built above a hollow grown up with sunflowers and ironweed, he sniffed with delight the rank odor, familiar to the prairie-bred man" (266). This is Cather's familiar experience, inflected through the eyes of the "prairie-bred" *man.*

As the train presses on, the townmaking becomes more pronounced: "Down the curve of the track he could see the old railroad 'eating house,' painted the red Burlington color; on the hill above the town the standpipe towered up from the treetops" (266). These details are hardly necessary to the story's plot, but they matter a great deal to the inventor of Sandy Point. Like the territorial colorist Whitman imagined, Cather is creating a view of the town that inspires her work. No revolt from the village, this description looks more like old-fashioned booming. The image is complete as Douglass runs "for the shabby little street car which ever since he could remember had been drawn by mules that wore jingling bells on their collars" (267). The passage recalls the streetcar in Red Cloud that was necessary because of the way the railroad had divided the town years before. Cather calls attention to the hero's memory in this sentence—almost as if she needed to advertise her mental process in the telling. The author is obviously describing her own excitement on returning to Red Cloud, perhaps more particularly after her first year in Pittsburgh.

Across all of Cather's Nebraska fiction, this scene would become her most satisfying motif. She reinvented it in "The Sculptor's Funeral," "The Joy of Nelly Deane," "The Bohemian Girl," *My Ántonia, The Song of the Lark, One of Ours,* and "The Best Years." Cather eventually confessed her loving, even obsessive, fascination with this moment of return in her poem "Going Home

(Burlington Route)": "How smoothly the trains run beyond the Missouri; / Even in my sleep I know when I have crossed the river" (*CSP,* 806). If in her fiction Cather often returned by railroad to Red Cloud, it was because she was always returning in her dreams.

In this first version of the reverie, Cather quickly sketches a reunion. Getting off the train, Douglass sees Rhinehold Birkner—the same old Rhine who operated the tombstone business in Speckleville. We know Cather loved to indulge in the territorial pleasure of renaming, but some things were sacred. The Divide was always the Divide, and in these two stories Rhine represents the real Rhine Birkner who grew up on 61 North Seward in Red Cloud. It would be fascinating indeed to know what made Rhine so special in Cather's imaginative townmaking. Years later, Birkner appears again in *A Lost Lady* as Rheinhold Blum. Why Cather felt the need to change his name at this point is yet another mystery. But what we know for sure is that Rhine was a compass point in her vision of Red Cloud.

Perhaps it was his good heart. Bennett tells how Rhine appeared at the Miners' house when Mrs. Miner died. He offered "a large box of roses, saying: 'For your mother, from me and the boys'" (*WWC,* 168). Rhine embodied the best of boy life. Or perhaps Cather valued Rhine simply because he was there to present the roses, because he could never imagine leaving Red Cloud. In "The Treasure of Far Island," Margie explains how Rhine once went to Arizona for his health, "but his family never could tell where he was for he headed all his letters 'Empire City, Nebraska,' from habit" (277). No matter where he went, Rhine was always at home in Red Cloud and Cather felt she needed him.

Margie Van Dyck hearkens back to Margie in "A Resurrection" and Margaret in "Eric Hermannson's Soul." The name anticipates a number of other "Marg's" in later short stories, although it is not prominent in the novels.[74] In fact, at this point in Cather's evolving imagination, it is the author's favorite name for a heroine. At times, she may have been thinking of the Cathers' maid, Margie Anderson. But there was one remarkable Margie in Cather's life. Margie Miner sold tablets, pencils, and whistles from her store in Sandy Point. In the 1888 production of *Beauty and the Beast,* she played Beauty while her sister Mary played the prince and Cather the father. "Willa and Margie scorned domesticity," Bennett remarks, and it was Margie who cut her hair before Cather did (*WCW,* 173, 45).

Margie was an important childhood ally, but she was also something of a rival, a fact that biographers seem to have missed. When Cather invented Sandy Point, Margie campaigned against her for mayor. Although Bennett

MARY Miner, dressed as the Prince; Margie Miner, dressed as Beauty in production of *Beauty and the Beast.* Source: Willa Cather Pioneer Memorial Collection. Special Collections & Archives at the National Willa Cather Center Special Collections & Archives at the National Willa Cather Center in Red Cloud, Nebraska.

assures us that Margie was eventually content to serve as an alderman, the competitive act stands out in the annals of the "country town" (*WCW,* 172). And it was Margie who married Fred Gund, the Blue Hill banker who had so delighted Cather at the dance in 1896.

In Cather's story, Douglass announces Margie's complexity soon after his arrival. He asks his mother: "But is she a girl? I somehow always fancied she would grow up a man—and a ripping fine one" (268). Read in the context of the territorial imagination, this jocular question seems to echo Beecher's (aforementioned) vision of the West as a *she* rushing to *manhood.* Within this context, it adds nuance to the foreclosed rivalry between the masculine Tommy and the feminine Jessica in "Tommy, the Unsentimental," while pointing toward the tomboy Sally in *My Ántonia.* Suffice it to say, when Cather named a character "Margie," she was thinking of her childhood friend, who embodied a certain gender fluidity that inspired a mix of admiration, envy, rivalry, desire, and nostalgia. Some of this magic was surely on Cather's mind when she sent Margie Miner Gund the (aforementioned) postcard from Venice in 1908.

Another mode of recollection plays out at home when Douglass greets his mother, waiting for him on a porch—with "bittersweet vines"—that sounds exactly like the Cather home on Cedar Street. Decades away from writing about her mother in "Old Mrs. Harris," Cather keeps her sketch of Mrs. Burnham simple. The mother is distinguished by her wish to hear her son read at a reception given by Mrs. Governor. He jokingly offers to perform one of his "old stunts," and we realize that Douglass (like Cather) may have once been advertised as a "child elocutionist." The writer knows that his talents have been celebrated here in the past. With all of his Eastern sophistication, he cannot appear to take it seriously, even though he cares passionately about his welcome. Studying Cather's many homecomings, Burgess explains, "The homecomer has the option of slipping into the childhood self or of insisting that the family at least acknowledge, if not adopt, the adult self."[75] Douglass is clearly experimenting at this point in the story.

On his way to the reception, the famous author runs into the house, and Cather stages one of the more fascinating reunions in all of her fiction: "In the vestibule he bumped up against something large and splendid, then stopped and caught his breath. A woman stood in the dark by the hall lamp with a lighted match in her hand. She was in white and very tall. The match burned but a moment; a moment the light played on her hair, red as Etruscan gold and piled high above the curve of the neck and head" (270). The moment is clearly supposed to be erotic, but it sounds rather nautical as the hero *bumps* "against something large and splendid." Or is it a little experiment in human interaction, a rare moment of erotic darkness that temporarily seems to transcend sex and gender? In the next instant of flame, Douglass fathoms the situation, but the match goes out again, "leaving Douglass to wonder whether, like Anchises, he had seen the vision that should forever blind him to the beauty of mortal women" (270). The paragraph resolves itself neatly with a mythological "vision," a now characteristic nod to Old World nuance, but the complexity lingers for the reader—as it did for Cather, who in *One of Ours* sends Claude to World War I on a ship named *Anchises*.

Douglass enjoys his reading, but Cather probably enjoyed it more because she could use the occasion to describe the citizens of Empire City, who mattered to Douglass over the years, expanding on the assay she began in "Tommy." In doing so, she begins to tap directly into country town memories that were highlighted by the Red Cloud newspapers as she was growing up. For instance, the audience includes the "old deacon" who chased Douglass out of his watermelon patch (270). Cather would have remembered a memorable summer of "watermelon sniping" in 1885, when boys swam the river just to creep into the best watermelon patches.[76] She would also have remembered that some girls were just as ready as boys to demonstrate their daring. On September 18, the *Chief* complained, "The young ladies who go water mellon 'cooning' and making a peep show of other people's houses ought to be ashamed of themselves. This must not happen again" (5). As her narrator explains in "The Way of the World," some girls make the best boys and the most disruptive peeping toms, but there is more going on here. As Cather experiments with her literary town-making, echoing stories she once read in print, her characters come to life as palimpsests, figures with rich "pasts" to which she can simply allude. Down the long road of her career, this allusive and layered way of writing about people in Nebraska would pay huge dividends.

The reception is also important because it allows the author to reflect with genuine honesty on her own homecoming habits. Unlike Douglass, Cather had been making the event a yearly ritual in her life. She knew that her arrivals were hardly as momentous as the return of Douglass, but they could be newsworthy. The August 21, 1898, *Chief* reported: "Miss Willa Cather of Pittsburg, Pennsylvania, arrived in the city Tuesday evening for a visit with her parents Mr. and Mrs. C. F. Cather and other friends" (5). The winter before she wrote "The Treasure of Far Island," Red Cloudians noted in the January 4, 1901, *Chief* that "Miss Willa Cather who is now located in Washington, D. C. returned home for a visit this week" (5). The young author enjoyed this bit of notoriety and valued the people with whom she reconnected. She was still the same person who had always been conscious of her special abilities while living in Red Cloud.

Cather seems to admit her feelings in the story. The narrator reveals Douglass's conclusion that "the reading was just as stupid as he had said it would be, but his audience enjoyed it and he enjoyed his audience" (270). This seems kindly enough, but a later impression is less flattering. Douglass stays for thirty minutes after the reading, "chatting with the nice tiresome old ladies who reminded him of how much he used to like their teacakes and cookies, answering labored compliments with genuine feeling" (271). The adjectives "tiresome" and "labored" would raise a few eyebrows back home, and it is worth remarking that at this early stage in Cather's career the citizens of her hometown could be forgiven for nurturing a bit of resentment, some of it earned, some of it mere envy. Margie tells Douglass that she has followed his career in the local newspapers, which "were full of interesting details about your being so busy that you ate and got shaved at the theatre" (271). This is how Cather returned to and lived on in the larger conversation of Red Cloud.

After the reception, Douglass and Margie begin to talk about childhood and art. Although Cather had already written a great deal about art and artists in her journalism, this scene stands as her first serious exploration in fiction of the artist's emergence and it just happens to occur in a story set in her hometown. Margie demands: "I want to know how you did it" (272). When Douglass cannot follow the question, she explains, "you have done it as they used to do it in the fairy tales, without soiling your golden armor" (273). The reader might expect Douglass to tell stories or speculate about his art, but the narrator does most of the talking. It is almost as if Cather cannot share the authority, even with the character who represents her interests. Or perhaps she wants to be sure to frame the famous author's mindset with her own honest appraisal: "As he talked he felt the old sense of power, lost for many years; the power of conveying himself wholly to her in speech, of awakening in her mind every tint and shadow of vague association that was in his at the moment. He quite forgot the beauty of the woman beside him in the exultant realization of comradeship, the egoistic satisfaction of being wholly understood" (273). This feels like revelation and confession. Artists are driven by a variety of impulses, but Cather seems to suggest that the primal, "egoistic" one is all about conveying oneself wholly. Aristotle might have called it the final cause of her art. The former mayor of Sandy Point calls it "comradeship."

Turning to Margie, he manages to open up the real conversation about the origins of art. He asks, "What plays have you been playing?" (273). Margie is saddened by the question, quickly reminding him that she has grown older in Nebraska and long ago stopped playing. Douglass responds, "I don't believe it, you play still, I can see it in your eyes" (273). Cather has reached her formula. Imagination becomes creativity and merges with craft when artists remember how to play.

And the artist's best sense of play comes from her memories of childhood. To make the point, Douglass begins to reminisce about the cattails in the "Salt Marshes." Margie remembers her fancy of smelling the salty air along the river in the middle of Nebraska. She wonders why they called them Salt Marshes in the first place. Douglass offers an answer quite in keeping with the territorial imagination: "Because they were the Salt Marshes, and couldn't have had any other name any more than Far Island could" (274). Peck is surely right to emphasize Emerson's influence here and conclude that "Cather was able to justify her own acquisition of Nebraska for her art."[77] More than anything else, the founder of Speckleville, like the founder of Sandy Point, has confidence in his power to rename the outward objects on the Great Plains. It is the supreme confidence of the child, the territorial settler, and the artist.

Romantic reunion and artistic manifesto come together in this scene as Cather anticipates the final part of the story. Douglass explains to Margie that he has come home after finding one of their old maps that promised "great treasure and his heart's desire" to anyone digging at the right spot on the tenth of June (274). The magical day is a week from Friday. Douglass tells Margie that they will set out for the island.

Romance has always depended on deferral, a fact that Cather understood perfectly. So she postpones the adventure as Douglass walks "about the old town, treading the ways he trod when he was a founder of cities and a leader of hosts" (275). With this bit of plotting and platting as her frame, Cather offers another manifesto that deserves mention alongside her famous essay "The Novel Démeublé":

> A child's normal attitude toward the world is that of the artist, pure and simple. The rest of us have to do with the solids of this world, whereas only their form and color exist for the painter. So, in every wood and street and building there are things, not seen of older people at all, which make up their whole desirableness or objectionableness to children. There are maps and pictures formed by cracks in the walls of bare and unsightly sleeping chambers which make them beautiful (275).

In this striking passage, Cather is answering, in part, the question that has haunted so many of her sophisticated critics: how does a girl raised in a small town in Nebraska at the end of the nineteenth century become a major figure in the canon of American literature? The mature artist must be able to tap into the "child's normal attitude."

With the kind of bracing honesty that could make the folks back home uncomfortable, the narrator concludes that for children "people and places alike were merely stage properties, contributing more or less to the intensity of their inner life" (276). O'Brien has pointed out that Cather promoted two models of the artist in her journalism of the 1890s—the heroic warrior and the divine creator (*WCEV,* 147). "The Treasure of Far Island" offers a third model that applies to artists no matter where they come from: the artist child.

The problem, of course, is how to keep this awareness living. At the end of her first decade of fiction writing, Cather had discovered an answer.

Writing to Canfield back on October 10, 1899, the author described her return to Pittsburgh: ". . . Isabelle met me, looking as though all the frieze of the Parthenon ought to be tripping after her, and I began to have a better opinion of Pittsburgh. She's so darned good to me that she's making me positively kiddish. She'll have me playing with dolls next."[78] Great love can make a person "kiddish" enough to create great art.

At this point, Cather could easily have transitioned from manifesto to adventure. She could have written, *The week passed slowly . . .*, or something like it. But she breaks the story into a second segment at this point, and the move highlights her evolving notions of literary creation. Cather is pursuing a more complex notion of composition that depends on the kind of abutments that playwrights traditionally create as they move from scene to scene and from act to act. Perhaps it is no coincidence that the artist figure in this important story who resembles Cather in so many ways just happens to be a playwright. The author of "The Westbound Train" would never compete with Douglass Burnham for space on a stage, but she certainly shared his understanding of imagination and craft.

To heighten the sense of juxtaposed parts, Cather returns to a now familiar technique, framing each segment with verse, once again suggesting that the two genres are linked in some sort of generative fashion. But rather than use her own poetry, she opens the story with lines from Robert Louis Stevenson's "Where Go the Boats":

> Dark brown is the river,
>   Golden is the sand.
> It flows along for ever,
>   With trees on either hand. (265)

As she did in "The Way of the World," Cather is using verse to invite the reader to cross a threshold into a realm of nostalgia. In this case, however, the poetry comes from a famous poet who lends an aura of authority to the nostalgia. Indeed, many of the story's readers would have recognized the poem from *A Child's Garden of Verses* (1885) and would have been able to supply the final stanza:

> Away down the river,
>   A hundred miles or more,
> Other little children
>   Shall bring my boats ashore.[79]

With the imprimatur of Stevenson, Cather frames her story with a thesis: the children who come after will carry on the imaginative journey, but they will always be "other."

Cather, I think, is ready to reverse these expectations dramatically. What if adults, with the right amount of imagination, can have a second act—even in Nebraska? Cather underscores her bold notion by framing the final part of the story with the second stanza of Stevenson's poem:

> Green leaves a-floating,
>   Castles of the foam,
> Boats of mine a-boating—
>   Where will all come home?

These are lines of elaboration, opening up the initial, nostalgic meditation. Instead of closure and plodding, inevitable continuation, they hint at possibilities—as second acts usually do. Perhaps Cather, having grown up in a world shaped by freewheeling territorial divisions, had come to associate division with opportunity. With a kind of religious zeal, she understood by this point in her life that every end announced a beginning.

She captures the joy of this understanding at the beginning of the second section with Douglass singing the lines from Stevenson as their boat slips into the river's current. When the boat runs upon the sand, he is thinking of *The Tempest* as he invites "Miranda" to disembark. The arrival, Douglass claims, is its own fantastic performance with all the attendant exhilaration. He declares, "None of my first nights have given me anything like it" (278). All art may be a mere shadow of what we once accomplished as children, but we may still have the power to revisit islands and enact new scenes.

Like Shakespeare before her, Cather is also thinking—one could argue for the first time in her Nebraskan fiction—of pastoral. Nodding back to Hesiod, Theocritus, and the Virgil she had studied in her youth while elaborating on the territorial pastoral of Gilpin and Colton, the two characters enter a liminal space of green seclusion, idleness, and pleasure. In his important discussion of pastoral in Cather's fiction, Stouck calls it "a retreat expressing man's dream of a simplified, harmonious existence from which the complexities of society and natural process (age, disease, and death) are eliminated. The passage of time in activity gives way to a kind of Epicurean leisure time or *otium.* Mythically, pastoral seeks to recover a 'Golden Age' when existence was ideally ordered. . . ."[80] Structurally, pastoral unfolds as a series of idylls, brief and relatively static scenes of rustic delight. As Shakespeare made abundantly clear in plays such as *A Midsummer Night's Dream* and *As You Like It,* the pastoral space is marked by transformation, play, and erotic dalliance. As Richard Giannone reminds us, it is often tinged with elegy.[81] When she hit upon pastoral, Cather's craft began to evolve in striking ways.

Everything depends on the imagination. Margie confides that their childhood "imaginings" seem like "realities, things that I actually lived through" (280). Douglass opines, "To people who live by imagination at all, that is the only life that goes deep enough to leave memories. We were artists in those days, creating for the day only; making epics sung once and then forgotten, building empires that set with the sun" (280). It is hard to imagine that the former mayor of Sandy Point and creator of Empire City could be any more earnest as she wrote these words. More than simply reiterating the notion that children are artists, she is extending the conversation from the first part of the story. Memories, in and of themselves, may be works of art.

The implications of this statement mean everything to a faithful reading of Cather's emergence. If the memories that matter are works of art, then Cather has just explained how she wrote "The Treasure of Far Island." The story is art made of art about art. Perhaps even more important to the author was the implicit (almost Jungian) notion that adults must know how to redeploy and rearrange these artifacts if they want to live satisfying lives. Cather had been doing precisely this with Isabelle McClung ever since she moved into the McClung household.

Inspired in this way, Douglass tells Margie, "If there is to be any Eden on earth again for us, dear, we must make it with our two hearts" (281). The result looks very much like the end of a traditional romance: "As her eyes and then her lips met his in the dying light, he knew that she had caught the spirit of the play, and that she would ford the river by night with him again and never be afraid" (282). Rooted in memory and imagination, Douglass and Margie's feelings seem worthy and genuine. It seems crotchety, then, to follow Woodress and denounce the story as "mawkish." I would rather follow Stouck, who describes the ending as "brilliantly ambiguous" and the effect "wholly moving."[82]

For her part, Cather leaves her lovers together on the island, ending the tale by noting that the "dinner hour in Empire City was long past" (282). No conventions have been shattered, and we know that Margie and Douglass realize they cannot remain on the island forever. But the narrator also makes it clear that these two adults do not have to obey the old conventions. There are advantages to growing up with imagination.

Growing old, for Cather, would be much harder. Decades later in *The Professor's House,* Godfrey St. Peter tells his wife, "it's been a mistake, our having a family and writing histories and getting middle-aged. We should have been picturesquely shipwrecked together when we were young" (92). I suspect that Douglass and Margie crossed Cather's mind as she wrote these words.

This is how Cather ended her first decade of serious fiction writing. In matters of craft, the importance of the decade cannot be overestimated. Far from damaging her writing, the early fiction and poetry allowed the author to experiment in ways that would be essential to her ultimate success. She deployed old territorial strategies of naming and division. She discovered the power of allusion in a Western setting. Embedding and juxtaposing stories like a country town newspaper editor, she tinkered with simple arrangement until it became artistic composition. She experimented with gender.

Through it all, Cather was never "overcoming Nebraska." Although it is tempting to identify a precise moment when Cather changed her mind about her home country, she was (in fact) always returning to it physically and imaginatively for inspiration. She wrote about Nebraska as the West, and she liked to write there. In some stories, she was foregrounding hardship, indulging in hyperbole about suicides on the Divide. On other occasions, she was celebrating the wild character of the place, its wind or its heat. Or she was exploring the imaginative possibilities of the place. It does not seem to have occurred to her during this period that the village should inspire a "revolt."

Ultimately, Cather was never writing about a single "Nebraska" during this decade. In fact, she was writing about at least three distinct versions of her home country. The first version is the harsh prairie world of early settlement that we find in "Peter," "On the Divide," and "El Dorado." The second version is the "live western town" of the 1880s and 1890s that appears in "A Resurrection," "Tommy," "The Way of the World," and "The Treasure of Far Island." The third version is just coming into view in "Eric Hermannson's Soul." It is the prairie world of settled Nebraska infused with Old World sensibilities that Cather would fully realize in *O Pioneers!*. Like a painter, the author was filling her studio with *studies* of Nebraska. When it was done, each story represented a palette of possibilities for her own emergence and the evolution of her craft.

Notes

1. Mark J. Madigan, "Cather and the Short Story," *The Cambridge Companion to Willa Cather,* ed. Marilee Lindemann (Cambridge: Cambridge University Press, 2005), 132.
2. Rosowski, *Birthing a Nation,* 77.
3. Marilyn Arnold, *Willa Cather's Short Fiction* (Athens: Ohio University Press, 1984), xiii.
4. Polly Patricia Duryea, "Paintings and Drawings in Willa Cather's Prose: A Catalogue Raisonne," PhD diss., University of Nebraska, Lincoln, Nebraska, 1993, 2.
5. Melissa J. Homestead and Anne L. Kaufman, "Willa Cather and Edith Lewis's Creative Partnership," *Western American Literature* 43.1 (2008): 50–53.
6. Downs, *Becoming Modern,* 41–44.
7. The June 15, 1888, *Chief* had described how "a Bohemian tailor, aged forty-seven committed suicide by hanging himself Sunday morning" (8). The October 11, 1889, *Chief* reported that "Frank Smolk, a Bohemian . . . committed suicide the other morning by hanging" (6). Bohemians do seem to have had a higher rate of suicide. See, among others, Howard I. Kushner, *American Suicide: A Psychocultural Exploration* (New Brunswick: Rutgers University Press, 1991), 158. For a discussion of popular images of Czech immigrants, see Prchal, "The Bohemian Paradox," 5–13. Prchal points out that Bohemians were also noted for their love of music (17).
8. Downs, *Becoming Modern,* 51–52, offers a fascinating glimpse of Cather's "days at the office."
9. Stout, *Willa Cather: The Writer and Her World,* 72.
10. Andrew Jewell, ed., "One Way of Putting It," November 5, 1893, *Willa Cather Archive,* http://cather.unl.edu/j00050.html.
11. "Willa Cather to Grace Broady," August 29, 1894, Special Collections & Archives at the National Willa Cather Center.
12. Ibid.
13. Ibid.
14. "Mariel Gere to Mildred Bennett," February 6, 1956, Special Collections & Archives at the National Willa Cather Center.
15. Downs, *Becoming Modern,* 52–53.
16. "Willa Cather to Ellen Gere and Frances Gere," July 30, 1895, Special Collections & Archives at the National Willa Cather Center.
17. Stout, *Willa Cather: The Writer and Her World,* 47.
18. Ibid., 49.
19. For a detailed description of these figures and Cather's arrival, see Slote, *KA,* 24–25.
20. Phyllis Robinson, *Willa: The Life of Willa Cather* (New York: Holt, Rinehart and Winston, 1983), 71; *WCLL,* 103-04; Downs, *Becoming Modern,* 59.
21. Stout, *Willa Cather: The Writer and Her World,* 49.
22. See, for instance, *Nebraska State Journal* (March 5, 1894): 1–2.
23. "To Mariel, Ellen, and Frances Gere; Althea 'Allie' Roberts; and Mary 'Maysie' Ames," January 2, 1896, *SLWC,* 25.
24. Murphy, "Nebraska Naturalism in Jamesian Frames," 232.
25. Rosowski, "Willa Cather's Ecology of Place,"39. For more on Cather's ecological perspective, see Cheryl C. Swift and John N. Swift, "Willa Cather and American Plant Ecology," *ISLE* 8.2 (2001): 4–6.
26. Arnold, "Poses of the Mind," 4.
27. "To Mariel Gere," *SLWC* June 16, 1894, 22.
28. James C. Olson and Ronald C. Naugle, *History of Nebraska,* 3rd ed (Lincoln: University of Nebraska Press, 1997), 224, 250. Many years later, when Cather wrote about the history of the state for the *Nation,* she argued that "these years of trial, as everyone now realizes, had a salutary

effect upon the new State. They winnowed out the settlers with a purpose." With enough distance, Cather found the Darwinian notion palatable, but at the time she was writing "On the Divide" the sense of recent hardship was uppermost in her mind.

29. Reynolds, *Willa Cather in Context,* 1–25.
30. Eudora Welty, "The House of Willa Cather," *Miracles of Perception: The Art of Willa Cather* (Charlottesville: Alderman Library, University of Virginia, 1980), 10. On this technique of juxtaposition, see also Middleton, *Willa Cather's Modernism,* 47–49.
31. James Woodress, "Willa Cather: American Experience and European Tradition," *The Art of Willa Cather,* ed. Bernice Slote and Virginia Faulkner (Lincoln: University of Nebraska Press, 1974), 43–62.
32. Reynolds, *Willa Cather in Context,* 68.
33. Bernice Slote, "Willa Cather: The Secret Web," *Five Essays on Willa Cather: The Merrimack Symposium,* ed. John Murphy (North Andover, MA: Merrimack College, 1974), 1–19; Marilyn Arnold, "The Allusive Cather," *Cather Studies* 3 (1996): 137–39.
34. Willa Cather Collection (RG2639.AM), Nebraska State Historical Society, Lincoln, NE.
35. *WCLL,* 111; *KA,* 29; Downs, *Becoming Modern,* 13.
36. Debra Seivert, "Responding to Romance with Realism in Cather's 'Tommy, the Unsentimental,' *American Literary Realism* 33.2 (2001): 104–5.
37. Noting this practice, Downs, *Becoming Modern,* 93, points out that Cather used the pseudonym of Helen Delay for her conventional nonfiction contributions.
38. Rosowski, *Birthing a Nation,* 66–67. See also O'Brien, *WCEV,* 229; Debra Seivert, "Responding to Romance with Realism in Cather's 'Tommy, the Unsentimental,'" *American Literary Realism* 33.2 (2001): 104–105; Jennifer Bradley, "To Entertain, To Educate, To Elevate: Cather and the Commodification of Manners at the *Home Monthly,*" *Willa Cather and Material Culture: Real-World Writing, Writing the Real World,* ed. Janis P. Stout (Tuscaloosa: The University of Alabama Press, 2005), 58; Judith Butler, "'Dangerous Crossing': Willa Cather's Masculine Names," *Bodies That Matter: On the Discursive Limits of Sex* (New York and London: Routledge, 1993), 161; Michelle Ann Abate, "Constructing Modernist Lesbian Affect from Late Victorian Masculine Emotionalism: Willa Cather's 'Tommy, the Unsentimental' and J. M. Barrie's *Sentimental Tommy,*" *Women's Writing* 18:4 (2014): 470, DOI: 10.1080/09699082.2011.600044, http://dx.doi.org/10.1080/09699082.2011.600044.
39. Stout, *Picturing a Different West,* xviii.
40. Butler, "Dangerous Crossing," 155.
41. Woodress, *Willa Cather,* 56.
42. Virgil Albertini, "Willa Cather and the Bicycle," *Platte Valley Review* (Spring, 1987), argues convincingly that Pound is the prototype for Tommy (16).
43. The spring before Cather left for Pittsburgh, she could have read about the "Towns of Webster County" in the April 12, 1895, *Chief,* which praised Blue Hill as "a very substantial and progressive place" populated by citizens "in good financial circumstances, and many of them are wealthy" (4).
44. Albertini, "Willa Cather and the Bicycle," 13, describes Pound's accomplishments: "It was not uncommon for her as a member of a Century Club to ride one hundred continuous miles in one day. This active, ambitious, and talented woman earned her first Century Road Club bar in 1895 and her second in 1896, and in 1896 she received the Rambler Gold Medal for riding five thousand miles in one year."
45. Roger Welsch, "Introduction," *Nebraska Folklore* by Louise Pound (1959; Lincoln: University of Nebraska Press, 2006), tells the story of Pound racing on her Rambler to rescue her brother Roscoe: "At any rate, the story, which I treasure as the truth, goes that Pound jumped on her bicycle and pedaled as fast as she could to the den of iniquity to warn her brother before the arrival of the

police, only to find when she arrived that Roscoe had already left the establishment. But she herself did not leave in time to escape being detained by the police, who would probably have been amazed and even scandalized to find a woman present . . ." (x). For more on Pound's cycling accomplishments, see Robert Cochran, *Louise Pound: Scholar, Athlete, Feminist Pioneer* (Lincoln: University of Nebraska Press, 2009): 80–82.

46. On cycling fiction, see Hallenbeck, *Claiming the Bicycle,* 79–87. For more on the concerns over women and cycling, see Sally Sims, "The Bicycle, the Bloomer and Dress Reform in the 1890s," *Dress and Popular Culture,* ed. Patricia A. Cunningham and Susan Voso Lals (Bowling Green: Bowling Green State University Popular Press, 1991), 130; Evan Friss, *The Cycling City: Bicycles and Urban America in the 1890s* (Chicago: University of Chicago Press, 2015), 176; Hallenbeck, *Claiming the Bicycle,* 35–36, 132–34.
47. See, for example, "Escape from the Fetters of the Skirt," *Pittsburgh Post-Gazette* (July 4, 1896): 8; "For the Fair Cyclist," *Pittsburgh Press* (August 16, 1896): 11; "For the Wheelwoman," *Pittsburgh Daily Post* (August 23, 1896): 14.
48. Bradley, "To Entertain, To Educate, To Elevate," 55. On the presumed sexuality of bicycle riding, see, among others, Sue Macy, "The Devil's Advance Agent," *American History* 46.4 (2011): 44.
49. Albertini, "Willa Cather and the Bicycle," 18.
50. Seivert, "Responding to Romance," 108.
51. Bergson, *Creative Evolution,* 7.
52. Baker, "Nebraska Regionalism," 21–22.
53. Seivert, "Responding to Romance," 108.
54. Stout, *Willa Cather,* 86.
55. Arnold, *Willa Cather's Short Fiction,* 10.
56. Rosowski, *Birthing a Nation,* 67.
57. Haywood, *Victorian West,* 131–32.
58. O'Brien formulates the challenging conundrum that continues to puzzle readers of the later fiction: "In reading Cather's fiction we need to develop interpretive strategies for determining when a male character is a 'mask' rather than an opposite-sex character whom Cather created by drawing, in part, on herself" (*WCEV,* 217).
59. The most powerful instance of this fascination is "Coming, Aphrodite!." See, for instance, Susan J. Rosowski, "Cather's Manifesto for 'Coming, Aphrodite!,'" *Willa Cather Pioneer Memorial Newsletter* 38.3 (1994): 51–56; Mary R. Ryder, "Looking for Love in All the Wrong Places: Voyeurism in Cather's 1920s Fiction," *Willa Cather Newsletter and Review* 49.1 (2005): 3–8; Richard C. Harris, "Barbusse's L'Enfer: A Source for 'Coming, Aphrodite!' and 'The Novel Démeublé,'" *Cather Studies* 7 (2007): 106–18.
60. Jeane Harris, "A Code of Her Own: Attitudes toward Women in Willa Cather's Short Fiction," *Modern Fiction Studies* 36.1 (1990): 85.
61. Arnold, *Willa Cather's Short Fiction,* 20.
62. David Stouck, *Willa Cather's Imagination* (Lincoln: University of Nebraska Press, 1975), 11.
63. On the violin as symbol of cultural values, see Bruce Baker, "Nebraska's Cultural Desert: Nebraska's Early Short Stories," *Midamerica: The Yearbook of the Society for the Study of Midwestern Literature* 14.1 (1987): 13–14.
64. Handley, "Willa Cather," 80–81.
65. Bloom and Bloom, *Willa Cather's Gift of Sympathy,* 35.
66. Cather's Allegheny High School student Fred Demmler may have inspired the evolution of Eric into Claude. For a discussion of Demmler's place in Cather's imagination, see Timothy W. Bintrim, "The Outlandish Hands of Fred Demmler: Pittsburgh Prototypes in *The Professor's House,*" *Cather Studies* 11 (2017): 190, 204.

67. Rosowski, *Birthing a Nation,* 67, points out that *Wyllis* also may imply *Willa.*
68. The article was reprinted back home in "Indignant Kansas," *Courier* (June 22, 1901): 2. Slote quotes the passage in "Willa Cather as a Regional Writer," 13.
69. Susan J. Rosowski, "Willa Cather and the Fatality of Place: *O Pioneers!, My Ántonia,* and *A Lost Lady,*" *Geography and Literature: A Meeting of the Disciplines,* ed. William E. Mallory and Paul Simpson-Housley (Syracuse: Syracuse University Press, 1987), 82.
70. "To George Seibel," July 17, 1901, *SLWC,* 60.
71. "To Preston Cooke Farrar," February 4, 1901, *SLWC,* 55–56 ; "To Dorothy Canfield," March or April, 1901, *SLWC,* 59.
72. "To George Seibel," July 17, 1901, *SLWC,* 60.
73. Stouck, *Willa Cather's Imagination,* 42. Demaree C. Peck, "'Possession Granted by a Different Lease': Alexandra Bergson's Imaginative Conquest of Cather's Nebraska," *MFS* 36.1 (1990): " Modern Fiction Studies, 5, identifies it as "the first story in which Cather idealized Nebraska and thus [it] can be seen as a rehearsal for her extended celebration of the prairie in *O Pioneers!.*"
74. March and Arnold, with Thornton, *A Reader's Companion to the Fiction of Willa Cather* (Westport: Greenwood, 1993), 464.
75. Burgess, "Willa Cather's Homecomings," *Willa Cather: Family, Community, and History,* 50.
76. *Chief* (September 4, 1885): 5.
77. Peck, "Possession Granted by a Different Lease," 6. Peck goes on to argue that "the Nebraska landscape that Cather wanted to possess in 'Far Island' was important not as local color but as the backdrop upon which she could recreate the world as a reflection of the spirit" (9). This argument seems to hearken back, with more sophistication, to Cather's early critics, who thought of Cather "overcoming" Nebraska. I would urge a more holistic interpretation of "Nebraska" and "imagination" in the story of Cather's emergence. The child in this formulation may also be, as Shaw, *Willa Cather and the Art of Conflict,* 4, has suggested, "an image of sexual guiltlessness and the time when sexual pleasures could be pursued and enjoyed." On this notion, see also O'Brien, *WCEV,* 111.
78. "To Dorothy Canfield," *SLWC,* 52–53.
79. Robert Louis Stevenson, *A Child's Garden of Verses* (London: Longmans, Green, and Co., 1885), 18.
80. Stouck, *Willa Cather's Imagination,* 35. Stouck's extended discussion of pastoral is well worth reading and still, perhaps, the definitive discussion of the mode in relation to Cather's fiction, but it should be pointed out that he stretches and adjusts the "standard" definition of the mode in order to obtain a perfect fit with Cather's fiction. His emphasis on memory, for instance, is a contested, rather than essential, ingredient. Compare and contrast Richard Hardin's "The Pastoral Moment," *Survivals of Pastoral,* ed. Richard F. Hardin (Lawrence: University of Kansas Publications, 1979), 1–17. For a more comprehensive treatment of the mode, see also Harold E. Toliver, *Pastoral: Forms and Attitudes* (Berkeley: University of California Press, 1971). For a succinct survey of Cather and pastoral, see John H. Randall, "Willa Cather and the Pastoral Tradition," *Five Essays on Willa Cather: The Merrimack Symposium,* ed. John J. Murphy (North Andover, MA: Merrimack College, 1974), 75–96. For a discussion of Cather's pastoral fiction in the larger context of American literature, see Louise H. Westling, *The Green Breast of the New World: Landscape, Gender, and American Fiction* (Athens and London: University of Georgia Press, 1996), 57–82. A number of other scholars have discussed Cather and pastoral in particular works, and their voices appear in the pages that follow.
81. Richard Giannone, *Music in Willa Cather's Fiction* (Lincoln: University of Nebraska Press, 1968), 30
82. Stouck, *Willa Cather's Imagination,* 43, 44.

Chapter 3.

The Road from *April Twilights* into the Far Country

I want you to be surer of your backgrounds, you have your Nebraska life. . . .
—Sarah Orne Jewett

I really love the "Far Country."
—Willa Cather

As the second decade of her career began, Willa Cather was, in Thacker's apt phrase, "a one-woman literary industry."[1] In 1902 she traveled to Europe for the first time, and it is no exaggeration to say that her adventure changed everything—not so much for any particular experience she had but for the way she felt about her career after she got home. As Woodress points out, she knew only too well that she "already was older than Keats, and as old as Shelley and Crane when they died" (*WCLL,* 165). The years were passing, and Cather wanted to create something more substantial, prestigious, and permanent (*WCEV,* 256).

This chapter traces a more ambitious phase of experimentation in Cather's career that made it possible for her to write *O Pioneers!*. Building on her early experiments with territorial remapping and renaming, Cather extended her Western vision in a letter to her brother Roscoe on February 12, 1910: "I really love the 'Far Country.' I get there so seldom that it seems about the farest and most restful country in the world" (*SLWC,* 128). Embracing her own deep anxieties over her career and her Western roots, the author wrote speculative stories about the ugliness of life on the Great Plains, offending readers back home while imagining alternative lives for herself. Inspired by Sarah Orne Jewett, Cather transposed her own cherished assumptions about heroines and heroes, all the while trying to add depth to her Western settings. In ways that pointed to a minimalism she had not yet invented, Cather began to free herself from plot. As Rosowski has pointed out, the editor in her began to mature into an artistic presence ready to shape every aspect of the print medium.[2] By the end of the decade, Cather had written five stories that were crucial to her emergence: "A Death in the Desert," "A Wagner Matinee," "The Joy of Nelly Deane," "The Enchanted Bluff," and "The Bohemian Girl." She also produced *April Twilights,* a collection of poetry, *The Troll Garden* (a collection of short fiction that included the first two aforementioned stories), and *Alexander's Bridge,* a novel. All in all, it was a remarkable decade that began with verse.

When opportunity came knocking in the person of Richard Badger, who wanted to publish a volume of her poetry, Cather leapt at the chance (*WCLL,* 165). As Slote has pointed out in her scholarly edition of the volume, "Nothing in her work is unrelated to the whole. In the poems (as in the first stories, some of which she rejected), we find the early sketches, the first motifs, the suggested design of her major work."[3] Jessica G. Rabin has described the complex way that this generative relationship unfolded over the decades as Cather revised her volume in 1923 and then continued to revise and rearrange the verse in subsequent editions.[4] Thacker sums up the relationship: "What Willa Cather's poems do reveal, when taken as a small body of serious work seen in relation to her indisputable accomplishments in prose, is another way of understanding the development of this literary genius."[5]

Viewed in the larger context of the territorial imagination that Cather inherited, this "serious work" seems practically inevitable. From the first days of white settlement, literary societies had encouraged their members to pursue both fiction and poetry. In keeping with this spirit, the territorial editors of the *Nebraska Advertiser* and the *Huntsman's Echo* created front pages that combined poetry with nonfiction, reporting, and fiction, convinced that a mingling of genres would produce a more valuable text. On June 7, 1856, the first edition of the *Advertiser* offered an entire column of "POETRY" on the front page, including G. W. Cutter's "The Press":

> Soul of the world—the press, the press—
> What wonders hast thou wrought?
> Thou rainbow realm of mental bliss—
> Thou starry sky of thought! (1)

Perhaps, as Cutter proclaims, the mingling of "press" and verse really could engender a cosmic realm of cogitation. Cather was, in a manner of speaking, following this formula, and her ambitions were every bit as lofty.

For the aspiring author, the volume contained a series of starry experiments in both theme and craft. As Slote points out, "The subjects of the poems show Willa Cather's rich interests—literature, art, music, places of the world, memories of home—and her ready response to the particular emotional aura of the experience."[6] In "Grandmither, Think Not I Forget," the poet echoes "The Night Express" (which appears in the volume) and "The Treasure of Far Island," revisiting the idea of homecoming:

> Grandmither, think not I forget, when I come back to town,
> An' wander the old ways again an' tread them up an' down.[7]

Testing pastoral invocations as frames for landscapes, Cather becomes increasingly conscious of herself as a Western writer. So "White Birch in Wyoming" begins with a bold simile:

> Stark as a Burne-Jones vision of despair,
> Amid the painted glare of sand and sky,
> She stands. . . .[8]

Perhaps European art and artists could be invoked legitimately in her home country?

In the imagistic "Prairie Dawn," the writer who has often been described as struggling to come to terms with the Great Plains "catches in eight exact lines of remarkable swiftness the look and feel of the open prairie."[9] The poem deserves to be quoted in any conversation about Cather's relationship to the West:

> A crimson fire that vanquishes the stars;
> A pungent odor from the dusty sage;
> A sudden stirring of the huddled herds;
> A breaking of the distant table-lands
> Through purple mists ascending, and the flare
> Of water ditches silver in the light;
> A swift, bright lance hurled low across the world;
> A sudden sickness for the hills of home.[10]

Far from being confounded by the place, the poet seems to fulfill the starry ambition of Cutter in his aforementioned poem. In fact, Cather seems to be answering Whitman's call for "some superior landscape painter, some fine colorist" who will be worthy of the Great Plains and the aesthetic challenges they embody. In ways she had not managed before in prose, Cather pays homage to the natural order of things on the prairie.

We also hear, in this poem and throughout the whole collection, a poetic voice that has left the village wit behind and is now intent on claiming authentic feelings, ambitious to say more than the forms will hold, a voice that would be essential to the author's mature fiction.[11] In "Prairie Dawn" it is easy to *hear* how Cather was already moving toward "The Bohemian Girl" and *O Pioneers!*.

Less obvious but no less significant in this pattern of experimentation is the "Dedicatory" she addresses to Roscoe and Douglass that frames the whole collection. Summoning the moon, the speaker proceeds to conjure:

> Let it work again its old enchantment.
> Let it, for an April night, transform us
> From our grosser selves to happy shadows
> Of the three who lay and planned at moonrise,
> On an island in a western river,
> Of the conquest of the world together.[12]

"Dedicatory" describes the Nebraska she shared with her beloved brothers, a story that has yet to be told in all of its complexity. It also describes the Nebraska of "The Way of the World" and "The Treasure of Far Island." By explicitly recalling the latter story, the poet seems to be reassuring herself and anyone else in the know that her imaginative relationship with Nebraska will always ground her ambition. Books will be made, and the artist in touch with childhood will make them.

April Twilights appeared, appropriately enough, in April 1903, and the book gave Cather immense satisfaction.[13] Still, the author wanted more. Even before the poetry collection appeared, the industrious English teacher was working on a group of stories that might form a volume. In fact, Cather was already calling the collection *The Troll Garden*. As Thacker has suggested, the book is, among other things, a fascinating experiment in mixing Old World influences with Western experience.[14]

In "A Death in the Desert," the experiment unfolds in territorial terms that eventually helped Cather write *The Song of the Lark*. Recounting the final days of Katharine Gaylord, former pupil of the famous composer Adriance Hilgarde, the story centers on the unexpected arrival of Hilgarde's twin brother, Everett. Setting her work in the sand hills of Cheyenne, Wyoming, Cather establishes the Western border of the anthology's fictional universe, a desert region just beyond the limits of the old Kansas-Nebraska Territory, which of course included the eastern half of present-day Colorado.

As if to emphasize the old territorial consciousness, Cather introduces her readers to Everett as he crosses the sand-hills of northeastern Colorado. Everett is joined in the stifling railroad car by a traveling man and two girls headed home from the Exposition in Chicago. Cather's narrator describes "the sage-brush and sand-hills," noting that "the grey and yellow desert was varied only by occasional ruins of deserted towns" (512). The two men strike up a conversation in a scene that seems to anticipate the opening of *My Ántonia,* but this is not the author's home country. In the novel, the train passes grassland; this train passes sagebrush. In the novel, the train passes country towns that inspire free masonry; this train passes "ruins" that recall Cather's vision of Brownville and Kansas in "El Dorado." This part of Wyoming is, in short, a "confusing wilderness of sand" (512).

According to modern definitions, this country is still part of the Great Plains, part of the same region as Cather's Divide. In fact, the boundary line would usually run just west of Cheyenne and then jog farther west on its way past Billings and Calgary to the north. Cather may have recognized this definition, but in this story she is working like an aggressive territorial colonizer, boldly revising the demarcations and denominations of Stephen Long's famous 1820 expedition report that first identified the Great American Desert. This is territorial art practiced with a large brush as the writer marks off an outback where the artist can go to die. "Nebraska," as far as Cather's imagination was concerned, was a series of different places and times. Years later, when she wrote *The Song of the Lark,* the author used this "study" to create a Western setting that seemed to account for her own emergence.

The rest of 1903 was often idyllic and memorable. Cather may never have been happier. She was in love, settled—and all the great rewards shimmered in the future, perfect in their possibility. During the summer, Cather was exploring the West. On July 13, she wrote Canfield from Cheyenne, which seemed nothing like the desolate place she invented in "A Death in the Desert." "It is fine and cool here," she reported (*SLWC,* 74). She also described her election to chair of the English department at Allegheny High School back in Pittsburgh, her physical discomfort in the altitude, and her love for her brothers. But her mind always returned to Nebraska: ". . . I do believe that its *[sic]* my duty to be here and in Red Cloud" (*SLWC,* 75). While visiting her old comrade, Sarah Harris, in Lincoln later that summer, she met Edith Lewis (*WCLL,* xxvii). A Thanksgiving letter to Canfield on November 27 gives us a sense of Cather's domestic bliss on the occasion (*SLWC,* 75–76).

But Cather's idyll would soon be unsettled by family and friends. In a letter to Canfield written in either March or April of 1904, Cather reported, "My family have moved into a big, comfortable house they have just built, and are more comfortable than they have ever been. They would like me to go home this summer to help them" (*SLWC,* 82). Cather demurred. For years, she had been happily returning to Red Cloud, soaking up the memories of the place, writing stories, playing with the children. Now, the house on Cedar Street was lost, and with it the yard that once defined the town limits of Sandy Point. The brothers who meant so much to her were "out West."

Someone interested in Cather's imagination might be inspired to return to the author's musings in "The Treasure of Far Island." In that story, the narrator had explained how the "external world" of Douglass and Margie "had been valued solely for what they suggested to the imagination, and people and places alike were merely stage properties" (*CSF,* 276). But Cather's response to her family moving into a new house suggests that external world of Red Cloud was no mere "stage property." It was precious. In fact, the idea of losing outward things was painful enough that she would go out of her way to avoid dealing with the loss. She would go to New York and seek diversion and even consolation in more substantial accomplishments.

Cather was certainly thinking about Nebraska, loss, and compensation that winter when "A Wagner Matinee" appeared in the February edition of *Everybody's Magazine.* A young man living in Boston, sounding very much like the author, recounts the visit of his Aunt Georgiana from Red Willow, Nebraska. After a long life on the prairie, the woman who had once taught at the Boston Conservatory is stunned by the great city filled with life. When the nephew takes her to an afternoon concert, she bursts into tears. All in all, it is a well-crafted little story with a deceptively simple surface that disguises a more experimental work than most readers have imagined.

When the story appeared, folks back in Nebraska, family and friends included, were appalled. Anyone who knew Cather and her family could see the resemblance between Aunt Georgiana and the author's Aunt Franc, and the portrait was far from flattering. The woman is "stooped" and "sunken," and she wears "ill-fitting false teeth" (*CSF,* 236). In Cather's words, her family was "insulted."[15]

Other people near to Cather were more concerned about the way Nebraska was depicted in the story. In his column for the *Journal,* her old mentor Jones wrote, "The stranger to this state will associate Nebraska with the aunt's wretched figure, her ill-fitting false teeth, her skin yellowed by the weather. . . . If the writers of fiction who use western Nebraska as material would look up now and then and not keep their eyes and noses in the cattle yards, they might be more agreeable company."[16] The *Chief,* which was paying cursory attention to her visits and her career and had not received its copies of the magazine with the story, reprinted the *Journal* review on the front page under a headline that sounded like a command: "Don't Like Miss Cather's Story."[17] Having shrugged off the complaints of readers in Brownville and Kansas when she seemed to denigrate their country, Cather was taken aback. As Romines points out, the story "threatened estrangement from the approval and support of the family and friends and from the orderly, supportive female world of 'Miss Jewett.'"[18]

The author chose to respond to this entanglement by focusing on the problem of Nebraska. She wrote to Jones on March 6: "That was a ringing slap you gave me in your more or less personal column. I wonder whether you really mean it, or whether it was for the benefit of the Red Willow contingent. I never even had an idea of disparaging the state" (*SLWC,* 80). The declaration of pain is clear. The nod to the people of "Red Willow" recalls the fictional town in "Tommy, the Unsentimental" and so reveals her consistent investment in a larger project of renaming the old territory. Has Jones really lost track of the difference between fiction and reality? It is worth pointing out that the March 11, 1904, *Chief,* after some reflection, thought the complaints were "much adoo about nothing" (5). The author may well have felt encouraged by this support, but Jones was an old friend and mentor.

Cather felt the need to make her case in ways that clear up all sorts of confusion about her artistic relationship to the American West. "Now my good friend," she writes, "didn't I take the pains to date the story back in the pioneer times?" In other words, this story has more in common with "On the Divide" than it does with "Tommy" and "The Treasure of Far Island." She adds, "I though[t] everyone admitted that those pioneer days were desolate, and I was misguided enough to think the story a sort of respectful tribute to the courage of those uncomplaining women who weathered them. Farm life in the territory when I knew it fifteen years ago was bad enough, what must it have been before?" With this letter, the author is laying explicit claim to the territorial imagination on her own terms. Pioneer women, in their letters, diaries, and reminiscences, really do agree that the early days were much harder.[19] Elia W. Peattie had made precisely this point about "On the Divide" when it appeared in the *Overland Monthly* back in 1896.[20] In other words, Cather knows what she is talking about and wants the freedom to write honestly about different phases of settlement and the settlers' recollections of their experiences.

In doing so, she offers a new bit of nomenclature that will apply to the important novels to come: Cather was writing about "farm life." This term refers not to a particular time or place, but to a particular way of life that Cather's father and mother could not embrace. In her early interviews, Cather talked about moving from Virginia to a *ranch.* In the promotional material she created for *April Twilights,* she described her early blissful days on the ranch.[21] By the time she published *O Pioneers!,* she was describing her arrival on her grandparents' "homestead" (*WCP,* 2, 3, 9). Over the years, she talked about riding her pony over the prairie and listening to neighbor women tell stories. Although she knew her Uncle George and Aunt Franc's farm well, she never had much to say about the hard work of farm life. Her feelings are clear in this important letter and utterly consistent with her public remarks: farm life in earlier times "was bad enough." Cather may have had to struggle to come to terms with the openness of the prairie, but it required all of her imaginative resources to transform farm life into literature. When she finally accomplished this feat, it felt like emergence.

Aunt Franc was another matter. Readers of the story then and now have found it difficult to identify the "respectful tribute." Many will find it touching and sad. Some will find it pathetic. In Cather's words, her family was certain that it was not "nice to tell such things."[22] But Cather was still very much the same person who reported a visit to her Aunt Franc's farm in 1893—the same visit in which she and her brother Roscoe climbed the windmill. In a letter to Mariel Gere on August 1, Cather describes, with pride, her aunt's degrees from Smith and Mount Holyoke, and her work with the local "literary": "By the way I must tell you about that aunt of mine some time, she is one of the ugliest, smartest, and most eccentric of human kind,—they say I am like her in ugliness and eccentricity" (*SLWC,* 20). In this brash moment of confession, Cather helps us understand how she may have really felt about her portrayal of her aunt in the story.

What, we can only speculate, would the story have been like if the author had attempted to infuse some of the smart and eccentric facets of this woman's character into Aunt Georgiana? I suspect that the work's sharp focus would have been lost, and it goes without saying that Cather had no desire to identify overtly with the old lady. The author felt too old already. Nevertheless, the narrator does confess, "I owed to this woman most of the good that ever came my way in my boyhood" (*CSF,* 236).

Cather was, of course, always coming back to herself, often to her "boyhood," in her fiction, and this fact is central to the importance of "A Wagner Matinee." As Woodress smartly observes, the story is "lean and compact, narrated with skill from a young man's point of view, the same perspective Cather used later in *My Ántonia* and other works" (*WCLL,* 177). In a story that caused so much heartache and furor, Cather was assaying the voice for one of her masterpieces.

If Jones and company had been able to step back from their love of Nebraska, they would have noticed the narrator's limitations as an "evaluator." They would have noticed his youthful fastidiousness and need for superiority as he carefully identifies the music in the concert. They would have noticed his attempt at honest self-examination as he remarks "how superficially I had judged her" (238). They would have noticed that the narrator's limited perspective "evokes nothing of the rhythm of her life as *she* perceives it."[23] Above all, they might have recalled that first-person narratives tend to be about the narrator. Neither history nor report, this is a fictional assay, a poignant sketch of a person who has left Nebraska, trying to hold on to someone who mattered dearly to him during his childhood.

THE farm of George and Frances Cather.

Source: Willa Cather Pioneer Memorial and Educational Foundation.

With all this in mind, I would set aside the false teeth, and focus on the way memory and imagination coalesce in the narrator's mind during the concert. During the *Tannhäuser* overture, the narrator paints the picture: "With the battle between the two motives, with the frenzy of the Venusberg theme and its ripping of strings, there came to me an overwhelming sense of the waste and wear we are so powerless to combat; and I saw again the tall naked house on the prairie, black and grim. . . . The world there was the flat world of the ancients" (239). The point in this passage is not to capture some definitive picture of life in Nebraska. Cather is interested in how an image of pioneer life on the prairie might emerge out of and in juxtaposition to great Romantic music from the Old World in the mind of a young man who thinks as she does. Employing European allusions with new sophistication while sketching the consciousness of the artist from Nebraska, "A Wagner Matinee" represents a crucial step in Cather's evolution as an author.

Nevertheless, Cather recognized that she had committed a serious faux pas even as she was writing something with a future. Imbued with this clarity, she closed her letter to Jones by confiding that the publication of her stories would be delayed a bit. With a certain touch of dignity, she added, "Maybe it will relieve you to know that the one under discussion is the only Nebraska tale in the lot."

No one who has read "The Sculptor's Funeral" will be fooled by this covenant. The story appeared the following January in *McClure's* in anticipation of the book's publication in March. To many, it has seemed to sum up Cather's early attitude toward her home country, perhaps because the story is so well made and so satisfyingly critical of life on the Great Plains. On the other hand, if we read the story in the context of Cather's emergence, against the backdrop of her experiment in "El Dorado" and her ongoing experiments with alternative renderings of her own life, not to mention her incorporation of Pittsburgh experiences, the "The Sculptor's Funeral" looks more like a tour de force of geographical imagination.

At the beginning of this often-discussed story, Henry Steavens accompanies the body of Harvey Merrick, a gifted sculptor, back to his hometown. Townspeople gather, taking the opportunity to scoff at the successful man's fortunes. Steavens recognizes that Jim Laird, the local hard-drinking attorney, seems to be the only one who understands the sculptor's worth. Steavens and Laird share an important conversation before the attorney stands up to the hypocritical citizens, finally setting the record straight.

When Cather assured Jones that only one story about Nebraska would appear in her book, she was disingenuously counting on the power of this story's opening sentence: "A group of townspeople stood on the station siding of a little Kansas town, awaiting the coming of the night train" (*CSF,* 173). Like "El Dorado" before it, this is a story set in Kansas. It is a tale of regional despair rooted in a locale south of Cather's Webster County. But anyone who knew anything about the territory or about Cather's fiction would immediately see through this pale Kansas-Nebraska act. The author had to recognize all this, especially as she wrote to Jones. Perhaps she thought she was telling the truth, but telling it slant, as Emily Dickinson recommended.[24]

The story was definitely familiar. A talented man is returning to a town that looks very much like Red Cloud as a train winds past a river that resembles the Republican. After the arrival at the train station, the passengers and townspeople head uphill to the center of town, as people in Red Cloud always did. As everyone gathers, figures echoing the citizens of Red Cloud gradually come into view. We seem to be revisiting the arrival of Douglass Burnham in "The Treasure of Far Island."

As it often was for the newspaper editors of Red Cloud and for Cather in her Nebraska fiction, boy life frames the arrival: "A number of lanky boys of all ages appeared as suddenly and slimily as eels wakened by the crack of thunder" (174). The detail is hardly haphazard. We know that Cather was thinking once more of Amos Cowden's return in 1901. She had already reinvented the scene in "The Night Express" in *April Twilights:*

> With restless heart of boyhood we watched that headlight when
> The whistle seemed to call us to dare the world of men (36).

In the poem, she focused on her response. Now, she was ready to rework her recollection of the experience. The simile of boys as eels works on at least three levels. In the fourth act of Shakespeare's *Pericles,* the brothel keeper Boult invokes the old notion that eels respond to thunder.[25] Cather seems to intend a paradoxical effect of highbrow allusion and feral galvanism that contributes to the story's dissonance. There is also a touch of Cather's youthful sense of humor, a glance back to the sardonic young letter writer describing vivisection. Finally, the simile is a witty way to imply that the boys who come to see the body function as primitive life forms. Hosmer and Warren, the old editors of the *Chief* and the *Argus,* would have approved.

By the time Steavens notices a crayon drawing of the artist in "kilts and curls" in the parlor, we realize that Merrick was once one of these boys (176). The author of "The Treasure of Far Island" has made her point again: children are artists, and artists are children who grow older but hold on to their childhood. Like a newspaper editor, Cather juxtaposes this cherished vision with a little story from one of the ignorant neighbors who recalls "Harve" as "a big feller in long pants and [how] his mother used to whale him with a rawhide" (182). In country town life, comeuppance and irony were always lurking between the columns of the "City News." Knowing only too well that this kind of talk is about both the sculptor and the town, Laird tells off his neighbors: "There was only one boy ever raised in this borderland between ruffianism and civilization, who didn't come to grief, and you hated Harvey Merrick more for winning out than you hated all the other boys who got under the wheels" (184). In the perfect summing up we would all wish for the maligned artist, the attorney frames the man's successful life in terms of boyhood.

Anyone familiar with life in Red Cloud had to admit that such scenes really did occur in this "borderland between ruffianism and civilization," but they hardly encapsulated life in the live western town.[26] In fact, Laird's presence in the story underscores that this sad tale is radically perspectival. Just as she explicitly nodded toward the real Rheinhold Birkner in previous stories, Cather was invoking a well-known attorney from southern Nebraska who just happened to be named Jim Laird. On the occasion of his death, the August 23, 1889, *Chief* remembered a man who might have defended Harvey Merrick: "He was a brilliant speaker and his conversational charm was exceedingly great. His influence over those with whom he came in contact was immediate and strong. Naturally aggressive, he was a frank and a manly fighter, a forgiving enemy and a loyal friend."[27] Cather's explicit casting of this man in her story attests to her recognition that the same country that could produce pettiness could also produce Laird and Merrick.

Perhaps Cather imagined writing a story called "The Attorney's Funeral." Her ending hints at such a notion by reporting how Laird died just beyond the limits of the old Kansas-Nebraska Territory, "across the Colorado mountains" (185). Summing up the life of the real Jim Laird, the August 23, 1889, *Chief* should be read alongside Cather's story: "There is no need for reading a homily over his coffin. He was what the Almighty made him, and training would have had little influence in modifying his chaotic nature. He lived every moment of his life up to the time he was stricken down. If he had been in any way different he would not have been Jim Laird. Nebraska loved and admired him for what he was" (5). This is the story behind Cather's angry Jim Laird in "A Sculptor's Funeral." It is the story of a brilliant but difficult man who was loved by Nebraska "for what he was." A story juxtaposed in the adjoining column reports that "a large number of G.A.R. boys went to Hastings Monday to attend the funeral of Hon. James Laird." Some eel-like boys grow into loyal friends. Cather goes out of her way to invoke these stories when she makes Jim Laird the moral center of Sand City.

Sand also helps us comprehend "A Sculptor's Funeral" in its Kansas-Nebraska context. Red Cloud newspaper editors often described the sand of Webster County as having arrived on a strong southern wind from Kansas. The October 22, 1886, *Argus* suggested goggles for its readers "by reason of the frequent blasts of Kansas sand coming rapidly in this direction" (8). It was territorial sand, after all, that Cather asked her father to have delivered to their yard on Cedar Street when she was building a town in her backyard on Cedar Street. "A Sculptor's Funeral" is built on the same sand.

In this story, Cather is thinking about "the end" as she invents a palimpsestuous nightmare of returning to Red Cloud, a grim companion piece to "The Treasure of Far Island." Not unlike Frank Capra in the classic film *It's a Wonderful Life,* she imagines an alternative universe during winter, a version of the familiar hometown where familiar faces have devolved into base versions of themselves. Like Scrooge in the Dickens novella, she pays a nocturnal visit to her own still corpse. But unlike the aforementioned holiday classics, Cather's vision unfolds in a collection of short stories under no obligation to offer holiday cheer.

Reviewers of *The Troll Garden* were less than enthusiastic. One particularly harsh critic, perhaps hoping for a bit of conventional cheer from a female author, described the book as a "collection of freak stories that are either lurid, hysterical or unwholesome, and that remind one of nothing so much as the coloured supplement to the Sunday papers" (qtd. in *WCLL,* 179). Writing with a keener sense of value, the reviewer in the *New York Times Book Review* saw the collection as "more the work of promise than of fulfillment" (qtd. in *WCLL,* 179). A little article in the *Bookman* described the author as "a hard-headed, clear-visioned, straight-forward young woman" (*WCP,* 5). Sales of *The Troll Garden* were unremarkable. Cather carried on with her teaching.

Meanwhile, something was percolating among the readers of her stories. Undeterred by "freakish" elements, they were intrigued by Cather's depiction of the American West. Letters came flowing into *McClure's.* Witter Bynner, the energetic office boy at the magazine, passed the inquiries along to Cather, who sat down to respond to them in early June. Her letter is a remarkable document of memory work and stocktaking. There is no preamble, no formal shaping of the document for her reader. She simply takes up a question.

Where did she get her information? She had lived there. With no paragraph break, she takes up the next question. Why is there such a "curious lack of a sense of beauty in the tales"? [28] Jones might have asked the same question. Cather admits that it is "true enough."

Warming to her subject, the author writes with unusual candor. "I had never thought of it before," she explains, "but I suppose one's early experiences rather cling to one, and the years when I first began to note my surroundings at all were pretty much devoted to discovering ugliness." Defending "A Wagner Matinee" to Jones, she had merely implied such feelings. Now, she is forthright: "If you've never been about in that part of the West, you simply can't imagine anything so bleak and desolate as a Nebraska ranch of eighteen or nineteen years ago." Even here, the confessing author cannot write "farm." She goes on to admit, "During the first year that we spent in the West I came about as near dying from homesickness as a healthy child well could." Of course, Cather had been writing about this experience all along, using her own personal code. Without missing a beat in the aforementioned paragraph, she illustrates her bitter despair as a child by describing the "one miserable little sluggish stream about eighteen miles from our ranch." Readers of Cather's "Kansas" story "El Dorado" will recognize this stream and suspect that it is personified in that story because a child's imagination haunts the telling.

Cather explains that her writing has also been influenced by the drought and financial difficulties that Nebraskans experienced in the early 1890s. She calls it "a rather grim chapter of human history to have lived through." Then she illustrates her point: "I knew one little Norwegian girl whose sister committed suicide by drinking carbolic acid. The girl herself thought that was wrong but she was always praying to die. I don't believe you could imagine how sincerely she wished to die." Cather knew dozens of stories of hardship from this era, but the story she tells is about two sisters who want to die because they are so depressed. It is as though Laura and Lizzie of Christina Rossetti's "The Goblin Market" had been abducted and forced to live on a Nebraska farm in a time of drought. In this alternative history, stories of high adventure would seem faraway and even irrelevant. Cather goes on to tell how the girl was "cured" by her father, who sent her to visit family back in Iowa where she saw "how beautiful the world was." Cather knows these details because the girl "told my little sister and me." Laura and Lizzie. The Norwegian girl and her sister. Cather and her sister. The grim chapter of human history becomes, in this letter, a story of sisters.

By this point in her career, Cather had assembled a number of Nebraska templates in her imagination, but this letter reveals that one had been left out, even repressed. It was the story of a young girl, a sister, on a prairie farm in the early days of settlement. In this story, we see Nebraska through the eyes of the suffering girl. The honesty of the writing, the mixture of integrity and deep feeling, would make any complaints about promoting or not promoting Nebraska moot. "I suppose," she writes, "the wild soil has to be reclaimed and subdued in that way, and always at pretty much the same cost." Having just completed a "cycle" of stories, the author is here describing a much grander cycle of settlement that would help her structure a novel. Cather was truly on the road to *O Pioneers!*.

The tug of the West was particularly strong that summer. Mariel Gere wrote to her during this period, but it was late September before Cather got around to responding with a newsy letter describing her time in Wyoming and South Dakota with her brothers and a month in Red Cloud "helping father fix up his new house, which is the pride of his heart."[29] She went on to mention family and friends before declaring, "I think, more than ever, that the West is the only place I want to live, and I am planning to get home to Red Cloud for a year before very long. There are many people there of whom I am very fond." Cather was ready for a renewed commitment to Nebraska, both as inspiration and studio.

Less than eight months later, she was living in New York, having accepted a position at *McClure's Magazine*. She seems to have left Isabelle in Pittsburgh with the notion that their relationship would continue. She never did get around to spending a year in Nebraska. Moreover, as Woodress points out, "After making her way by stages from the Divide, to Red Cloud, to Lincoln, to Pittsburgh, and finally to New York, she never left the city to live elsewhere" (*WCLL*, 189). In her early thirties, Cather could not have planned this outcome. It simply worked out this way with the kind of motion that suggests destiny. Through it all, Cather was always "planning to get home."

The hot summer in New York came and went, and Cather did not make it home for a visit. Caught up in the whirlwind of office life that defined *McClure's*, she barely noticed the months flying by. As Christmas approached, she wrote to her father on December 17: "I feel so badly about not getting home to spend Christmas with my sick daddy. Until today I have thought that I might be able to make it, and I have shed a good many bitter tears over giving it up. For eight years it has been my dream to have a Christmas at home, and this year I thought I would make it" (*SLWC*, 99). More than a plan, the holiday visit to Red Cloud was the kind of "dream" that stretched out over the passing years, lending a certain structure to the author's displaced imaginative life. Fiction did not necessarily follow. After the publication of "The Sculptor's Funeral" in 1905, Cather did not return to Nebraska in fiction until she wrote "The Enchanted Bluff," which appeared in *Harper's* in April 1909.

These were years of intense labor, exhaustion, exhilaration, frustration, and personal discovery. While giving everything she could to the magazine, Cather did manage to write and publish five stories, the best being "On the Gull's Road." She moved to Boston for a little over a year to work on a revision of Georgine Milmine's *Life of Mary Baker Eddy.* It was there that Cather met Sarah Orne Jewett. After another trip to Europe in the spring of 1908, she returned to New York. She and Lewis moved into an apartment at 82 Washington Place. They would remain together for the rest of Cather's life.

She had, in many respects, made it, but she was hardly satisfied. Lewis remembers "it as a period of uncertainty and change, and of somewhat troubled housekeeping. Willa Cather was even then considering whether she ought to leave *McClure's,* and give all her time to writing" (*WCL,* 74). Everything began to bubble over during the final months of 1908, when Cather sent Jewett copies of "On the Gull's Road" and "The Enchanted Bluff," referring to the latter as a "scorned tale," S. S. McClure having pronounced it "*all introduction.*"[30] Cather thought the story's focus on the West would intrigue Jewett. At this uncertain moment in her career, the author's keen intuition was on display. After a hiatus, she had returned to her memories of Nebraska with an inspiration that seems to have come quite out of the blue. Turning her back on the plotting that was so important to realism, she conjured up a new way of writing about Nebraska. McClure dismissed it, but she knew better.

Although Baker rightly calls it "a germinal story,"[31] the innovation is not obvious. Cather is once more using a first-person male narrator to look back and remember life in Nebraska. Like the editors of the country town newspapers she knew so well, the author is telling yet another "boy story." Once again, she is returning to a sandy island in a prairie river that "was brown and sluggish, like any other of the half-dozen streams that water the Nebraska corn lands" (*CSP,* 64). For Cather, the descriptions of the river and boy life have become conventional, but the reference to "corn lands" is important because it emphasizes that this is not a tale of early settlement. Working in the period of Nebraska history she knew so well, Cather experiments with a relatively static narrative in order reimagine the significance of storytelling rooted in 1880s Nebraska.

A hint that things will be different is buried in the sand, the ubiquitous prairie alluvium that she always connected with creativity. These are "the

Sandtown boys," and they come from "Sandtown folks" (64, 68). The narrator recalls that the boys built their fire "on the level terrace of fine sand which had been added that spring; a little new bit of world, beautifully ridged with ripple marks, and strewn with the tiny skeletons of turtles and fish, all as white and dry as if they had been expertly cured" (65). The new sand and old skeletons suggest a different sort of time at work in this story. More particularly, the combination of "little new" is either accidentally awkward or intentionally foregrounded, perhaps implying that innovation in this imaginative milieu is subtle, sedimentary, and seasonal. The story of emergence and imagination that follows grows out of this sand.

At the distance of some twenty years, a male narrator remembers sitting around a campfire on the night before he left home to teach school. As she does in previous stories, Cather introduces a cast of boys, but this group seems rather remarkable. They are not the primitive herd she sketches in "The Sculptor's Funeral," and they are older and more cerebral than the boys of Speckleville in "The Way of the World." As she did in that story, Cather musters the boys. We meet Fritz and Otto Hassler, sons of the town's tailor. They live the river boy life that Cather describes in "A Resurrection" and know a bit of astronomy. Percy Pound reads "boys' story-papers" and knows something about the Aztecs. Tip Smith collects cigarette cards and artifacts from the Holy Land and knows about a mysterious rock in New Mexico called the Enchanted Bluff. The tall Arthur Adams leads the group, and his most striking feature is the pleasant voice he uses to read poetry aloud at school in such a convincing fashion that no one laughs. He knows something authoritative about many things.

Their conversation flows with a mature quality of reflection and speculation, shifting from Columbus and Coronado, to astronomy and Native Americans. When a dog barks, Fritz suggests someone is stealing melons. Many of Cather's readers familiar with life in Red Cloud during the 1880s would have thought of this scenario when they began to read "The Enchanted Bluff." In fact, they would have expected to read about it. But these boys are too busy speculating about Coronado and planning adventures in New Mexico to concern themselves with the family Cucurbitaceae. Stout suggests that Cather was "constructing a gender-neutral aesthetic of the West."[32] I agree with this notion, but would qualify it by suggesting that we think of this aesthetic as one of a number of gender experiments that Cather was tinkering with on the road to *O Pioneers!.*

If this were one of her previous stories, Cather would shift to action at this point or introduce a vignette, either in the present or in the past. In this story, conversation is enough, especially when Tip captures everyone's attention by talking about the Enchanted Bluff. The boys try to imagine how it could be climbed. A single, long paragraph ends the boys' conversation, and it is no coincidence that Cather uses a bird to signal closure. The narrator recalls, "Suddenly we heard a scream above our fire, and jumped up to see a dark, slim bird floating southward far above us—a whooping-crane, we knew by her cry and her long neck" (71). As Red Cloud newspaper editors liked to do, Cather marks the changing season by paying attention to a migratory bird.

A glance back at Cather's community helps us appreciate the surprising reverence of the boys who race after the bird simply hoping to "see her alight" (71). Red Cloud boys were not always so regardful. During the spring of 1888, the April 20 *Chief* reported, "On Sunday, Ed. Cook shot and wounded a pelican that measured 7 feet and 9 inches from tip to tip and 6 ½ feet from end of tail to end of beak. His bill was 13 inches long. It is a rare bird in this section. The bird could not fly after being wounded but fought three boys for about two hours before they killed it" (5). As a rule, people in nineteenth-century Nebraska liked to watch and wonder at wildlife. Other folks liked to kill what they encountered, no matter how rare. Cather's boys may not be typical of Red Cloud, but they certainly embody its higher motives. The former editor of the "High School Items" who had chastised her male classmates for their lax behavior was reimagining Red Cloud boy life as depicted in the newspapers. It is probably no coincidence that these boys share the spirit of Sylvia, who protects the bird in Jewett's famous story "The White Heron." When Cather sent Jewett her bird story, she emphasized that the work would help the Eastern writer appreciate the distinctiveness of the West.

Perhaps more than any fiction she wrote before *O Pioneers!,* the perspective is ecological. Moving deftly from the opening description of how "our clean sand-bar grew fresher and smelled of the rank ironweed and sunflowers growing on the flatter shore" to the "spring freshets and flooded bottoms" to the whooping crane, the narrator describes the cyclical life of a river on the Great Plains (64). Rosowski observes, "Interaction of species with the soil influenced by wind, water and humidity, and culminating in a triumphant emergence or climax—this is a narrative structured by the ecological model evolving at [the University of] Nebraska during the years that Cather was a student there."[33]

The night of talk ends when the boys agree that whoever gets to the top of the Enchanted Bluff first will report what he finds. The boys can sleep after the agreement is reached, and Cather has an end to her story, but she was already committed to working with sections, segments, and scraps at this point in her career. She could give up traditional plotting, but not the pleasure of juxtaposition. After a break on the page, the narrator speaks in the present, reporting the boys' various destinies as a series of miniature vignettes that echoed the side-by-sidedness of her first "One Way of Putting It" column back in 1893.

Now she was ready to make use of the technique in the service of a more nuanced sort of storytelling. Percy is a successful businessman in Kansas City. Otto and Fritz are "the town tailors" (72). Arthur led a dissolute life in Sandtown, dying when he was only twenty-five. Tip married badly and runs the town grocery store. None of the boys has ever made it to the Enchanted Bluff. In turn, each vignette suggests that the boys who used to contemplate the stars have all suffered a serious diminution of vision.

It seems a sad fate and certainly could be cited as an indictment of "village life" were it not for Tip's confession at the end of the story. He still plans to set out on the old quest, but "will wait until his boy, Bert, is old enough to go with him. Bert has been let into the story, and thinks of nothing but the Enchanted Bluff" (73). There is something hopeful about this ending. Perhaps it is the simple notion that dreams do not die, that they can be passed along to the generations that follow.

Or Cather is being bolder. Like Speckle in "The Way of the World," Tip had the power to tell a story that made his listeners want to inhabit the world he described. Speckle, as we know, went on in Cather's imaginative universe to be a successful playwright, a professional storyteller. It is no surprise that he continues to invite other people into his invented worlds. Tip embodies another radical notion. Even though he never left the country town and even though he spends his days selling groceries, he still has the power to tell a story that his listener can "enter." The implicit message for Bert may be summed up in the famous lines from Whitman quoted back in chapter 1: "the powerful play goes on, and you may contribute a verse."

More hopeful still is the shadowy figure of the narrator, who sounds a lot like the author. We know that, unlike the other boys, he left Sandtown. We know he went to college, and we have been let into one of his stories. It seems reasonable to assume that he would have honored the promise and told the other boys if he had ever made it to the Enchanted Bluff. So, the magical place waits for him, just as it does for Tip and Bert. When the time is right, he can tell that story, too.

This, of course, is exactly what Cather eventually did, and the story that was "all introduction" stands as a prologue to the rest of the career. She would not be tied to plot, and she would visit the places that called to her imagination. In 1912, she made her first trip to the Southwest. In the novels that followed, she returned time and again to the thematic material announced in "The Enchanted Bluff," beginning with *Alexander's Bridge.*[34] In *O Pioneers!* (1913), Ivar cares for the migratory birds that stop at his pond. Thea finds inspiration by visiting the Southwest in *The Song of the Lark* (1915). In *My Ántonia* (1918), Jim puzzles over the Native Americans who used to live in Nebraska. In *The Professor's House* (1925), Tom Outland finds out what is on top of the Blue Mesa. Two decades later, Cather was still writing about "rocks" in *Death Comes for the Archbishop* (1927) and *Shadows on the Rock* (1931).

Near the end of November, Jewett responded to this remarkable story with encouragement and wisdom: "Do not hurry too fast in these early winter days,—a quiet hour is worth more to you than anything you can do in it." Recognizing that her advice would be difficult for a woman committed to motion, the older author wrote again in December: "I want you to be surer of your backgrounds, you have your Nebraska life, a child's Virginia, and now an intimate knowledge of what we are pleased to call the "Bohemia" of newspaper and magazine-office life."[35] At this stage in Cather's career, Jewett clearly envisioned several roads for the younger author's energies. There was nothing inevitable about Nebraska, but Cather had to do better when she wrote about it. Jewett's language is deceptively simple. Nebraska is a "background," and the author needs to be "surer." A reader might assume from these terms that Cather was misrepresenting Nebraska in some way, or failing to choose the right details to conjure up the milieu. These were adjustments in craft, but Jewett had something far more powerful and complex in mind that had to do with the writer's emergence.

Everything depended, she explained, on Cather feeling responsible to her "literary conscience." And this sense of responsibility would come from how she lived her writing life. Jewett urged,

> you must find your own quiet centre of life, and write from that to the world that holds offices, and all society, all Bohemia; the city, the country in short, you must write to the human heart, the great consciousness that all humanity goes to make up. Otherwise what might be strength in a writer is only crudeness, and what might be insight is only observation; sentiment falls to sentimentality—you can write

> about life, but never write life itself. And to write and work on this level, we must live on it—we must at least recognize it and defer to it at every step. We must be ourselves, but we must be our best selves.[36]

This was radical advice. It was not enough to publish and work on the craft of writing. The gifted artist could only emerge as a great author by living each day on a high plain of integrity.

Cather wrote back immediately, grateful for the encouragement and advice but hesitant about what to do next. McClure sent her on another trip to Europe the following spring, and she was in London on June 26, 1909, when she got the news that Jewett had died of a stroke at the family home in South Berwick, Maine. Crushed by the news, she made a brief trip back to Nebraska in the summer. As she tended to do, the hardworking editor got sick just before Christmas and spent the holidays thinking about the folks back home, haunted by Jewett's wisdom.

In a reflective mood, Cather began to describe yet another change in her relationship with Nebraska. On January 5, 1910, she wrote to Aunt Franc, "I am hoping to get home next summer, and to run out for a little visit with you. The one this summer was such a satisfactory visit. It was the first time I've really seen you for years. Mother was so willing about my going into the country this time, and I went with a light heart and enjoyed every minute of it. There is no place in the world where I can be so happy or rest so well" (*SLWC,* 127–28). Cather's delight in "the Far Country" is palpable and probably crucial to the extraordinary and improbable burst of writing that was about to occur. "I had such a good visit with her this summer," Cather wrote to her brother Roscoe on February 13 (*SLWC,* 129). In this letter, she takes an important imaginative leap. Ever since she began writing fiction, Cather had cringed at the hardship and labor associated with farming and the life of her Aunt Franc. In the wake of Jewett's death, Cather had not simply gone home to Red Cloud. She had "gone into the country" to see Aunt Franc and become surer of what Jewett called her "background."

Now, like the territorial settlers who claimed and divided the land before her, Cather was ready to set this realm apart. She was ready to name it and claim it. By calling it "the 'Far Country,'" she was (whether consciously or not) linking it to the "edge of the world" in "Eric Hermannson's Soul" and to "The Treasure of Far Island." At long last, with enough distance and hardship and good feeling and Jewett's exhortation to become surer of her backgrounds, Cather was making a new imaginative map of Nebraska that included a farming region in "the country."

Working harder than ever at the magazine, Cather began to write "The Joy of Nelly Deane," another "Margaret story" that nods back to the vivacious but frustrated heroines of her early stories. As in "The Enchanted Bluff," a mature narrator recalls episodes of childhood before stepping back to tell the rest of the story. Nell is the prettiest and most popular girl in the town, but she marries a miserable fellow named Scott Spinny, who ruins her life. Margaret, the narrator, leaves town for college, but eventually returns to hear what happened to Nell. Red Cloud is once again rechristened, this time as Riverbend. The old Kansas-Nebraska Territory is acknowledged as flowers are delivered from Denver. In all these ways, the story fits comfortably alongside "A Resurrection," "The Treasure of Far Island," and "The Sculptor's Funeral."

Although "The Joy of Nelly Deane" has received scant critical attention, it deserves an important place in the history of Cather's creations because of the way it introduces a female narrator into Cather's Nebraskan experiments. Jewett probably deserves the credit here. Back in 1908, when the older author responded to "On the Gull's Road," she registered one serious objection. "The lover," Jewett explained, "is as well done as he could be when a woman writes in the man's character,—it must always, I believe, be something of a masquerade. I think it is safer to write about him as you did about the others, and not try to be he."[37] Cather, of course, liked very much to "be he" in her stories, but Jewett thought something far more honest was possible. It was yet another call for integrity. Grieving for her friend and filled with new visions of the Far Country, Cather seems to have taken her mentor's advice to heart as she wrote this unique story, which seems to signal her transition from a "male to female protagonist, from conventional man to natural woman."[38]

It must have felt like tightrope walking as she drafted the first paragraph: "Nell and I were almost ready to go on for the last act of 'Queen Esther' " (*CSP,* 74). This was bracing stuff for the experienced short story writer. She would tell the story of one woman's love for another, and she would tell it with her own mature voice. It is surely no coincidence that she returned to recollections of youthful performances in Red Cloud in order to do so. Remembering the latter as she wrote, she thought of the "City News" in her story: "We gave the cantata in the Baptist Church on Christmas eve, 'to a crowded house,' as the Riverbend 'Messenger' truly chronicled" (76).

In fact, *Queen Esther* was a perennial favorite in the Red Cloud Cather remembered. Giannone discusses the popularity of the oratorio and suggests that " 'Queen' is Cather's addition,"[39] but in fact the author's title is really just her acknowledgment that she is working from the matrix of memory recorded by the Red Cloud newspapers. For example, she probably recollected a May performance from 1885 in the M. E. Church. The May 22 edition of the *Chief* reported that "the house was literally packed, hundreds of people being unable to gain admission" (9). Below the performance review in the first column, the editor called attention to a new enterprise: "Mr. Cathers is a reliable thorough going business man. Under his efficient management the business of the abstract office will be conducted with accuracy and dispatch." Cather's father may have chuckled over his name and the newspaper's reliability, but we can see how his new venture took its place beside *Queen Esther*. Taken together, these juxtaposed snippets of Red Cloud life reveal how Cather's memory merged with public memory as she wrote this pivotal story.

The approach is apparent throughout the rest of the story as Cather lovingly sketches elements of Red Cloud life. Margaret recalls how the ladies of the Baptist sewing circle hovered over the girls during the show, how they competed with the Methodist women for Nelly's allegiance, and how everyone came to hear Nelly. Giannone comments, "The oratorio is all the more effective because it allows Nell to demonstrate in her singing the very virtuosity and rareness of spirit which the music honors and which the town condemns."[40] Giannone captures the significance of the performance for the story's heroine, but seems to invent a hostile country town that squares neither with the story nor Cather's own recollections of Red Cloud. Having once helped to do battle in the pages of Red Cloud newspapers, Cather has a laugh when Spinny wraps up the flowers in a copy of the Riverbend *Messenger* (78). Nelly's fate will have more to do with her choice of husband than with the malevolence of the village.

More in keeping with the mood of *The Song of the Lark* than "The Sculptor's Funeral," Margaret describes Riverbend on Christmas Eve: "Although it was after midnight, lights were shining from many of the little wooden houses, and the roofs and shrubbery were so deep in snow that Riverbend looked as if it had been tucked down into a warm bed" (78). As the town folk stomp home, calling out holiday greetings, it "all seemed to us very unusual and exciting" (78). Later in the story, Margaret meets Nelly's daughter as she sleds down "Lupton's Hill." Cather was remembering and renaming Indian Princess Hill along the Republican River.[41] Having stepped out of her comfortable pose as a male narrator, the author embraces the elements of Red Cloud with the kind of simple pleasure that, many years later, would infuse "Old Mrs. Harris" and "The Best Years."

Against this background, Cather envisions a fleeting moment of intimacy. Echoing the phrase from the opening sentence of the story, Margaret commences a long paragraph: "At last Nelly and I got up-stairs and undressed" (79). The girls stay up late: "Our light must have burned long after every other in Riverbend was out" (79). Like the night on the island in "The Enchanted Bluff," this moment is a distillation of youth. "We could not let go of life," Margaret explains, "even for a little while" (79).

As it does for the boys in "The Enchanted Bluff," the momentous night vanishes and life goes on. Once again, Cather creates a break in the story so she can juxtapose phases of life. Nelly's father loses his money "in a luckless venture in Cripple Creek," and Guy disappears. The narrator goes off to college, and her family moves to Denver. In this story, Cather anticipates her territorial approach in *The Song of the Lark,* turning "Colorado" into a liminal space of transformation. Nelly remains in Riverbend, where she finally succumbs to Spinny's advances. When Margaret happens to return to the town during the winter vacation of her senior year, she sees Nelly join the Baptist Church.

Perhaps we should call Margaret the heroine of this story because her second homecoming, years later, suggests something far more hopeful than Nelly's fate—an outcome that looks a lot like Cather's life. It seems that the storyteller has been living a full life beyond Riverbend. When she returns to Riverbend, she finds "comfort and completeness" as she visits with Mrs. Dow. More important, Margaret goes out into the snow to find her namesake. The younger Margaret (who also resembles Cather) is full of energy, "her sturdy little legs plowing through the trampled snow" (87). At the end of the story, Margaret is holding Nelly's baby, "so warm and tingling with life" (88). Cather could not have written a more confessional ending. Ever since she went away to college, her homecomings had been filled with the whoops and warmth of children, who offered an uncomplicated welcome. With no intention of having her two heroines ride off on their bicycles into the sunset together, Cather managed a conclusion that honored her mentor's vision.

As a long summer of labor wore on, the Cather of previous years would have planned a visit to the Far Country, but the author knew it was time for decisive change. On September 28, she escaped the magazine with McClure's blessing and with the help of McClung, who guided her to the woodsy solitude of Cherry Valley in upstate New York. It was a rescue worthy of the old romances and quite in keeping with the spirit of Jewett's letter, which affirmed a woman's power to rescue another woman in the name of love.

PRINCESS Hill, south of Red Cloud, n.d. Source: Nebraska State Historical Society.

In the peace of upstate New York, Cather started over in a story she called "The Bohemian Girl," a justly celebrated work that marks the final step toward *O Pioneers!*. Although I am hardly the first person to suggest this progression, I want to return to the story to explore the way so many of Cather's previous experiments come together in its pages. Stouck really began this project more than four decades ago when he described the story as "a blending of several imaginative modes," including romance, irony, pastoral, and epic.[42]

My own list of "blended" modes and strategies begins, not surprisingly, with Cather's territorial imagination, its sandy palimpsest, and her archetypal homecoming narrative of trains and depots. Cather envisions her hero on "The Trans-Continental Express [as it] swung along the windings of the Sand River Valley" (89). When the agent stores his trunk, the narrator informs us that the initials are "N. E." We learn that his name is Nils Ericson and realize we are following a hero whose initials stand for Nebraska: "He gave the town, as he would have said, a wide berth, and cut through a great fenced pasture, emerging upon a white dusty road which ran straight up from the river valley to the high prairie, where the ripe wheat stood yellow and the tin roofs and weather-cocks were twinkling in the fierce sunlight" (90). Up until this point in her fiction, Cather's homecomers have headed up the hill toward town. Nils has a different sort of visit in mind, choosing pasture over town. As Cather had done back in the summer of 1909, Nils is going "into the country." Unlike the forbidding landscape of "On the Divide," this settled land is planted with "yellow wheat" and defined by light. It is, from a painterly perspective, of a piece with the author's pastoral depiction of the glowing country in "Eric Hermannson's Soul."[43] When his brother Olaf asks him about his plans, Nils says he might just stay: "I like this country better than I used to" (92).

Cather makes this clear when she describes the hero's homesickness. The author had lived most of her life with this sense of yearning, first for Virginia, then for Nebraska. She wrote about it in her letters, but in this story she takes us inside the mind of the young man who shares her own surprise at the way a country road can conjure up longing. There are no islands out here. No brick opera house. What could produce the feeling? Nils speculates: "The mention of a name or two, perhaps; the rattle of a wagon along a dusty road; the rank, resinous smell of sunflowers and ironweed, which the night damp brought up from the draws and low places" (92). The woman on the wheel in 1896, pedaling along a dusty road, might not have been able to produce this reflection, but the former magazine editor at work in Cherry Valley was more than ready.

Stirred by these emotions, Nils views the country with surprising clarity. As the wagon climbs the upgrade, "The country, receding from the rough river valley, swelled more and more gently, as if it had been smoothed out by the wind" (92). The wind that was "the real thing" and "the keynote of this country" in "Eric Hermannson's Soul" has become a kindly presence in this story. Beneath this pastoral melody, the territorial imagination persists as Cather marks every significant movement with a crossing of "the sand creek." In fact, she goes out of her way to note six different crossings in the story, a strategy that underscores her faithfulness to a topography she loved to reinvent.

Put another way, Cather was ready to write about *the land.* In some of her previous stories, she had described *fields, pastures,* and *country.* In stories where the buying and selling of parts of that country mattered, such as "Tommy, the Unsentimental," "El Dorado," and "Eric Hermannson's Soul," she talked about *land.* Now she was ready to combine the terms in a single vision. After the barn dance, Nils and Clara meet in a world fit for romance: "The moonlight flooded that great, silent land. The reaped fields lay yellow in it. The straw stacks and poplar windbreaks threw sharp black shadows. The roads were white rivers of dust" (124). Nothing is gilded in this scene. Every detail is faithfully rendered by a gifted colorist intent on capturing this "great, silent land."

Against this canvas, the reunion of mother and son is particularly interesting. As she did in "The Wagner Matinee," the author once again sets her background by painting another "grim" version of the Cather farmhouse (92). Although this story is infused with homesickness, Cather has done nothing to spruce up the "grim" visage. It has endured over the years with the clarity of a Solomon Butcher photograph.

When Nils appears, the reunion unfolds with its own chilly grimness, enlivened only by the two characters' attempts to make sense of each other in ways that echo some of the author's deep anxieties about her roots. Mrs. Ericson assumes Nils never "got used to steady work," having left the farm. With this casual observation, the mother has introduced a theme that haunted Cather throughout her adult life: if real work happens on a farm, how do we value work that happens elsewhere?[44] It is, of course, precisely this question that stands behind the citizens' mockery of Harvey Merrick in "The Sculptor's Funeral." When Cather did not make it home to see her father at Christmas in 1906, she assured her father that she was "working night and day" and "doing just what you would do in my place and what you always taught me to do." We can imagine that Nils wrote letters like this to his father, but in this early scene he offers a simple declaration: "I'm sorry I didn't get back to see father" (96).

As the tension builds, in its steady Nordic fashion, the conversation centers on an irreconcilable conflict at the center of territorial (perhaps all of American) life and European romance: the conflict between those who stay and those who go, those who take routes and those who choose roots. For Mrs. Ericson and her kind, the reward is land. Nils seems confident enough to go along with his mother and admit, "Land's a good thing to have" (97). But Mrs. Ericson catches him again by snapping, "Only when you stay on it" (97). The mother speaks for the homesteaders who stayed put and proved their claims. In the tradition of romance, she speaks for all the villagers and people of the castle, who held their ground against the dragon. The son speaks for all the people who, like Huck Finn, lit out for the territory. The son stands for the knights errant, noble characters committed to wandering and service. Cather seems to endorse the wanderer's vision—until the very end of the story when Eric, with a ticket to Norway in his pocket, turns around and heads back home to his mother and the farm. Cather has no intention of trying to settle the old conflict in this story.

But Joe Vavrika, Clara's father, does embody an alternative. The Bohemian runs an upstanding saloon that is really a kind of household. He stays put in Nebraska, and his vision of happiness does not depend on accumulating land. He values his daughter, music, fine brandy, and good company. Nils recalls how he created an inviting world for "the boys'" imaginative energies, a place of singing, herring and pickles. It was not located in the county seat, "but in a cheerfuller place, a little Bohemian settlement which lay at the other end of the county . . ." (109). Like an island in the river, the settlement is a region set apart, a realm where magical interaction and transformation are possible.

Joe is "six feet four, with curly yellow hair and mustache," and his literary genetics deserve attention by anyone interested in Cather's emergence. A fiddle player, Joe is descended from the title character of Cather's first story, the broken Peter who finds no pleasure in the rough country of Nebraska. Joe is also descended from the tired fiddler in the first "One Way of Putting It" column for the *Journal.* And he owes something to the idea of Eric Hermannson, who becomes convinced that he must give up his fiddle for God. For each of these prototypes, fiddle playing is a source of joy that cannot be sustained in Nebraska. Joe, by contrast, is content. He represents the musical Nebraskans who also, not coincidentally, "have a capacity for pleasure."[45]

Recalling the spirit of Virgil and Gilpin, Joe has created a garden sanctuary: "On Sunday afternoon Joe Vavrika, in his shirt-sleeves and carpet-slippers, was sitting in his garden, smoking a long-tasseled porcelain pipe with a hunting scene painted on the bowl" (113). His daughter sits under a cherry tree, a black cat at her feet, reading Bohemian newspapers to him. When Nils appears, Joe produces a bottle of rare Hungarian Tokai that a friend has given him. The abundance and contentment of this scene are all heightened by knowing Joe's predecessors in the short fiction. Cather had discovered another way to like this country.

It is no coincidence that Joe's accomplishment has its roots in Red Cloud, where John Polnicky was a well-respected citizen. The June 26, 1885, *Chief* describes Polnicky as "one of Webster county's prosperous farmers, and one of the early settlers" (5). In 1892, Polnicky gave up farming to open a saloon called the South Side Sample Rooms. As Cather was preparing to leave for college, the saloon proprietor was becoming one of those country town citizens who appeared as regular characters in the pages of the newspapers. His health, travel, and mishaps were all reported. During election time in 1891, the *Chief* called Polnicky "one of our prominent Bohemians," but the story went on to explain that Polnicky had been overlooked as a candidate for sheriff because certain individuals "didn't want a Bohemian for sheriff."[46] Polnicky fashioned a good life for himself and his family in Red Cloud, but no one in town ever forgot that he was "a Bohemian." Cather's fictional tribute to the man must be read in this context.

Titling her story "The Bohemian Girl," Cather certainly invites this kind of contextualization. So, it seems important to recognize that Clara Vavrika may owe something to Polnicky's daughter Emma. During the autumn of 1894, a little item in the first column of the October 19 *Chief,* just below an advertisement for Doctor McKeeby, reported that Polnicky was in Omaha (5). Across the page, the *Chief* described "a very pleasant surprise" party given for eleven-year-old Emma (5). A year later, the October 18 *Chief* described "the numerous young friends" who celebrated Emma's twelfth birthday (5). But Emma died on November 30 and was buried in the Red Cloud cemetery. It seems that Emma Polnicky was the celebrated Bohemian girl who never left Red Cloud.

In "The Bohemian Girl," Cather imagines the girl's escape, and it comes as a surprise. In all sorts of ways, the author hints that this romance will have more in common with "Eric Hermannson's Soul" than the "The Treasure of Far Island." Clara's marriage to Olaf is the kind of obvious impediment that seems to doom the central characters. When Clara complains of how boring the Ericson family can be, she declares, "I'd almost be willing to die, just to have a funeral" (105). It is the kind of grim humor Cather liked to use in her letters from "the provinces," and it may conjure up an ironic and melancholy recollection of Emma Polnicky, perhaps foreshadowing Clara's extinction.

Stretching all the way back to "On the Divide" and "A Resurrection," Cather had been concerned with the ways in which women could become trapped in country towns. When Nils finally presses Clara about why she ever married Olaf, she attributes it to pressure from "the neighborhood": "You see, they have it on you, Nils; that is if you're a woman. They say you're beginning to go off. That's what makes us get married: we can't stand the laugh" (111). Laughter shared by lovers is bliss, but this other kind of laughter stands for the kind of communal contempt and bullying that inspired American writers to condemn the village. Cather does not explore it in this story, but she certainly acknowledges it. Romance and realism merge here as, once again, the author seems surer of her background.

A few lacunae remain. As pictures of farm life go, the one in "The Bohemian Girl" is still quite incomplete. When Nils's mother wants to take him out to see the threshing, he sneaks away to see Clara. We do not follow Eric on his chores. When the boy runs away, returning home late, his mother has done the milking. Nor do we see the rhythms of domestic ritual that ground farm life. Mrs. Ericson likes to tend her own stove, but we do not follow her as she does the work. As Romines has remarked, Cather seemed intent on avoiding domestic subjects early in her career and she largely maintains her resolve in this story.[47]

Olaf's magnificent barn-raising may be the only exception, but the scene is more like a generous serving of Webster County hospitality. It is also an important

JOHN Polnicky's Saloon, Red Cloud. Source: Willa Cather Pioneer Memorial and Educational Foundation.

transitional sketch in the author's career. Cather the colorist pays attention to Cucurbitaceae: "In the middle of each table was a big yellow pumpkin, hollowed out and filled with woodbine. In one corner of the barn, behind a pile of green-and-white-striped watermelons, was a circle of chairs for the old people . . ." (117). As they did in "The Enchanted Bluff," the gourds suggest abundance, the lateness of the season, and the rhythms of life in Nebraska.

Once again, Cather was dipping into the matrix of memory recorded in the pages of Red Cloud newspapers. A glance at the *Argus* during this season in 1885 underscores the point. Editor Warren was offering a free subscription to his newspaper for the largest watermelon one week and announcing a "melon sociable" the next.[48] Watermelons were everywhere, and they served as yet another occasion for communal hospitality founded on the labor of women. A little piece in the December 10, 1897, *Chief* captures the feeling from the homemaker's perspective: "How dear to my heart is the old yellow pumpkin, when orchards are barren of stuffing for pies" (5). Surer of her background, Cather takes care to place gourds where they can inspire this aura of Red Cloud hospitality and homemaking.

In this vein, the narrator describes the roasts and baked hams, the fat pies and cookies, and the old women who prepared the delicacies.[49] We view the women through the eyes of Nils. As he contemplates their years of hard work, he becomes dizzy. Romines observes that the passage is "determinedly celebratory, but "Nils is aware of the brutalizing as well as the nurturing potential of the old women's domestic energy."[50] Again, the author is surer of her background.

A locomotive headlight completes the effect while refining our understanding of Cather's Nebraska. Olaf brings the light to the party, but then spends all his time worrying about setting the barn on fire. As she included this detail, Cather was probably thinking back to November 1889, when the "railroad boys" hosted a grand ball at the Opera House in Red Cloud. They promised in the *Argus* "A lifelike representation of an engine with a flaming head light" that would fill "the entire stage."[51]

Whatever else we make of Olaf—and he usually comes in for hard treatment—we must admit that the man knows something about the aesthetics of prairie hospitality. He knows hospitalities do better with illumination, and he knows that light (like passion) will burn things down. Like any red-blooded American male or railroad boy, Olaf wants to outdo his neighbors by implementing industrial-strength lighting at his barnraising.[52] In so doing, he confuses light with the warmth of hospitality—something the railroad boys did not do. As the *Chief* reported shortly after the event, "Much has been said about railroad boys, but when you find a class of men that have bigger hearts, more liberal, and enjoy life better than they do, we want to see them."[53]

Nils knows how to enjoy life. Gallantly dancing with Evelina Oleson, Olena Yenson, and little Hilda, he eventually finds his way to Clara. She recalls the way they used "to waltz on rollers at the old skating-rink in town" (123). With this reference, Cather nods back to the Red Cloud rink, which was always being mentioned in the newspapers. Skaters such as Clara and Nils spent countless hours there, and the rink was used for all sorts of entertainments, including a performance of *Queen Esther* early in 1885, about the time rink masquerades were becoming all the rage.[54]

With her memory of skating, Clara is recalling one of the important stages for display and extravagant role playing in country town life. She is remembering how their relationship thrived as a kind of performance. Stirred by this recollection, Nils sings to Clara on the dance floor. When she becomes embarrassed, he tells her, "We're making a legend" (124). This sounds like more bravado, but in the register of romance Nils can make this sort of claim. Having honed their performance skills at the skating rink, the lovers can reach out for a mythic life that breaks the bounds of literary realism and local color. If Cather saw herself through the masculine eyes of the hero, it was perhaps because the habits of masquerade she had learned in Red Cloud were still intoxicating.

At the end of the story, as Nils pleads with Clara to join him, as he reminds her that she only has "one life, one youth," he confesses his successful life with the shipping line: "There, I hadn't meant to tell you; I wanted you to come on your own nerve" (127). Does the confession sway her? She says it does not matter. Later when we hear of the couple's happiness in Norway, we have no way of knowing whether they could have been just as happy without their wealth. Perhaps literature does not need to settle such things when the author aims at what Jewett called "new and more shining ideals."[55]

Cather is clearly working at a higher level at the end of this story and prepared to invent a new sort of heroine. As Clara struggles to make up her mind, the author's ambition yields an important breakthrough. When the heroine says worldly wealth is not the issue, she goes on to confess, "something seems to hold me. I'm afraid to pull against it. It comes out of the ground, I think" (127). Nils thinks he knows what she means, but Clara is describing something more organic and profound that the narrator shares with us: "The great, silent country seemed to lay a spell upon her. The ground seemed to hold her as if by roots. Her knees were soft under her. She felt as if she could not bear separation from her old sorrows, from her old discontent. They were dear to her, they had kept her alive, they were a part of her" (128). This is Cather's new protagonist, a woman rooted in the prairie. Another writer might turn this moment of recognition into a bit of pastoral promotion, a ringing endorsement of the Great Plains in the style of Gilpin. But Cather quite honestly acknowledges that this magical rootedness is bound up with "sorrows" and "discontent." Like all great characters in literature, Clara's strength is inextricably linked to weakness and suffering. Thacker astutely points out that there is no precedent for this epiphany in the stories Cather wrote before "The Bohemian Girl" (*GPF,* 150). Clara is an innovation, and she marks a huge turning point in Cather's imaginative relationship with Nebraska. After writing "The Bohemian Girl," Cather could write "The Swedish Woman."

It is tempting to claim even more for Clara. Rosowski argues for a radical conclusion: "The awakening of 'The Bohemian Girl' is of a woman's desire shattering and freeing itself from gendered codes." Cather certainly sets us up for such notions. When we see her for the first time (through the eyes of Nils), she seems to ride her horse right out of the emerging genre of Western fiction (90–91). As Rosowski notes, "Cather appropriates qualities of the male hero: she is tall, dark, and brooding, possessed of a wild spirit that is forever restless."[56] Readers of *The Virginian* or Cather's "El Dorado" might expect this heroine to ride off into the sunset at the story's end.

Clara is lifted into the saddle by Nils, and they ride off together in an ending that feels more like resistance than code shattering. A far more radical ending, one that Cather's mentor Jewett might have imagined, would center on a woman riding off with another woman. For all sorts of understandable reasons, Cather was not ready to go so far. In this remarkable story, we are left with the man's grand gesture of sweeping the heroine up into his arms. A knight out of the tradition of romance, Nils is a far more civilized version of Canute in "On the Divide." He looks a bit like the male rescuer in "Eric Hermannson's Soul" when Margaret is surrounded by wild ponies. Most important for anyone interested in the evolution of Cather's craft, his action stands as a sketch for the transcendental lifting up of Alexandra in *O Pioneers!*.

There is much that is triumphant here, but an air of belatedness hangs over this story, a combination of white dust and sunlight creating an autumnal glow. It is the yellow of the Tokai, the pumpkins, and the wheat in the moonlight. In this world, the threshing is done and fat pies are all baked. An automobile chugs up and down the white roads. One son leaves for Norway with his true love, "two dark shadows going over the hill" (128). Romines observes that Cather's "language suggests that the lovers' plot, which will climax when they catch the train, lacks substance, compared to the cyclical story of the land."[57] Meanwhile, the other son returns to the land and to his mother on the farm, her fingers tangling in his hair.

Notes

1. Robert Thacker, "Foreword," *April Twilights and Other Poems* by Willa Cather (New York: Everyman, 2013), 11.
2. Susan J. Rosowski, "Willa Cather Editing Willa Cather: From Houghton Mifflin to the House of Knopf," *Studies in the Literary Imagination* 29.2 (1996): 9–25, describes the full flowering of his capacity in Cather's later career.
3. Bernice Slote, "Willa Cather and Her First Book," *April Twilights (1903)* by Willa Cather, rev. edition, ed. Bernice Slote (Lincoln: University of Nebraska Press, 1968), ix. Woodress, *WCLL*, 166 and O'Brien, *WCEV*, 256–57 have echoed this point.
4. Jessica G. Rabin, "'Honey, do we really need five copies of this?': *April Twilights* Revisited," *Willa Cather: New Facts, New Glimpses, Revisions* ed. John J. Murphy and Merrill Maguire Skaggs (Madison: Fairleigh Dickinson University Press, 2008), 117–37.
5. Thacker, "Foreword," *April Twilights*, 19. Rabin, "April Twilights Revisited," *Willa Cather: New Facts, New Glimpses*, Revisions," 122, points out that critics have offered conflicting accounts of Cather's motivation and success as a poet.
6. Slote, "Willa Cather and Her First Book," xxv.
7. Willa Cather, "Grandmither, Think Not I Forget," *April Twilights (1903)*, rev. edition, ed. Bernice Slote (Lincoln: University of Nebraska Press, 1968), 11.
8. Cather, "White Birch in Wyoming," *April Twilights*, 29.
9. Slote, "Willa Cather and Her First Book," xxx.
10. Cather, "Prairie Dawn," *April Twilights*, 38.
11. Slote, "Willa Cather and Her First Book," xxxv; Rabin, "April Twilights Revisited," *Willa Cather: New Facts, New Glimpses*, Revisions," 130–31; Thacker, "Foreword," *April Twilights*, 17.
12. Cather, "Dedicatory," *April Twilights*, 3.
13. Cather made this point succinctly in a 1925 letter to Alice Hunt Bartlett, *WCP*, 179. Her satisfaction is evident in a letter to Jones: "To Will Owen Jones," January 2, 1903, *SLWC*, 68.
14. Thacker, "Foreword," *April Twilights*, 14. See also Rosowski, *Voyage Perilous*, 22.
15. "To Will Owen Jones," March 6, 1904, *SLWC*, 80.
16. Qtd. in *WCLL*, 177.
17. *Chief* (March 4, 1904): 1. A rare report of Cather's doings during this period described her work in Washington, D.C., and a recent visit in the *Chief* (January 4, 1901): 5.
18. Romines, *The Home Plot*, 133.
19. On women's evolving responses to the early phases of settlement, see Glenda Riley, "Women's Responses to the Challenges of Plains Living," *Great Plains Quarterly* 9 (1989): 177. In a passage entirely apposite to Cather's defense of her story, Jeffrey, *Frontier Women*, 87, quotes pioneer Phoebe Judson: "the inconveniences of our environment and the constant drudgery eventually took all the romance and poetry out of our farm life."
20. Slote, "Willa Cather as a Regional Author," 12.
21. Porter, *On the Divide*, 4.
22. "To Will Owen Jones," March 6, 1904, *SLWC*, 80.
23. Romines, *The Home Plot*, 131.
24. Emily Dickinson, *The Complete Poems of Emily Dickinson*, ed. Thomas H. Johnson (Boston: Back Bay Books, 1976), 506–07.
25. I thank Timothy W. Bintrim for pointing out the Shakespearean allusion.
26. Slote, "Willa Cather as a Regional Writer," 11.
27. *Chief* (August 23, 1889): 5.
28. "To Witter Bynner," June 7, 1905, *SLWC*, 88.
29. "To Mariel Gere," September 30, 1905, *SLWC*, 90.

30. "To Sarah Orne Jewett," October 24, 1908, *SLWC,* 117.
31. Bruce P. Baker, " 'The Enchanted Bluff': Dream and Disillusion," *Nebraska English and Language Arts Journal* 37.1 (1991): 29.
32. Stout, *Picturing a Different West,* 136.
33. Rosowski, "Willa Cather's Ecology of Place," 40.
34. Lewis notes Cather's affection for stories about boys and campfires (*WCL,* 79). On this point, see also Judith Fryer, *Felicitous Space: The Imaginative Structures of Edith Wharton and Willa Cather* (Chapel Hill: The University of North Carolina Press, 1986), 224.
35. "To Willa Sibert Cather," November 27, 1908, *Letters of Sarah Orne Jewett,* ed. Annie Fields (Boston: Houghton Mifflin, 1911), 247; "To Willa Sibert Cather," December 13, 1908, *Letters of Sarah Orne Jewett,* 248.
36. "To Willa Sibert Cather," December 13, 1908, *Letters of Sarah Orne Jewett,* 249–50.
37. "To Willa Sibert Cather," November 27, 1908, *Letters of Sarah Orne Jewett,* 246.
38. Rosowski, *Birthing a Nation,* 67.
39. Giannone, *Music in Willa Cather's Fiction,* 47.
40. Ibid., 48.
41. "Indian Princess Hill," *Walk Red Cloud,* Suzi Yost Schulz, http://walkredcloud.com/?p=79, July 30, 2016.
42. Stouck, *Willa Cather's Imagination,* 19.
43. In the earlier story, the narrator describes "a scented sea of cornland bathed in opalescent air and blinding sunlight" (*CSF,* 363).
44. Downs, *Becoming Modern,* 34–36, discusses the birth of this theme during Cather's days in Lincoln.
45. Giannone, *Music in Willa Cather's Fiction,* 52.
46. *Chief* (August 21, 1891): 1.
47. Romines, *The Home Plot,* 128.
48. *Argus* (August 27, 1885): 3; *Argus* (September 3, 1885): 3.
49. For some of the recipes that stand behind this catalog, see Romines, *At Willa Cather's Tables: The Cather Foundation Cookbook.*
50. Romines, *The Home Plot,* 136.
51. *Argus* (November 28, 1889): 8.
52. It is strange indeed how certain notions in American culture endure. In this instance, many people will conjure up images of Clark W. Griswold lighting his home in the popular film *Christmas Vacation.*
53. *Chief* (December 6, 1889): 4.
54. *Chief* (February 6, 1885): 5; *Chief* (February 20, 1885): 5. For a particularly lavish account of one of these festivities, see the *Chief* (March 6, 1885): 5.
55. "To Willa Sibert Cather," December 13, 1908, *Letters of Sarah Orne Jewett,* 249.
56. Rosowski, *Birthing a Nation,* 72–73.
57. Romines, *The Home Plot,* 139.

Chapter 4.

"a ride through a familiar country": The Different Process of *O Pioneers!* and the Emergence of Willa Cather

Here there was no arranging or 'inventing'; everything was spontaneous and took its own place, right or wrong. This was like taking a ride through a familiar country on a horse that knew the way.
—Willa Cather

A crucial difference, I think, between successful and unsuccessful artists is the ability to survive disappointment. Logically, after the failure of Alexander's Bridge, *Cather should have given up. She had always figured she couldn't make it as a novelist. Here, apparently, was the proof. But for some reason that no one has ever been able to explain, she immediately sat down and wrote a second novel,* O Pioneers!
—Joan Acocella

Something profound happened to Willa Cather as she wrote *O Pioneers!,* and the author's biographers and critics have never quite explained it. Until Cather wrote "The Bohemian Girl," it would have been very hard to anticipate *O Pioneers!* with its focus on farm life and a farming heroine. *The Song of the Lark* would have seemed more likely, with its rich depiction of a live Western town and its focus on the growth of a female artist in that environment. But a number of powerful influences and events coalesced during Cather's time in upstate New York. There was the firm voice of Jewett urging surer backgrounds and a focus on female experience. There was Cather's epiphanic experience of "going into the country" during the summers of 1909 and 1912, and her reading of Bergson's *Creative Evolution* in that year. There was the remarkable experience of writing "The Bohemian Girl," with its country background and its "rooted" heroine. And there was Cather's life-changing trip into the Southwest in 1912 that seemed to clarify her whole being as an artist. These and a number of other elements discussed below inspired a creation that confounded the author. Talking to Sergeant well after the fact, Cather recalled "a sudden inner explosion and enlightenment."[1]

Looking back in 1931, with decades of hindsight, Cather knew that her decisions to focus on Nebraska and to write for herself were crucial to her success, but she barely had words for the actual endeavor. It seemed "a different process altogether. Here there was no arranging or 'inventing'; everything was spontaneous and took its own place, right or wrong. This was like taking a ride through a familiar country on a horse that knew the way" (*WCW,* 92–93). The author seems to be describing a mixture of trance, alchemy, and automatic writing, but we can avoid all talk of thaumaturgy here. *Emergence* is a perfectly good word for what Cather experienced because it names a cumulative effect that greatly exceeds the amalgam of the individual elements.

How and why this emergence happened are the subjects of this chapter, which moves through the novel, pausing to consider the writer's process while making frequent references to the first two decades of short stories, which line the road like so many sunflowers. My hypothesis, at the outset, is that Cather's process imitated the early settlers of Nebraska who embraced motion and stasis as the defining elements of their territorial existence. Never satisfied with mere "local color," Cather worked self-consciously in the manner of all great novelists whose stories are imbued with a critical consciousness. In so doing, she remapped the American West while reflecting on cherished notions of gender, prairie, love, friendship, imagination, and economics.

Inscribing a copy of *O Pioneers!* to her childhood friend Carrie Miner Sherwood, Cather suggested how to understand her creative endeavor: "This was the first time I walked off on my own feet—everything before was half real and half an imitation of writers whom I admired. In this one I hit the home pasture."[2] This talk of "pasture" is surely, as Handley suggests, a claim of authenticity.[3] But the implicit idea of a different process understood as a movement through the country deserves more attention. In this metaphorical description, it is a motion untied to roads, perhaps a ramble allowing even more opportunities for inspiration. Taken together, the two accounts recall the way Nils returns home in "The Bohemian Girl," first walking into the pasture, then climbing on a wagon for a ride into the country.

Motion, then, was part of the novel's formula, but so was stillness. Indeed, it was Jewett's suggestion to write from a "quiet center" that seems to have inspired Cather to free herself from magazine work in the waning months of 1911. Relishing the pleasures of her own mind, Cather began to write about a woman in touch with her own quiet center who just happened to grow up on a farm in Nebraska.

Cather called the story "Alexandra" and seems to have written it with no intention of producing a novel. Once again, she was preparing herself (quite intuitively) for a great leap forward in her craft by starting with what she knew how to do: write a short story about a Nebraskan heroine. The project still qualified as an experiment in a number of ways. She would return to what she called "the early times" of "On the Divide." She would finally focus on farm life that seemed so brutal to the narrator in "A Wagner Matinee" and to Nils in "The Bohemian Girl." And her protagonist would be a female farmer rooted in the great, silent land.

In *O Pioneers!,* this transmuted story begins with "one of the most powerful expressions in American literature of the need for spatial order."[4] We recognize it as townmaking, the process familiar to territorial folk and readers of Cather's short stories: "One January day, thirty years ago, the little town of Hanover, anchored on a windy Nebraska table-land, was trying not to be blown away" (11). Anyone familiar with Cather's work would assume that she is preparing to plat yet another version of Red Cloud, but the reference to "table-land" suggests a different town, perhaps Bladen or Blue Hill.[5] As she goes on with her work, it becomes apparent that this is a humbler place than Red Cloud. As she did in "Tommy, the Unsentimental," Cather stretches from the first sentence to embrace a larger portion of the old territory. The instinct for early Nebraska townmaking that took hold when she visited Brownville back in 1894 informs the work.

A knowing reader might expect to hear the mordant voice from "On the Divide," but two tiny cues in the opening sentence announce a different narrator. The phrase "One January day" conjures up old-fashioned storytelling, the kind that could delight a child with a fable or a fairy tale.[6] Meanwhile, the personification of the town suggests a note of whimsy that implies a *certain* hopefulness. We know that Cather had been personifying miserable creeks and rivers in previous Nebraska stories, but this bit of fancy suggests courageous effort on the part of the little hamlet. The result of this whimsy, as Rosowski puts it, "is to move a historical reality into a realm that has the potential for the unexpected, even the miraculous."[7]

In previous stories, Cather would already be pushing toward her protagonist, anxious to introduce him or her, but here she takes her time. The humble town matters not because the author wants to recall Red Cloud but because it embodies the challenge of the early days with its "deeply rutted road" and "uneven rows of wooden buildings" (11). Cather's patience for platting is palpable, the orientation of the station to the town underscoring that this is not a reworking of Red Cloud. Protagonists will emerge on these streets, but only in their own good time. As Cather wrote the first paragraphs of the story that would become a novel, she seemed to be hearing Jewett's advice to slow down on a winter day and value the "quiet hour."

Against this surer background, the author places a series of four vignettes that represent refinements of the now-familiar strategy of side-by-sidedness. There is the sketch of the "little Swede boy" and his frightened kitten, the "strong girl" with extravagant "reddish-yellow curls" who crushes the spirit of the "little clothing drummer," the kitten rescue, and Joe Tovesky and his cronies in a circle around "a little Bohemian girl, Marie Tovesky" (12–13, 17). The Bohemian men drink "raw alcohol, tinctured with oil of cinnamon" (20). As Laegreid points out, the juxtaposition of "good" and "bad" immigrant cultures is striking. Swedish hardiness is set against Bohemian unruliness.[8] Like her vignettes for Nebraska newspapers, each of these pieces is remarkably visual.

The pieces seem to follow each other with a certain inevitability, but there is no necessary order for them. A few sentences of transition would make other arrangements work. To put the matter mathematically (which we need to do in order to appreciate Cather's craft), the opening vignettes of *O Pioneers!* feel like *permutations* (groups of things with strict order), but they are simply *combinations.* Cather could have arranged the chapter in twenty-four different ways.

Appreciating this fact helps us understand a bit more about the author's distinctive process. Here we return to Cather's fantastic notion in the 1931 essay that the writing of these pages was "spontaneous," requiring "no arranging or 'inventing.'" It sounds like simple hyperbole, but Cather's claims become more intriguing later in the essay when she talks about trying to stuff too much detail into *Song of the Lark.* In retrospect, she recognized that *My Ántonia* was more successful because "it took the road of *O Pioneers!*" and so preserved "a very satisfying element analogous to what painters call 'composition'" (*WCW,* 96–97). In this account, I think Cather was describing the virtual quality of the novel's many distinct parts, an imaginative disposition announced in this opening gambit of vignettes. Whether we view the approach toward "composition" as snipping and pasting or cutting and stitching, whether we locate its origins in the packing crates of Sandy Point or the practices of nineteenth-century newspapering, in metaphors of quilting or music, this process of cration clearly energized the writer as she moved ever closer to her first Nebraska novel.

Among these first mobile vignettes, this first glimpse of Alexandra deserves study because of the way Cather experiments with gender. The heroine is "a tall, strong girl, and she walked rapidly and resolutely, as if she knew exactly where she was going and what she was going to do next. She wore a man's long ulster . . . carried it like a young soldier" (13). The sketch sounds a great deal like Cather at a similar age, who signed her name "William" and once posed for a photograph wearing a stylish "Confederate" outfit.[9] In ways that also echo the title character from "Tommy, the Unsentimental," Alexandra is adopting *certain* elements of masculinity, but not trying to pass as a man.[10] When the traveling salesman admires her hair, the girl "stabbed him with a glance of Amazonian fierceness" (15).

We glimpse the depth of Cather's experiment when we mark the narrator's qualification that the girl walked "as if she knew exactly where she was going." In this state of locomotion, she marches right past her crying brother. "She did not notice the little boy," the narrator explains, "until he pulled her by the coat" (14). The foreshadowing is emphatic. The intense, perhaps masculine, focus that will carry her forward through great difficulties means she is prone to overlooking details in front of her. With these deft touches, Cather has turned the static newspaper vignette into art, a vibrant structural device that ensures complex psychological revelations later in the novel. Pinpointing the author's innovation in the novel, Thacker explains that "the advance made by Cather lies in the extent to which she *dramatizes* what others had merely observed" (*GPF,* 152).

For twenty years, Cather had been writing stories set in Nebraska that unfolded either in town or in the country. Until she wrote "The Bohemian Girl," the author tended to introduce either one of these backgrounds and stick with it. But *O Pioneers!* is the product of a different process that is like riding into the country. So Alexandra, Carl, Emil, and cat climb into the wagon. The motion has a sudden and startling effect: "The little town behind them had vanished as if it had never been, had fallen behind the swell of the prairie, and the stern frozen country received them into its bosom" (21). After scrupulously platting Hanover, Cather allows it to dissolve like a stage effect. Townmaking is over. This novel is about human relationships with the land. The heroine rides into the female country, a stern presence that, rather paradoxically, offers comfort.[11]

In her early fiction, a journey into the country would be accompanied by talk of madness and suicide, perhaps in the sardonic tone of the narrator in "On the Divide" or "El Dorado." This narrator is wiser and ultimately focused on the land. Unwilling to either idealize or sneer, she reports the young people's suffering, noting "the eyes of the girl, who seemed to be looking with such anguished perplexity in the future; upon the sombre eyes of the boy, who seemed already to be looking into the past" (21). The narrator leaves no doubt about the cause-and-effect relationship. The country is frozen in all sorts of ways: "It was from facing this vast hardness that the boy's mouth had become so bitter; because he felt that men were too weak to make any mark here" (21). As it did to Canute, the land has damaged the settler and there seems to be little hope for such men.

But what about women? With all the forthrightness of an experienced magazine writer, the author announces a major theme of this work: "But the great fact was the land itself, which seemed to overwhelm the little beginnings of human society that struggled in its somber wastes" (21). As she wrote, Cather recognized that this focus on the relationship between a heroine and the land was original.[12] Acknowledging her innovation, scholars have been quoting this sentence for decades. It rings like a manifesto, a testament to the territorial imagination that endures in living memory.

It was, of course, an autobiographical moment for the author. Shortly after the publication of *O Pioneers!,* she told an interviewer about her arrival in the West: "As we drove further and further out into the country, I felt a good deal as if we had come to the end of everything—it was a kind of erasure of personality" (*WCP,* 10). This story of "erasure" is surely behind the first section's conclusion as Alexandra drives on toward home: "The rattle of her wagon was lost in the howling of the wind, but her lantern, held firmly between her feet, made a moving point of light along the highway, going deeper and deeper into the dark country" (24). Cather was finally ready to confront this experience through fiction, imagining, as she had often done in her Nebraska stories, an alternative version of her own life on the Divide.

Ever since her first stories, Cather had been aware, to some degree, of the territorial imagination that flowed through her craft. She welcomed the countless associations, habits of mind, and general aura that made the American West a lively place. But as we know, there were elements of the early past that she avoided, perhaps because she had not experienced them herself. None of these lacunae is more surprising than the missing fiction devoted to the woman homesteader. As historians remind us, women homesteaders existed in the old Kansas-Nebraska Territory. They did not simply inherit homesteads. They filed and proved their own claims.

If Cather had wanted to tell a revolutionary story about Nebraska history, she could have begun with a character named Alexandra, who files and proves a claim in the heart of Nebraska. With this in mind, Peck argues, "At its deepest level, *O Pioneers!* tells not the dramatic story of the pioneer's conquest of the prairie but rather the imaginative story of an artist's conquest of her true literary material."[13] There is much truth in this comment, but the privileging of artistic consciousness over Western materials seems unnecessary. The two were intertwined in countless ways that came to inform this great work of emergence.

For instance, Cather felt that the quality of the present work depended on her ability to engage the long perspective of colonization by white settlers in the territory. She needed, in some fashion, to incorporate this epoch without trying to dramatize it. So she hit upon the notion of the dying John Bergson, in "the low log house," conjuring up early homesteading as a montage—and generations of readers have *felt* that *O Pioneers!* tells the story of "frontier life." Moved by this strategy, scholars have viewed the Bergson home as a "shanty" and suggested that Alexandra and her family live in "abject poverty."[14] One can imagine Cather recalling "the ringing slap" from Will Owen Jones about her depiction of Nebraska and her passionate response to her old friend, "I though[t] everyone admitted that those pioneer days were desolate. . . . Farm life in that territory when I knew it fifteen years ago was bad enough, what must it have been before?" We do not know if Jones ever responded directly to this query, but Cather lets Mrs. Bergson settle the matter once and for all. When asked, later in the book, about the early days, she answers, "Oh, worse! Much worse" (60). Cather was writing a memorial version of pioneer life and claiming the last word in her own story of emergence.

In the glow of "authentic hardship," the author deftly returns to the present of her story as the father calls his three children around him. It is not *King Lear*, but Cather was a fan of Shakespeare and she knew that she was creating her own version of a dramatic situation that was worthy of great literature. His message is simple: "keep the land together and . . . be guided by your sister" (31). After her managerial experience at *McClure's*, Cather must have derived particular pleasure from imagining the scenario. Most of her readers will join her in appreciating the feminist implications of the situation.[15]

Writing with unprecedented confidence in a way that felt distinctly her own, the author ends the chapter with a vignette about Mrs. Bergson, her insistence on "household order," and her near "mania" for preserving (33–34). Most readers probably smile at this portrait today, but they probably do not realize that they have encountered the author's idiosyncratic vision of early farm life on the Great Plains. Romines argues that Cather "celebrated domesticity only when it managed to get beyond the limits of dailiness; improvising, inventing, overcoming, and imagining in ways that popular culture was more likely to sanction in men (who 'saw a better way')."[16] Alexandra's appreciation for Crazy Ivar's advice on hogs fits this disposition perfectly (46–47).

Chapter Three begins on a Sunday, six months after the father's death as the Bergsons and Carl drive deeper into the country to visit Crazy Ivar. At some point in her writing, Cather realized that Sundays might serve as a pattern for her quilted narrative. Important elements could repeat on these Sundays. In "Winter Memories," we learn that Alexandra's dream of being carried away "most often came to her on Sunday mornings" (185). Probably feeling something like spontaneity, the author realized that she could announce another Sunday at any place in her novel and move forward.

In this first Sunday vignette, the riders share their impressions of Ivar, who feels the pain of animals, healing them with prayer. Learning about Ivar, we also learn about Emil, who is at first frightened but quickly fascinated. Lou and Oscar laugh at the old man. It is an accretive method of characterization that flows easily out of dialogue, ending when the narrator shifts to territorial mapping: "The road to Ivar's homestead was a very poor one. He had settled in the rough country across the county line, where no one lived but some Russians" (37–38). In this way, characterization flows into territorial consciousness as we see how humans have divided the prairie into roads and lines that stand as imaginary boundaries between us and them. In a novel that makes so much of Swedish and Czech homesteaders, these divisions relegate the Volga Germans (Russians) to the margins.[17] Because these lines coincide with geological and botanical features, the settlers acknowledge the divisions without question. Their wagon enters "Crazy Ivar's country [where] the grass was short and gray, the draws deeper" (39).

Capturing this ride into the country, the prose turns increasingly botanical and even ecological, expanding as a catalogue of the plant species as they pass: "shoestring, and ironweed, and snow-on-the-mountain" (39). For centuries, ever since Coronado and his company arrived in present-day Kansas in 1541, writers had lacked the words for bluestem, buffalo grass, cordgrass, grama, needlegrass, sweetgrass, and switchgrass. If they registered the tenacity of the grasses' roots, they rarely wrote about it, even as they overlooked the prairie turnip, paintbrush, and milkweed. At long last, a writer was chronicling the botanical wonders of the prairie. Charles Bessey, the famous botanist at the University of Nebraska, would have been proud. Cather, for her part, was clear that this novel of emergence had come "out of the long grasses."[18]

Ivar's homestead is a major site in Cather's fiction, an extended vignette that comes straight out of Red Cloud newspapering. The August 15, 1884, *Chief* offered an investigative look at the life of W. H. Delancy: "On Saturday last our reporter in company with Dr. Mosena went to see the Prairie Hermit, living if living it may be called about three miles north of Inavale. On arriving at the den, surrounded and almost hidden from view by Nebraska's native kindling wood, the golden sunflower, a scene of destitution rarely if ever witnessed in a civilized country appeared."[19] Delancy was Cather's inspiration, and the newspaper's critical appraisal has much in common with Lou and Oscar's version of the man. On the other hand, Cather's narrator describes no destitution in her portrait of a hermit. Ivar's "little cave house" is "clean as a cupboard" (44). If his homestead is unconventional, it is nevertheless praiseworthy: "Ivar had lived for three years in the clay bank, without defiling the face of nature any more than the coyote that had lived there before him had done" (39–40). By giving this simple judgment to her trustworthy narrator, the author makes her values clear. Long before anyone was ready to talk about environmental awareness on the Nebraska prairie, Cather goes out of her way to endorse a "wild homestead" that preserves the natural world around it (41).[20] If the author had accomplished nothing else in this novel, she would deserve celebration for introducing ecological awareness into our vision of the Great Plains.

Emil, Carl, and Alexandra appreciate the vision, asking about the pond and the birds that come there. In doing so, they recall the people of Webster County who paid attention to birds and liked to read about them in the newspapers. At the same time, the young people reveal their kinship to the boys who watch the whooping crane in "The Enchanted Bluff." As if to highlight the resemblance, Cather has Ivar tell of a crane that came the previous week quite out of season. Carl asks about a seagull that visited, and Ivar remembers her cries (43). Lou and Oscar merely grin as Ivar shares his conviction: "Yes, I know boys are thoughtless. But these wild things are God's birds" (43). The moment feels like a culmination for a number of reasons. Boy life really has become central to her art, stretching from her youth to "The Way of the World" to "The Enchanted Bluff" to this first Nebraska novel. Some boys are better than others, and how we respond to wild creatures reveals a great deal about who we are.

As I suggested in chapter 1, territorial creation was inevitably defined by expediency and division. The same can surely be said of Cather's leap into the fourth chapter of her novel. More than a simple skip forward, it announces the vision that will hold the novel together. By the time she reached this point in her narrative, the author had written more about farm life than she had in the previous twenty years combined. Had she shared Garland's love of farm and ranch detail, she might have plunged forward with a chapter about the building of the pig corral. That chapter would certainly have included details about farm chores and perhaps something about Emil's new fascination with the birds around their pond. It might have marked the changing of the season, with a reference to the migratory birds of late summer and autumn.

But Cather had no desire to write this kind of local color. She needed a way of efficiently getting to a story she wanted to tell that was rooted in her own memory. It was time to divide and advance. So the opening sentence tells us about the Bergsons' three years of prosperity after the father's death, and then the three years of "hard times that brought every one on the Divide to the brink of despair; three years of drouth and failure, the last struggle of wild soil against the encroaching plowshare" (49). The separation into a fourth chapter allows Cather to describe the family's difficulties in a montage. Quite efficiently, she establishes the boys' increasing frustration—and the fact that this is "the last" great difficulty that the white homesteaders will face.

In other words, the vision governing this novel is the same one she would use in writing her article about the history of Nebraska for the *Nation* in 1923: this is the story of the first cycle. Reynolds has analyzed how the novel builds upon this ancient sense of time by reckoning the way "chronologies of migration and settlement run up against other timescales" such as the geological and the prehistoric realm of the early human.[21] For two decades, ever since "On the Divide," Cather had been experimenting with mixtures of past and present, visions of territorial imagination, modern making on the Great Plains, historical motion, and stasis.[22]

Cather needed nearly twenty years of experimentation and practice before she was prepared to write in this fashion, but her enthusiasm is apparent as she locates the chapter's opening idyll. Even in the midst of a "barren" summer, the garden frames the story's heroine in pastoral beauty. As Carl arrives, he finds Alexandra "standing lost in thought, leaning upon her pitchfork, her sunbonnet lying beside her on the ground. The dry garden patch smelled of drying vines and was strewn with yellow seed-cucumbers and pumpkins and citrons" (50). Joe Vavrika's garden in "The Bohemian Girl" served as a preliminary sketch for this moment, but this scene suggests an evolution. Cather the colorist splashes the yellow of the Cucurbitaceae family, adding the "feathery asparagus, with red berries" and "gooseberry and currant bushes," "zinnias and marigolds, and a row of scarlet sage" (50). Cather practiced many years in order to block and paint this little world. When she finally did, it felt like emergence.

Conjuring up images from Breton, Millet, and Homer, the heroine's painterly pose suggests something more than tranquility. It is, as Peck points out, Alexandra channeling the imaginative power and authority of Emerson and Whitman.[23] It is also a rarefied vision of farm life in repose that is essential to Cather's picture of Alexandra as the heroine of Jewett's "quiet hour."

In this autumnal setting, Carl tells Alexandra that his family is leaving. As James Hillman has observed, *leaving* and *being left* define human being,[24] but Cather had been avoiding stories about leaving until she began to dramatize the event in "The Bohemian Girl." Now, as the two old friends try to put their intimacy into words, they come to a profound understanding of their friendship. Carl laments that he and his family will not be around to help Alexandra and her family. Alexandra corrects him: "Oh, it's not that. Nothing like that. It's by understanding me, and the boys, and mother, that you've helped me. I expect that is the only way one person ever really can help another" (53).

Understanding is, of course, one of the great themes of this novel, and no author has ever written a more heartfelt declaration for one of her characters. In Alexandra's wise words, we hear the anguish of the author's letters from Red Cloud during college, afterward when home felt like Siberia, and during her first lonely days in Pittsburgh. In the same key, we hear the romantic, even Schumannian, outburst of Margaret in "Eric Hermannson's Soul" as she longs for "one thing that would warm me when I am alone!"

The chapter ends with a sketch of settled farm life in Nebraska that echoes Cather's experience. Carl and Oscar play checkers while Lou goes off to court Annie Lee. As Cather did with her siblings, Alexandra reads *The Swiss Family Robinson* to Emil and her mother. The checker players soon begin to listen. Readers of "The Way of the World" and "The Treasure of Far Island" will recall Cather's notion that children are artists, and certain adults manage to hold on to this sensibility. In a moment of domestic harmony, Alexandra invites the rest of her family back into this magical realm.

"The Wild Land" might have concluded with Carl's departure or his decision to stay near Alexandra. It could have unfolded through her conversations with neighbors during her trip with Emil. The experimenting author imagines her heroine consulting with "one young farmer who had been away at school, and who was experimenting with a new kind of clover hay" (63). But this long "story" is about the heroine's deep understanding of the territory. As brother and sister drive through the country toward home, the narrator declares: "For the first time, perhaps, since that land emerged from the waters of geologic ages, a human face was set toward it with love and yearning" (64). Everything in the story comes down to this powerful expression of the territorial imagination. Eliding Native American experience, the narrator announces the definitive American romance.

Of course, Cather was not the first to undertake this kind of mythmaking. Back in 1893, as she was writing her first stories about the harsh world of early settlement in the territory, Mary Pillsbury Weston painted *The Spirit of Kansas* for the World's Columbian Exposition in Chicago. In this brightly colored vision, the spirit resides in a young woman with impressive hair, riding a white horse into the lush country. In the first decades of statehood, with the Civil War still fresh in everyone's memory, the painting answered a deep need for a female image of peaceful prosperity on the prairie.

Two decades later, Cather was creating a more enduring and forward-looking portrait of a strong female farmer who rode into the country with both exuberance and wisdom. In a muted palette, more akin to Breton and Millet, the narrator announces the truth Cather had known for some time: "The history of every country begins in the heart of a man or a woman" (64). Alexandra explains her decision to stay put and buy more land: "When you drive about over the country you can feel it coming" (66). Knowing is *feeling*—which philosophers would probably call *intuition*—on a ride into the country. The result, the narrator explains, is nothing less than "a new consciousness" (68).[25] This is Cather's triumphant announcement in *O Pioneers!*.

WILLA Cather reading to her brother Jack and sister Elsie, c. 1900.

Source: Archives & Special Collections, University of Nebraska–Lincoln Libraries.

It is tempting to paint this dénouement in Weston's bright colors, but that would misrepresent the mystery of Cather's heroine, a quality that she clearly inherited from Clara in "The Bohemian Girl." During her epiphanic ride through the country, Alexandra "felt as if her heart were hiding down there" in the land (69). This is not Weston's vision, and one wonders whether any young person should have to live with her heart hiding deep in the earth. Even in moments of joyous epiphany, Alexandra is, like her creator, a darkly divided creature.

Thacker rightly points out that the author is adding "a new kind of 'romance' element to prairie fiction" by depicting "Alexandra's love *for* the prairie itself" (*GPF,* 156). In terms of craft, the author had been preparing for this invention for a long time. As far back as "El Dorado," she had personified corn and rivers, experimenting with ways to voice bitterness and heartache rooted in the soil. Now, in this first Nebraska novel, she attempts something different. When she tries to explain to Carl how Nebraska has changed, Alexandra says, "It had its little joke. It pretended to be poor" (108). In this context of intimate disclosure, the author's penchant for personification has been repurposed in a new sort of romance that Cather called "Alexandra." The story was finished.

Or so the author thought. An extraordinary trip into the Southwest during the spring of 1912, echoing the boys' long-anticipated adventure in "The Enchanted Bluff," transformed her imaginative relationship with the West. In the well-known 1931 essay, Cather described the time: "The longer I stayed in a country I really did care about, and among people who were a part of the country, the more unnecessary and superficial a book like *Alexander's Bridge* seemed to me. I did no writing down there, but I recovered from the conventional editorial point of view" (*WCW,* 92). This story of revelation seems simple enough. The author realized she should write about people out West because she felt deeply connected to them and their country. It turned out to be a crucial step in her emergence. When *O Pioneers!* appeared, Gardner Wood marveled over the result in the pages of *McClure's Magazine.* "The West," he declared, "seems inexhaustible."[26]

On closer inspection, the explanation is puzzling. As we have seen, Cather had been writing about a territory she "really did care about" for more than twenty years, celebrating "the live western towns" in "Tommy," the "wind" in "Eric Hermannson's Soul," and dusty moonlight in "The Bohemian Girl." Was Cather once again offering a partial version of her interior life for public consumption? What really happened down there?

Cather's surviving letters tell us what we need to know. Writing to Sergeant on April 20, 1912, from Winslow, AZ, the author confessed, " 'Bigness' is the

MARY Pillsbury Weston, *The Spirit of Kansas,* 1893. Source: Kansas State Historical Society.

subject of my story. The West always paralyzes me a little" (*SLWC,* 150). She goes on to recall her "fright" as a child, remembering, "I used always to be sure that I'd never get out, that I would die in a cornfield. Now I know I will get out again, but I still get attacks of fright. I somehow feel that [if] one were really a fit person to write about a country they wouldn't feel that." In the Southwest, Cather finally faced this sense of inadequacy, and there was a kind of liberation in the confrontation. The author was free to rediscover the country of cornfields.

A precedent for what followed can be found in Coronado's sixteenth-century journey of "discovery" that began in present-day Mexico and crossed the Southwest before reaching its farthest northern point in the Kingdom of Quivira in present-day Kansas. When the expedition arrived in the heart of what would become the Kansas-Nebraska Territory, they viewed the country in juxtaposition with every stage of their journey and with their recollections of home. Pedro de Castañeda de Nájera, the great chronicler of the expedition, declares, "this land was seen to be very much like the [land] of Spain, in regard to its types of plants and fruits."[27] Juan Jaramillo, one of the chronicler's comrades, was even more enthusiastic: "This land has a very beautiful appearance, such that I have not seen better in the entirety of Spain, nor in Italy or part of France, nor even in other lands where I have traveled in

His Majesty's service."[28] Jaramillo thought the next step was obvious: "you could bring many people from Spain, I understand, to settle the land without misgivings, owing to the appearance and indications that the land shows."[29] Centuries after Coronado's expedition, Cather experienced the same sense of revelation by juxtaposing the Great Plains and the Southwest. Not unlike Coronado and his chroniclers, she was able to overlay her perceptions of the West with her experience of Europe, particularly in the south of France and her memories "of her time at Lavandou."[30]

By late June, her imagination buzzing with visions of Cliff Dwellers and Mexican songs, Cather was back in Red Cloud, "soaking herself in the scents, the sounds, the colours of Nebraska, the old memories—and a new vision of it all" (*WCL,* 84). Soon she was planning another voyage into "the Bohemian country for a week to see the wheat-harvest. That is always a splendid sight, and there is much merry-making among the people." Describing her plans to her reader in the East, she explained, "The whole great wheat country fairly glows." She and her father had been "motoring about the country," "but when I go up into the Bohemian township I shall drive, and saunter about from farm to farm in the old-fashioned way." Cather was living the different process that would enable her to complete *O Pioneers!,* already planning a return to Pittsburgh, where she would work on a story entitled "The White Mulberry Tree."[31]

In this letter, she enclosed nineteen lines of verse, beginning with "Evening and the flat land. . . ." Just as she had done in Red Cloud when she watched the night express bring the body of Amos Cowden home, Cather rushed to capture her awakening in verse. Looking back at the territorial settlers' desire for panoramas, we can see her finding a way to transform this longing into an aesthetic approach she could share. As Thacker explains, "These lines define both the primacy of prairie space and human struggle within it" (*GPF,* 152). Foregoing rhymes, Cather discovered simple lines of attention that pointed to prose as rich as the "fresh-plowed soil." *McClure's* would publish the poem as "Prairie Spring" in December, and Cather would place it at the beginning of *O Pioneers!* The lyric impulse to share pure feeling was too intense to resist—and she knew she had it right this time (*SLWC,* 159).

At the bottom of the poem, Cather wrote: "This is how the wheat country seemed to me three weeks ago when I first came back from the Southwest. There's another note in it now." In ways no trip to England, for instance, could ever do, the juxtapositions of Arizona and New Mexico to Nebraska transformed Cather's creation. Again, I would emphasize that it is not that she suddenly cared about the place and the people back home. Cather's realization was something far more subtle and valuable that could only be suggested in musical terms. Cather was now thinking of Nebraska as a musical composition—as melody, harmony, rhythm, tone, and tempo. More than anything else, this Nebraska offered itself up for modulation. After her momentous trip, Cather the composer could create freely. It felt like a ride through the country.

Back in Pittsburgh, she set to work on "The White Mulberry Tree," which seemed a successful and independent work when she finished it. In a quiet hour, she pulled out the manuscript of "Alexandra," and something extraordinary happened. Cather picked up the two stories, held them side-by-side, and realized that they might be combined to make a novel. Sometime later, Sergeant asked the author to explain what had happened: "She said she could only describe this coming together of the two elements that made the book as a sudden inner explosion and enlightenment."[32] The pyrotechnical language suggests a kind of marvel.

There was no reason to be amazed. Cather had been rearranging "elements," with pieces and parts of stories, ever since her name appeared in the *Chief* and *Argus* as editor of "High School Items." Is it any wonder that the experienced editor suddenly realized that stories created for one purpose could be repurposed in the name of a larger project? Having juxtaposed versions of the West on her recent trip, Cather almost inevitably juxtaposed manuscripts. Pushing herself to incorporate more in a single narrative structure, the author created the conditions that made it possible to finish a novel. "More," as P. W. Anderson wrote of emergence back in 1972, really was "different."[33]

From her first stiff attempts at Old World allusion in "On the Divide," Cather had been experimenting with ways of incorporating venerable echoes and frames in her Nebraska stories. With this reservoir of experience behind her, she was ready to take advantage of her experimentation. Writing to Sergeant on September 12, Cather announced that she was "making a two-part 'pastoral'" (*SLWC*, 167). Hearkening back to the idylls of Theocritus and the territorial rhetoric of Gilpin, Cather realized that her large composition, made up of many juxtaposed pieces, could achieve a kind of profundity through pastoral.

Bergson's *Creative Evolution* was the other important influence that autumn. Responding to a recent letter by Sergeant, Cather answered on September 12, "Yes, I think the first two chapters—or books?—of 'Creative Evolution' glorious." By this point in his career, Bergson was an international celebrity embraced by people who wanted an alternative to popular celebrations of mechanized life. In *Creative Evolution,* Bergson offered a vision of life as ceaseless becoming, impelled by an *élan vital,* informed by intuition. In language that must have made Cather gasp with recognition, he called human beings "artisans," declaring, "that we are, to a certain extent, what we do, and that we are creating ourselves continually. This creation of self by self is the more complete, the more one reasons on what one does."[34] Perhaps I state the obvious, but it is a crucial point for understanding Cather's relationship to her art. With her fiction and poetry, Cather was always trying to "reason on" her own life. The problem, as Bergson saw it and Cather recognized, was that human beings can easily become stuck in this process.

Over the years, a few scholars have noted the importance of this vision to Cather's fiction. In the definitive discussion of the subject, Quirk rightly observes, "The enabling circumstances that encouraged the creation of *O Pioneers!* were several, but it is not incidental that the 'inner explosion' that produced it occurred shortly after she had acquired firsthand her own sense of the new reality as it was revealed in an excited reading of *Creative Evolution* in 1912."[35] For two decades Cather had struggled to reconcile everyday life, the mundane world of farm chores and office tasks, with the kingdom of art where imagination joined with craft to engender beauty and truth. When Cather read Bergson, as Quirk demonstrates, she suddenly saw how everything fit together, and it is probably no coincidence that her heroine is named *Bergson.*[36]

Buoyed by this vision, Cather skips over sixteen years, sketching the changes in the countryside as a background for her pastoral portrait of Alexandra's farm. The narrator proceeds to sketch the familiar house on the hill and the "several miles across the fields" (80). Making no attempt to paint the open prairie, the narrator leans once more on her pastoral frame: "South of the hill, in a low, sheltered swale, surrounded by a mulberry hedge, was the orchard, its fruit trees knee-deep in timothy grass" (80). A curious stylistic shift in the final paragraph signals the author's urgency: "When you go out of the house into the flower garden, there you feel again the order and fine arrangement manifest all over the great farm . . ." (81). For many writers, this dip into second-person would represent a loss of concentration, but "you" works here to create a sense of immediacy and even communion. As if she cannot stress the experience enough, the author repeats the phrase again in the final sentence: "You feel that, properly, Alexandra's house is the big out-of-doors, and that it is in the soil that she expresses herself best" (81).

With classical symmetry, Cather has Carl return to Alexandra in the garden on this Sunday afternoon. It is an emotional event and part of the larger love story, but Carl also adds an analytical presence to the novel, one that Cather had slowly been embracing for decades. In her youth, the editors of the *Chief* and the *Argus* had imitated the editorializing of their territorial forebears who both boomed and criticized Nebraskan life, past and present. From her days in Lincoln, Cather had simply assumed that this critical labor was part of her job description as a professional writer, even if it sometimes got her into trouble. In her several assays of Brownville, we see her experimenting with analytical postures. In "Eric Hermannson's Soul," she invents outsiders, who see the territory with fresh eyes. Eventually, she would write "The End of the First Cycle," her definitive nonfiction version of this labor. Now, in the middle of *O Pioneers!,* Cather was ready to write her definitive version in fiction, and Carl's arrival helps her stay on track.

Like a figure out of a George Caleb Bingham painting, Lou sits down to whittle soon after Carl arrives. The old neighbor wants to know how William Jennings Bryan is viewed back in New York, but what he really wants to do is make a point about the region he calls home: "The West is going to make itself heard" (104). The mix of pride, bravado, and inadequacy is palpable. Although she embraced progressive ideals, Cather followed her mentors back at the *Journal* in their distaste for Populist demagoguery (*WCL,* 208-10). Embodying a benign version of this attitude, Carl simply laughs. "But, surely, it did do that, if nothing else," he says. Lou turns red and claims that "We're waking up to a sense of our responsibilities, out here, and we ain't afraid, neither" (105). In the transition from struggling homesteader to proud farmer, Lou has become a blustering politician. Cather, as she will do so emphatically in "The End of the First Cycle," begins to wonder whether the West is a better place today than it was in the past.

After supper, sitting in the moonlit garden by the tall castor beans, Alexandra and Carl continue to take stock of past and present, Carl preferring the past over the present in a kind of nostalgia that frames his thoughtful declaration: "And now the old story has begun to write itself over" (110). Story and cycle. This is the eternal structure at the heart of *O Pioneers!,* and Carl just happens to describe it metaphorically as the song of a lark. Years before, Cather had described the stories of *The Troll Garden* as a "cycle," a structural principle for an editor producing a collection of short fiction.[37] Now she was ready to explain how the idea of a cycle encompassed everything she cared about. Inside this morphology, stories write themselves. No entropy occurs as story engenders story, each one as fresh as the last. It is a bold Bergsonian vision of life—of history and literature—that justifies the novel Cather was writing.

In this context, Cather returns to an old vignette. Alexandra describes the sister of one of her hired men who "tried to kill herself once or twice" but recovered after a visit to Iowa: "She said that anything as big as the bridges over the Platte and the Missouri reconciled her. And it's what goes on in the world that reconciles me" (115). Obviously, Cather was repurposing the story she told in her 1905 letter to Bynner.[38] As she began doing in the *Journal* decades before, the author recognized that she could use the vignette for reflection and a bit of moralizing summed up in a single word: "reconciliation." As the *Oxford English Dictionary* explains, the word comes from the Latin *conciliāre,* which means "to combine, unite physically or in thought or feeling, to make friendly or agreeable." So, Cather seems to be saying, through Alexandra, that changing the way one sees the world is not enough. In order to flourish on the Great Plains, a person must be united—on friendly terms—with the territory.

In a way, the rest of the novel unfolds as a series of variations on this notion of reconciliation, with each variation conjuring up parts of Cather's Nebraska, past and present. Echoing Cather's own anxieties over work and farms, we learn that "Emil, for all his track practice, did not stand up under farmwork very well" (116). Glancing back at the birds that mattered to people in Webster County, Nebraska, "The Enchanted Bluff," and Ivar's wisdom in the present novel, Cather creates a powerful bit of foreshadowing when Emil kills the five ducks. As far back as "Eric Hermannson's Soul," Cather had begun to portray the Nebraska grasslands in painterly terms. On his morning walk, Carl remembers Alexandra moving "over the close-cropped grass" in "the milky light of early morning" (117) that echoes the visual language of painters such as Breton and Millet of the French Rural Tradition.[39] Looking back at her first attempts to frame Nebraska with Old World allusions, the author elegantly transposes the tragic tale of Pyramus and Thisbe in the story of Emil and Marie, pinning it to the idea of the mulberry tree in Nebraska. In all of these ways, Cather imagines a new sort of unity with the Great Plains.

"The Neighboring Fields" concludes on another Sunday, with yet another family debate. Convinced that their old friend is angling for a piece of their property, Lou and Oscar demand that their sister send Carl away: "Everything you've made has come out of the original land that us boys worked for, hasn't it?" (151). The old questions of land and labor return in territorial terms. Who can claim the land, and how can the claim be preserved? Who can divide the land? Once divided, why can't the land be divided again and again? As she wrote this scene, Cather was probably thinking about real cases of family conflict in Webster County.

But the more she wrote, the more the scene came to center on deeply personal questions that had haunted her since her days in Lincoln. When Lou and Oscar dismiss her role in their success, Alexandra becomes angry: " 'And what about my work?' she asked in an unsteady voice" (153). Can the work of the mind, of imagination and intuition, count alongside physical labor? Can a woman's work ever count the same as a man's work? We know how Cather wanted to answer such questions, and we know she struggled with her conviction. It is no coincidence, then, that we learn the heroine's age during this exchange: she is forty. Cather turned forty soon after the novel was published. When Alexandra sends the brothers packing, Lou worries that Oscar went too far in bringing up their sister's advanced age. As he considers it more, Lou speaks the final words of the chapter: "Maybe she'd as soon be forty as not!" (156). Feeling both her age and her full power as a writer of fiction, Cather was wondering the same thing about herself and eventually produced an answer in *Not Under Forty,* published in 1936.

At this point in her composition, Cather inserts "Winter Memories." Not unlike the opening vignettes, these two slight chapters might have been dropped elsewhere in the text or left out entirely. But Cather's instincts are good. Thinking more of music than quilts, she employs the chapters as a kind of intermezzo. Like a composition by Schumann, the pieces invite the reader into a reverie that feels, in every way, transitional. Beginning with a lyrical description of the season, Cather conjures up the spirit of Schubert's *Winterreise,* the famous song cycle that would eventually inspire *Lucy Gayheart.* In a satisfying bit of recapitulation, she hearkens back to the novel's opening: "Winter has settled down over the Divide again; the season in which Nature recuperates, in which she sinks to sleep between the fruitfulness of autumn and the passion of spring" (169). This is winter in a pastoral key, the overwrought semicolon forcing the reader to notice the benevolent cycle of life on the prairie.

A classic vignette of Great Plains hospitality unfolds as Alexandra takes old Mrs. Lee to visit Marie. It is the kind of sociable event that the *Argus* and the *Chief* might have noted on their pages of local news if the editors had paid equal attention to the social lives of "Swedes and Bohemians." Once again, Cather was elaborating on the columnar vision of these country town institutions in a way that would attract the eyes of an artist. The Monet of *The Red Kerchief* might have painted the moment as "Marie saw Mrs. Lee's red shawl come bobbing up the path" (172). Part of the generation of women Nils admires in "The Bohemian Girl," the toothless old woman helps the reader appreciate Marie's kitchen as she looks "with great interest at the table, set for three, with a white cloth, and a pot of pink geraniums in the middle" (173).

More wonders await the old woman: "Her eyes lit up as Marie bent down and opened the oven door" (175). Marie produces "a pan of delicate little rolls, stuffed with stewed apricots" (174). If Marie's geraniums represent innovation, these *kolache,* as the Czech immigrants called them, represent tradition.[40]

With these striking gestures, Marie succeeds in creating an intimate moment of female friendship. As Fryer notes, "Cather's three women are immigrants: they are by definition uprooted, estranged; but together they can make a sense of place."[41] In telling this story, Cather captures the living memory of pioneer experience that stretched back to territorial days. Jewett would have been pleased, but probably surprised and even disappointed that in such a long work of fiction Cather could not conjure up any other comparable moments.

The intermezzo ends with a Bergsonian meditation on the novel's heroine, who lacks the "imagination" to see the relationship between Emil and Marie (183). What Alexandra prefers to do is "look back" (184). She recalls driving through the country with Emil and a wild duck "swimming and diving all by herself in the sunlight, a kind of enchanted bird that did not know age or change" (184–85). In Bergsonian terms, the past is "leaning over the present" for Alexandra. Instead of analyzing the feelings of those around her, she daydreams of water fowl, a particularly revealing choice for the author of "The Enchanted Bluff."

This is archaeological work for Cather, who seems intent on laying claim, once and for all, to her own archetypal consciousness—and perhaps her salvation as a female artist in the West. Digging deeper, the narrator describes Alexandra's most cherished fancy of "being lifted up bodily and carried lightly by some one very strong" (185). As she did with the vision of the wild duck, Cather was again looking back over her Nebraskan short stories, recalling Canute's lifting of Lena at the end of "On the Divide," nodding back to Nils boldly lifting Clara onto the horse at the end of "The Bohemian Girl." In both of these stories, a man resolves a woman's fate with a single, strong-armed gesture. Here, the heroine is carried away by a mythic power rooted in the country.[42]

"The White Mulberry Tree" begins with a series of vignettes of what the narrator calls "the rich French farming country" (189). Recalling the French-Canadian people who lived north of Red Cloud on the border of Webster County and Franklin County, Cather was also recalling her previous sketch of the place in "Eric Hermannson's Soul."[43] An avid sender of postcards, Cather creates a picturesque vision of the Church of Sainte-Agnès as a "red-brick building" standing "high above the rest of the landscape, with miles of warm color lying at its feet, and by its position and setting it reminded one of some of the churches built long ago in the wheat-lands of middle France" (189). Having grown up in a town nearly obsessed with its red brick architecture, the author emphasizes the brick church, a crimson edifice presiding over ripening fields. As the chapter unfolds, it becomes a perfect illustration of Cather's ability, described by Reynolds, to write about her home country as though it were a foreign land with a certain "doubleness of the prose, the sense of being both within and without the scene."[44] When the author recalled her own harvest drives through the country and described her "different process" in writing *O Pioneers!* in those terms, the idea of riding probably implied this sensation of doubleness, of passing through the world and the parish.

She is also, at the same time, boldly dipping into the matrix of memory and townmaking that defined her Nebraska. In her short stories over the last two decades, Cather had often indulged in the old territorial pleasure of rechristening places, and she certainly does this with Sainte-Agnès, renaming a church that everyone in Webster County would have known. As March and Arnold have chronicled, Cather was remembering the curious case of Wheatland, settled by French Canadians who often called their town St. Anne in honor of the church there.[45] In 1885, as Danker points out, "the post office was renamed St. Ann and transferred to a general store owned by Jean Baptiste LaPorte. . . ."[46] People in neighboring communities began referring to Wheatland/St. Ann as LaPorteville. As she wrote, Cather was recalling how this town with three names had been displaced by a new town named Campbell, invented by railroad interests and allies about a mile and a half west of the old village in 1886. In 1887, the *Argus* described a struggle between the parishioners of St. Anne who wanted to stay and those who wanted to go.[47]

Feeling that something was lost in the translation, Cather seems to be attempting a sort of restoration in this intricate work of townmaking. Whether consciously or not, she alludes to one of the town's names when she likens the setting to the "wheat-lands" of France. By renaming it Sainte-Agnès, she emphasizes that personality, repurposing the French Canadian New World in order to suggest the Old World of France. To further heighten the effect, Cather describes the brick church in Campbell (built in 1910) rather than the old wooden church in Wheatland, where the bishop had come for an impressive confirmation service in 1881. Danker suggests that the author "made this change because there was little either impressive or distinctively French about the earlier rude wooden structure, while the brick church was an

A conventional photograph of St. Anne's Church, Campbell, NE, n.d.
Source: Willa Cather Pioneer Memorial and Educational Foundation.

imposing edifice based on a French design."[48] In this way, the opening of "The White Mulberry Tree" stands as an imaginative project of both restoration and reinvention.

Against this backdrop, Cather focuses on the doomed romance that echoes in so many ways "The Bohemian Girl." Emil overtakes Marie as she walks home on "a night of warm wind and faint starlight, with the fireflies . . . glimmering over the wheat" (205). At first glance, Marie seems modeled on Clara from the short story, but Marie's situation is different in ways that must be remarked upon. She admits that she loved Frank and will not run away with Emil because she is a faithful Catholic: "How wickedly you talk! I am not that kind of a girl, and you know it" (207). If Marie is trapped on a farm in Nebraska like Clara, it has nothing to do with an oppressive culture of the Victorian West. No gossiping town has intimidated her. If Marie will not budge from her doomed life on the Divide, it is because she has made—and continues to make—conscious decisions about her life that are rooted in her values.

If Cather's vignettes of the "French country" allowed her to reinvent the past and explore the Bohemian woman's consciousness, they also allowed her to come to terms, once more, with farm life. When Emil goes to visit Amédée in the fields, we see the scene through his college-educated eyes:

> The six big work-horses that drew, or rather pushed, the header, went abreast at a rapid walk, and as they were still green at the work they required a good deal of management on Amédée's part; especially when they turned the corners, where they divided, three and three, and then swung round into line again with a movement that looked as complicated as a wheel of artillery. Emil felt a new thrill of admiration for his friend. (217)

More than any other element in this long sentence, the semicolon signals a transformation in Cather's writing. Although she could have been content with her description up to the heavy mark of punctuation, she had more to say. Viewed through Emil's eyes, which have much in common with the author's vision, a military simile comes to mind and the farmer becomes a modern Alexander in the field. Working through intense pain, Amédée is heroic in every traditional sense of the word. He is also distinctly modern, a fact that Emil only half-consciously acknowledges. Thinking over the farmer's admirable traits, the observer concludes, "I'll have to bring Alexandra up to see this thing work" (217). Emil admires and envies Amédée, but his mind has drifted toward the amazing piece of farm machinery.[49]

When Amédée dies, the loss reverberates in striking ways. The embodiment of noble farming, past and present, the farmer straddled the Old World and the New. Husband and father, he was also, in the language of the book, a "boy" (219). Poised to farm beyond what Cather would eventually call "the end of the first cycle," Amédée is a victim of simple biological destiny, a moving illustration of what the old writers used to call mutability. Of course, one of the classic responses to this awareness was *carpe diem,* so exquisitely expressed by Horace in his famous ode: "*carpe diem, quam minimum credula postero.*"[50] Alexandra says as much when Carl tells her he is leaving for the gold fields. "People have to snatch at happiness," she says, "when they can, in this world. It is always easier to lose than to find" (164). It is also easier to urge than to accomplish wisely. For centuries, Horace's injunction has been misread as a justification for rash indulgence, and all sorts of unhappy people like Emil have heard the argument.

In this way, the death of Amédée triggers Emil's muddled thinking as he listens to the confirmation service on the Saturday before his friend's funeral. As she wrote this scene, Cather was returning to a vignette she had been exploring in print since the first "One Way of Putting It" column, where she had described a broken woman watching a father and daughter at a concert. Like this woman and like Aunt Georgiana in "A Wagner Matinee," Emil is caught up in himself as he listens to the music, which seems to fuel his passionate reverie: "The spirit he had met in the music was his own" (229). Cather takes pains to underscore the youthful quality of this thought process: "And it did not occur to Emil that any one had ever reasoned thus before, that music had ever before given a man this equivocal revelation" (229). Giannone aptly remarks, "It is another of those total surrenders to musical enchantment which puts Emil in the company of Peter Sadelack and Paul in the kingdom of the unattainable."[51]

Fired by "revelation," Emil looks for Marie in the orchard, a pastoral space that has almost nothing in common with Cather's early Nebraska landscapes: "Long fingers of light reached through the apple branches as through a net; the orchard was riddled and shot with gold; light was the reality, the trees were merely interferences that reflected and refracted light" (231). Instead of *otium,* this idyll, with its sticky semicolons and disturbing imagery, promises entrapment and violence. As Rosowski points out, it is also a space of dreaming, of "pastoral transformation" and incipient loss, that owes much to Ovid and Keats. When Emil awakens Marie in the orchard, she sums up the moment: " 'I was dreaming this,' she whispered, hiding her face against him, 'don't take my dream away!' " (232). Sounding like the speaker in Keats' "Ode to a Nightingale," Marie captures the evanescence of the moment, but anyone familiar with pastoral already knows the idyll cannot last. A painful return to "reality" is at hand and a palpable sense, as Rosowski points out, of "open-endedness."[52] Cather opted for murder, and her readers back in Nebraska were probably not surprised.

Indeed, the tragic scene unfolds in ways that have as much to do with Cather's Nebraska as they do with Ovidian influence. As the author was growing up in Red Cloud and for years afterward, stories of husbands murdering their wives appeared with a certain regularity in the newspapers. A story from 1884 is typical as the *Chief* described Isaac Gatewood's murder of his wife with a club in St. Louis. Late that summer, a single page of national news juxtaposed three different cases of murderous husbands. Over the years, there were stories of drunken beatings, shotguns, and suicides.[53] By the time she was writing *O Pioneers!,* Cather probably felt that the stories were as archetypal as orchards and pastoral.

Among these tales of mayhem, a story from Brownville (the town that had long fascinated Cather) stands out as an illuminating contrast. Just before Christmas in 1898, the *Chief* described how a jealous husband named Frank Cheesman had surprised his wife, Minnie, and her lover George Ray in the Cheesmans' home. A gunfight ensued between the two men. Cheesman was wounded and eventually died. The newspaper reported that "the beautiful young widow" knew of Cheesman's jealousy but admitted that she "loved Ray more than her husband."[54] Now there is no way to prove that Cather read this story, but it is not unlikely. After moving away in 1896, Cather continued to peruse Red Cloud newspapers. She was inclined to read about Brownville, and she liked to repurpose found materials. Perhaps the name Frank stuck in her imagination, and perhaps she spent some time mulling over the motives of the beautiful young widow?

In so doing, her mind may have returned to stories of deranged Bohemian husbands.[55] The September 28, 1888, *Chief* reported this memorable tale: "In a crazy fit John Spilinek, a Bohemian, shot his wife three times at Omaha the other day and then killed himself. The woman could not live. He was fifty-three years of age and well to do but his mind had become disordered and he stood continually in fear of burglars and of being poisoned" (2). Less than a year later, the May 31, 1889, *Chief* told the story of "Frank Pekarick, a Bohemian, [who] suicided near Wahoo the other day by hanging himself in his barn" (2). Pekarick, it seems, feared further legal punishment for beating his wife. As she moved toward the end of her novel, Cather may have contemplated this amalgam of stories. The name "Frank" would surely have come to mind. Guns and jealousy must have seemed inevitable and intriguing. The newspaper's habit of identifying certain perpetrators with "a Bohemian" had to stand out. Perhaps the most fascinating element in these stories was the link between Bohemians and mental instability in the popular imagination.

For the emerging novelist, this prejudicial discourse may have suggested a distinctly modern way of writing about violence on the Great Plains: "But the stained, slippery grass, the darkened mulberries, told only half the story. Above Marie and Emil, two white butterflies from Frank's alfalfa-field were fluttering in and out among the interlacing shadows; diving and soaring, now close together, now far apart; and in the long grass by the fence the last wild roses of the year opened their pink hearts to die" (241). Instead of gunfights and tawdry motives, Cather is interested in the recollection of stylized agony. The narrator pays careful attention to composition, butterflies above, lovers below, wild roses in the background. Like her contemporaries the Fauves, the author exuberantly dabs color to heighten the primitive scene. This was not one of the *Chief's* murder stories.

Aptly named, the fifth section of the novel is called "Alexandra." A series of vignettes devoted to her central character as she moves from grief to understanding and reconciliation, the section is, in many ways, a tour de force in narrative closure. After a surreal soaking in the cemetery, lying in the darkness of her room, Alexandra experiences the "old illusion of her girlhood," the masculine figure, "his face was covered" with a white cloak (251). Seeing his strong bronzed arm, "she knew at once that it was the arm of the mightiest of all lovers" (251). Cather's readers have been uncertain about the identity of this "lover." But the most important thing about this figure is the utter surety it engenders in the heroine: "She knew at last for whom it was she had waited, and where he would carry her" (251). Recasting the familiar sensation from "On the Divide" and "The Bohemian Girl," Cather was probably describing what it felt like to write *O Pioneers!*.

Great romances find closure in reunions, and *O Pioneers!* is certainly a great romance. A telegram from Carl announcing his return to Hanover signals the finale. As he and Alexandra walk "across the fields," they make their way to "the pasture pond," where they work out their own explanation of all that has happened (266, 269). In this romance of the soil, it is the only setting for such important labor. The two old friends resolve to remain on the farm. "They went into the house together," the narrator concludes, "leaving the Divide behind them, under the evening star. Fortunate country, that is one day to receive hearts like Alexandra's into its bosom, to give them out again, in the yellow wheat, in the rustling corn, in the shining eyes of youth!"[56]

When she reached the end of *O Pioneers!,* Cather tried to explain what she had made. On the one hand, it was loosely structured and she agreed with Sergeant that it was a weakness: "The modelling is not bold. But the country itself has no skeleton—no rocks or ridges. It's a fluid black soil that runs through your fingers. . . . It's all soft, and somehow that influences the mood in which one writes of it—and so the very structure of the story." On the other hand, she told Sergeant the work "has been rather a pull because it's knit so much closer than anything I have ever done before."[57] In this seeming paradox of the closely knit narrative with no skeleton, Cather was coming very near the genius of her creation. She had solved the problem of making something substantial out of parts by marrying Bergsonian biology to her own sense of the novel as a visual and musical composition, moving forward as easily as a ride through the country through motion and rest. In 1927, E. M. Forster identified this form as *rhythm,* "which may be defined as repetition plus variation, and which can be illustrated by examples."[58]

What would it be like, Forster wondered, to encounter a truly remarkable example of "rhythm"? He speculated: "Is there any effect in novels comparable to the effect of the Fifth Symphony as a whole, where, when the orchestra stops, we hear something that has never actually been played? The opening movement, the andante, and the trio-scherzo-trio-finale-trio-finale that composes the third block, all enter the mind at once, and extend one another into a common entity. This common entity, this new thing, is the symphony as a whole."[59]

At the end of *O Pioneers!,* Cather felt something that she had never quite put on the page. Some of her first critics remarked the phenomenon. The reviewer for the *Boston Evening Transcript* concluded: "it is deep, thrilling, intense—and this intensity comes through the simplicity—one might say the severity, of treatment." Writing in the *Chicago Evening Post,* Floyd Dell knew the novel was "touched with genius" but could not explain how it produced its effects.[60] As far as Cather was concerned, she had written her first novel. Frankly amazed by her creation and by what she had become, she turned to exclamation marks—at the end of her title and at the end of her novel's final sentence. The marks may seem youthful, exuberant, and indulgent. They stand for emergence!

Notes

1. Sergeant, *Willa Cather,* 116.
2. Qtd. *OP,* 283.
3. Handley, "Willa Cather," 76–77.
4. Susan Rosowski, "Willa Cather and the Fatality of Place: *O Pioneers!, My Ántonia,* and *A Lost Lady,*" *Geography and Literature: A Meeting of the Disciplines,* ed. William E. Mallory and Paul Simpson-Housley (Syracuse: Syracuse University Press, 1987), 83.
5. Stouck, "Explanatory Notes," *OP,* 11.2.
6. Rosowski, "Fatality of Place," 81, argues that the novel is rooted in the fairy-tale tradition.
7. Rosowski, *The Voyage Perilous,* 49.
8. Laegreid, "The Good, The Bad," *Great Plains Quarterly,* 108.
9. Stout, *Willa Cather,* 16.
10. Stout, *Picturing the West,* 182.
11. On the traditional notion of male settlers entering a female land, see Kolodny's *The Lay of the Land,* 4.
12. "To Zoë Akins," October 31, 1912, *SLWC,* 169.
13. Peck, "Possession Granted by a Different Lease," *Modern Fiction Studies,* 5.
14. See, respectively, Bloom and Bloom, *Willa Cather's Gift of Sympathy,* 15, 23; Rosowski, "Fatality of Place," *Geography and Literature,* 84; and Sara Farris, "American Pastoral in the Twentieth-Century *O Pioneers!, A Thousand Acres,* and *Merry Men,*" *ISLE* (1998) 5 (1): 29.
15. Reynolds, *Willa Cather in Context,* 56; Farris, "American Pastoral," *ISLE,* 32.
16. Romines, *The Home Plot,* 144. Halverson, *Playing House in the American West,* calls it a kind of "alternative domesticity," 138.
17. Laegreid, "The Good, The Bad," 110.
18. Qtd. in Sergeant, *Willa Cather,* 92.
19. *Chief* (August 15, 1884): 5.
20. For more on Ivar's combination of Christianity and environmentalism, see Matthias Schubnell, "Religion and Ecology on the Divide: Ivar's Monasticism in *O Pioneers!, Willa Cather and the Culture of Belief,* ed. John J. Murphy, with Linda Hunter Adams and Jesse S. Crisler (Provo: Brigham Young University Press, 2002), 41–49.
21. Reynolds, *Willa Cather in Context,* 50–51.
22. Critics and scholars have not always been prepared for this structure. For a succinct history of this perception and for an elegant response, see Bruce P. Baker, "*O Pioneers!:* The Problem of Structure," *Great Plains Quarterly* 2.4 (1982): 219–20. Stouck, *Willa Cather's Imagination,* 23–34, suggests that the novel is informed by an epic structure. Harris, "Peck, Turner, and Willa Cather's *O Pioneers!,*" 45, has suggested that Cather's structure may have been inspired by the territorial prose of John Mason Peck.
23. Peck, "Possession Granted by a Different Lease," 14–17.
24. James Hillman, *The Force of Character* (New York: Random House, 1999), 155–60.
25. Mullins, "I Bequeath Myself,"129–30, persuasively links this epiphany to lines from Whitman's *Song of Myself.*
26. Wood, "Books of the Day," *McClure's Magazine,* 199.
27. Pedro de Castañeda de Nájera, *Relación de la jornada de Cíbola, Documents of the Coronado Expedition, 1539–1542,* trans. and annotated by Richard Flint and Shirley Cushing Flint (Dallas: Southern Methodist University Press, 2005), 423.
28. Juan Jaramillo, *Relación, Documents of the Coronado Expedition,* 517.
29. Jaramillo, *Relación, Documents of the Coronado Expedition,* 517–518. For more on the Spaniards' response to present-day Kansas, see Daryl W. Palmer, "Quivira, Coronado, and Kansas: A Formative Chapter in the Story of Kansans' Collective Memory," *Kansas History* 35.4 (2012–13): 251.

30. Mark Fackitz, "Character, Compromise, and Idealism in Willa Cather's Gardens." *Cather Studies* 5 (2003): 300.
31. "To Annie Adams Fields," June 27, 1912, *SLWC,* 163; "To Elizabeth Shepley Sergeant," July 5, 1912, *SLWC,* 164.
32. Sergeant, *Willa Cather,* 116.
33. P. W. Anderson, "More Is Different," *Science* 177.4047 (1972): 393.
34. Bergson, *Creative Evolution,* 7.
35. Quirk, *Bergson and American Culture,* 103. For a discussion of Cather's study of Bergson, see Quirk, 124–25. See also, for instance, Loretta Wasserman, "The Music of Time: Henri Bergson and Willa Cather," *American Literature* 57 (1985): 227–28; Daryl W. Palmer, "Ripening Claude: Willa Cather's *One of Ours* and the Philosophy of Henri Bergson," *American Literary Realism* 41.2 (2009): 114–19.
36. Quirk, *Bergson and American Culture,* 100, 124.
37. "To Dorothy Canfield," March 28, 1903, *SLWC,* 70.
38. "To Witter Bynner," June 7, 1905, *SLWC,* 89.
39. Fryer, *Felicitous Space,* 232-44; Susan J. Rosowski, "Willa Cather and the French Rural Tradition of Breton and Millet: *O Pioneers!, The Song of the Lark,* and *My Ántonia,*" *The Rural Vision: France and America in the Late Nineteenth Century,* ed. Hollister Sturges (Omaha: Joslyn Art Museum, 1987), 53–61.
40. Ann Romines, "Kolache Controversies," *Willa Cather Newsletter and Review* 49.2 (2005): 46–47. See also, Welsch and Welsch, *Cather's Kitchens,* 81–83. For the recipe, see Romines, *At Willa Cather's Table,* 148, 19.
41. Fryer, *Felicitous Space,* 257.
42. Urgo, *Willa Cather and the Myth of the American Migration,* 44, rightly calls this power "motion."
43. As Laegreid, in "The Good, The Bad," 106–7, explains, these homesteaders were "the good immigrants" celebrated in the popular discourse of the day.
44. Reynolds, *Willa Cather in Context,* 68.
45. March and Arnold, *A Reader's Companion,* 650–51.
46. Danker, "The Influence of Willa Cather's French-Canadian Neighbors," 38. For contemporary reports of this move, see the *Journal* (January 15, 1896): 5; *Chief* (February 5, 1886): 7; *Chief* (August 6, 1886): 3.
47. Ibid., 651. Danker, "The Influence of Willa Cather's French-Canadian Neighbors," 38–39, describes the controversy.
48. Danker, "The Influence of Willa Cather's French-Canadian Neighbors," 42.
49. William Conlogue, "Managing the Farm, Educating the Farmer: *O Pioneers!* and the New Agriculture," *Great Plains Quarterly* 21.1 (2001): 3, 11, argues that Cather embraces modern farming in the novel, but Cather's vision is more complex and subtle than he suggests.
50. Horace, *The Odes and Epodes,* trans. C. E. Bennett (London: Heinemann, 1921), 32.
51. Giannone, *Music in Willa Cather's Fiction,* 77.
52. Rosowski, *The Voyage Perilous,* 44–56.
53. *Chief* (February 22, 1884): 2; *Chief* (August 1, 1884): 2; see the following articles in the *Chief:* (July 6, 1888): 4; (May 30, 1890): 17; (October 11, 1895): 6; (August 30, 1889): 3; (November 27, 1908): 6; (December 15, 1910): 6.
54. *Chief* (December 23, 1898): 2.
55. For more on the popular link between Czechs and retaliation, see Prchal, "The Bohemian Paradox," 13–14.
56. Here, again, Mullins, "I Bequeath Myself, 132–33, links Cather's memorable prose to lines from Whitman's *Song of Myself.*
57. "To Elizabeth Shepley Sergeant," March 22, 1913, *SLWC,* 175; "To Elizabeth Shepley Sergeant," December 7, 1912, *SLWC,* 170.
58. E. M. Forster, *Aspects of the Novel* (New York: Houghton Mifflin, 1956), 168. See also E. K. Brown, *Rhythm in the Novel* (Toronto: University of Toronto Press, 1950), 3–9.
59. Forster, *Aspects of the Novel,* 168.
60. Qtd. in Stouck, "Historical Essay," *O Pioneers!,* 296–297.

Chapter 5.

Emergence, Experimentation, and Evolution: *Song of the Lark*, *My Ántonia*, and the Fiction that Followed Out West

I believe that the strongest need of your nature is to find yourself, to emerge as *yourself.*
—Harsanyi in *The Song of the Lark*

I am so happy *the West likes the book.*
—Willa Cather

With the publication of *O Pioneers!* in 1913, Willa Cather's emergence as a major American author was, in many ways, complete, but it would be a serious mistake to think that emergence meant the end of her evolution as an artist. The author was always, in some sense, actively becoming Willa Cather, *continually creating herself,* as the philosopher Bergson would put it.[1] Scholars interested in the phases of Cather's life and career, surveying the years from 1913 to 1947, could easily propose a number of important periods marked by growth and change. In a book focused on the author's emergence in the West, I think it is important to acknowledge this process by paying particular attention to the two so-called "prairie novels" that quickly followed *O Pioneers!*. It also seems important to say a few words about the decades of experimentation that came after these works as Cather explored a maturing and distinctly Modern vision of the West that returned, inevitably, to Sandy Point.

Working on *The Song of the Lark* in 1913 and 1914, Cather understood that something special was happening. In a letter on November 19, 1913, Cather told Sergeant, "The new novel took a bound before I left Pittsburgh, and I did about 28,000 words in four jolly weeks; did it twice, which means that it's in almost final form (*SLWC,* 185). Even for someone with a journalist's penchant for production, this was a stunning accomplishment. If *O Pioneers!* had engendered a different writing process, then something even more dramatic could be said for *The Song of the Lark.* The author told her friend that she was ready to lock herself up and "become a fountain pen and have done with it—a conduit for ink to run through" (*SLWC,* 185).

How did this happen? Cather's friendship with the famous opera singer Olive Fremstad may have triggered the process. Giannone explains, "She was Willa Cather's artist par excellence—powerful, passionate, daring, intellectual." Having sketched Western singer heroines in "A Death in the Desert" and "The Joy of Nelly Deane," Cather was ready to write about a performing artist who would mirror her own life. As Giannone puts it, the author was ready to explore "a singer's creative growth as an ideal analogy for the discovery and expression of all art."[2]

But particularly in the Moonstone chapters, Thea's story unfolds out of the author's memories, many of which echo through the newspapers of her childhood beginning in 1884–85, when Cather was eleven years old.[3] In their fine edition of the novel, Moseley and Ronning provide a detailed account of the many ways in which Thea's life imitates Cather's life.[4] Thea's mother resembles Cather's mother. Thea's little brother Thor resembles Cather's brother James. Thea's attic bedroom with the flowered wallpaper duplicates Cather's room. And the list goes on and on until a reader would be tempted to assume that this book is a simple autobiography.

In Cather's mind, it was a grand experiment in autobiographical fiction. Thea is not, after all, Cather. Thea is no elocutionist, and she does not write for the local newspapers. Thea does not want to be a doctor and lacks Cather's fascination with dissection and vivisection. The fictional heroine never seems to have played along the river. Thea does not dress in masculine ways and call herself "Theo." In all sorts of ways, Cather marks differences between herself and her character that free her from the constraints of autobiographical fidelity and so open up the novel as a genuine work of art. She probably understood this so clearly because she had just finished writing an "autobiography" before *The Song of the Lark.*

In 1912, while Cather was in the Southwest, McClure wrote to his successful protégé to see if she would be willing to write his life story. By this time, the old editor had been forced out of the publication he had created. The chance to publish a testament to his legacy meant everything to McClure. Given her feelings of respect and gratitude, Cather could hardly decline. In the end, the book she wrote pleased her mentor and garnered positive reviews.

For a long time, scholars tended to assume that the work was nothing more than a detour on the way toward *The Song of the Lark,* but Shaw corrects this assumption when he observes that "the biographer's impulse was as fresh and strong [in Cather as she wrote *The Song of the Lark*] as the fictionalist's."[5] Recognizing this impulse, Thacker has cogently explored the implications of *My Autobiography* for the fiction that followed. "Seen retrospectively," he reasons, "Cather's act in writing McClure's life was a crucial step in her aesthetic development." Honing in on the way Cather prepared to write by listening to McClure tell his story, Thacker describes what he calls a kind of "melding" process: "As she listened . . . Willa Cather made it her own and made it, too, part of the stories of the numerous characters who were to spring from her imagination. At the same time, Cather was defining a relation between storyteller and single listener, an audience of one motivated most explicitly by her own sympathies."[6] Figuring out how to meld her listening with McClure's storytelling prepared her to meld her story with Fremstad's. In so doing, she was able to write about intimate experience with the kind of distance that feels real and engenders sympathy.

With all this in mind, I want to offer another explanation for Cather's astonishing output. I believe that Cather's rush of creativity occurred because she finally and completely indulged the old passion for townmaking. In so doing, she tapped deeply into the territorial imagination with its emphasis on palimpsestuous experience, remapping and renaming parts of Nebraska, Colorado, and Arizona while deftly putting her own distinctive stamp on the American West. In the end, *The Song of the Lark* is a profound exploration of how she became Willa Cather.

With no obvious transition between thoughts in the aforementioned letter, the exuberant Cather made her vision clear. "Unless you had lived all over the West," she told Greenslet, "I don't believe you could possibly know how much of the West this story has in it" (*SLWC,* 199). At first glance, Cather seems to be stating the obvious. Ever since "Tommy the Unsentimental," she had been exploring the region with gusto, and scholars have always acknowledged the awakening Cather experienced when she visited her brother Douglass in Winslow, AZ, in 1912. But her point in the letter is more precise.

What made the writing of this novel different was that there was more of the West in this one, as though the region were a great sack of flour and Cather a baker adding scoop after scoop to the bowl. The author was surer of her Western backgrounds. Tony R. Magagna points out that "the plotting and planting that has taken place here among the Colorado sand hills is reminiscent of the efforts of her unvanquished settlers of the Nebraska plains who are celebrated for their successes in marking and defining the open space of the West."[7] Cather embraced the territorial imagination, and the ink simply flowed.

Cather's letters from this time confirm that she was thinking about her craft this way. In an August 1913 letter to Sergeant, Cather described her special delight in the Western reviews of *O Pioneers!*: "I am *so happy* the West likes the book" (*SLWC*, 179). When *The Song of the Lark* was published and Boynton called it a "great novel," Cather wrote to thank him for his understanding of her larger aims: "In that review you suggested some feeling on your part that the cow-puncher's experience of the West was not the only experience possible there, and you seemed to feel that one might give some truthful account of life in a new country without pretending to a jovial brutality which, however much one might like to have it, cannot be successfully affected—at least, not by women."[8] In Cather's mind, *The Song of the Lark* was transforming the West in radical ways anticipated by the short stories that had come before.

It was time for her boldest experiment with the territorial imagination. The narrator explains that it is "a very pleasant mile out of town toward the glittering sand hills" (24). As Moseley has suggested, the topography may owe something to Holyoke, CO, a town on the Burlington line that Cather knew from visiting her brother Douglass.[9] In order to reach these hills, Thea "followed the sidewalk to the depot at the south end of town; then took the road east to the little group of adobe houses where the Mexicans lived" (24).[10] Cather's readers back home must have been incredulous as they read this description. Readers familiar with Red Cloud today will have the same reaction if they have begun to assume that Cather is simply re-presenting her hometown. In the quoted passage, the semicolon indicates the rift. As the heroine's path runs beyond the punctuation mark, she walks out of Red Cloud and into Winslow, AZ. In a striking adaptation of the territorial imagination, Cather embeds a slice of Arizona in a Nebraskan landscape she has renamed Colorado.

In this bold Kansas-Nebraska act, Thea steps out of a version of the Red Cloud Cather knew as a youth and into a version of Winslow that Cather knew and loved as an adult. Childhood inspiration of the past merges with adult inspiration of the present in a kind of geographic melding that was neatly contained inside the boundaries of the old territory. For Cather the invention may have felt like psychic unity and surely represented unprecedented opportunities. In this imaginative world, the author could introduce characters who transcended the limited spheres of friendship that define a successful life. Old friends could live on through ascendancy, and new friends could reach back to stabilize the fleeting happiness of childhood. In the end, of course, it turned out to be a matter of townmaking for Cather and a brilliant opportunity for the palimpsestuous imagination she inherited from territorial times and first explored while inventing Sandy Point in her backyard. Her elegant solution in *The Song of the Lark* is to layer Mexican Town over the edge of her version of Red Cloud, now located in Colorado.

Cather makes her territorial vision clear a little later in the novel when Thea remembers how an old rancher showed her and her father the path of the Forty-Niners and Mormons. If the story of remembering is particularly vivid, it may be because Cather's trips to Wyoming had made a powerful impression on her: "the old man had told them that he was in Brownville, Nebraska, when the first telegraph wires were put across the Missouri River, and that the first message that ever crossed the river was 'Westward the course of empire takes its way.'"

The narrator concludes that "Thea remembered that message when she sighted the wagon tracks toward the blue mountains. She told herself she would never, never forget it" (60–61).

Two decades after her unforgettable trip to Brownville, Cather was still recycling and repurposing the experience, envisioning a westward line of expansion stretching from the territorial town in Nebraska out through the mountains of Wyoming. Emerging territory and emerging artist meet explicitly in this passage.

The cramped house on Cedar Street that Cather recalled from her childhood stands at the center of this project. With her earnings from music pupils, Thea "fit up a little room for herself upstairs in the half-story" (62). The passage has become famous because it so perfectly captures a young person's process of emergence. The narrator makes the point emphatically: "The acquisition of this room was the beginning of a new era in Thea's life. It was one of the most important things that ever happened to her" (64).

In a novel crammed with the details of Thea's emergence as an artist, this declaration of importance is remarkable. With the same Bergsonian understanding she invoked in her descriptions of Alexandra Bergson's mental world, Cather describes Thea's discovery of the artist's "double life" (64). Growing up in a territory that had been divided and doubled over and over again, Thea realizes what Cather had come to understand during her early years in Nebraska: imaginative freedom lies in doubleness. In the solitude that Jewett had urged Cather to embrace, Thea discovers mental faculties she did not realize she had.

Pilgrims visiting Red Cloud today can imagine this space of transformation when they see Cather's little room in the house on Cedar Street, but they have no way of conjuring up the amateur entertainments that enlivened Red Cloud life in the 1880s. Drawing on her first sketch of this material in "The Joy of Nelly Deane," Cather invents another Christmas Eve concert. In Moonstone, Lily Fisher ("the Baptist prodigy") manages (with the help of Mrs. Johnson) to outshine Thea and earn the lavish praise of the *Gleam* (66). To a degree she had not attempted before, Cather writes autobiographically. Like her heroine, Cather had seen her own performances announced in the newspapers. Like Thea, the author had seen her work praised in the same pages even as she followed the reviews of her rivals. More particularly, Lily Fisher seems to have been based on Lillian Smith, who performed at the same Baptist social that welcomed the brilliant piano playing of Professor Schindelmeisser (Cather's prototype for Wunsch) in 1885.[11] In the novel, a disconsolate Thea simply goes to bed on Christmas Eve to read and dream of "distant voices calling, 'Lily Fisher! Lily Fisher!'" (71).

Rivals mattered in Cather's matrix of memory, but friends mattered more. As far back as 1896 in "Tommy," Cather had written about the adult male friends of her youth in Red Cloud. With this matrix of memory in mind, Cather introduces Ray Kennedy as the noble conductor of Moonstone who dotes on Thea. Rehearsing his stories of travel through the West, he embodies the old territorial desire to "light out" for new adventures. He is, at once, an avatar of the boys in "The Enchanted Bluff" and the railroad boys of Red Cloud. When she was the age of Thea at the beginning of the novel, Cather could have read in the May 1, 1885, *Chief* about Charlie Kaley, Sam Garber, and

WILLA Cather's childhood home with Cather family and friends on front porch.
Source: Willa Cather Pioneer Memorial and Educational Foundation.

Will Brakefield, travelling to "Raton, New Mexico where they expect to carve Red skins and shoot the wild cactus over the plains, as all truly courageous cowboys have done, who have entered that land before them" (5). Ray has something of this Red Cloud spirit in him, a bit of Brakefield in the brakeman.

In Cather's melding imagination, Ray can transport her heroine from Nebraska into Colorado and Arizona. In railroad terminology, Ray is a switchpoint between the Red Cloud of the author's youth and the Winslow of recent memory that included Tooker, the storytelling brakeman Cather met there. In Ray's company, Thea can ponder "the line of many-colored hills; rich, sunbaked yellow, glowing turquoise, lavender, purple; all the open, pastel colors of the desert" (53). In this utterly fanciful recreation of her autobiography, Cather the mature artist is importing a whole new palette of Western colors into her childhood. It is easy to imagine Douglass Burnham, in his elaborate meditations on childhood and the imagination in "The Treasure of Far Island," endorsing the vision as a way of breathing new life into the aging artist.

On a picnic, Ray tells a story of growing up along Cherry Creek near the town that would evolve into Denver. Ray remembers how his father made him drive a load of melons "right up Capitol Hill! Pap got out and stopped at folkses houses to ask if they didn't want to buy any melons, and I was to drive slow. The farther I went the madder I got" (55). When a pretty girl noticed melons falling from the wagon and city dudes laughed at him, the embarrassed young man cracked the whip and took off. "I never looked behind," Ray recalls. It is precisely the kind of Western tale that Thea wants to hear. Ray even tells her, "You're stuck on that story, kid" (55). When she listens to Ray's story, Thea gets to imagine what it would be like to ride away from a Western town without looking back, not unlike Bywaters in Cather's "El Dorado" or Nils and Clara in "The Bohemian Girl." Years after publishing those stories, Ray allowed the author to indulge in another Western tale of escape.

If, as Cather confessed to Greenslet on March 28, 1915, "the death of the noble brakeman" was indeed the germ of the novel, it was probably because she imagined, from the outset, a dramatic final meeting between her heroine and the railroad man that would reveal the girl's deepest sympathies in an experimental blend of opera and Western (*SLWC,* 199). Once again, invention mingles with newspaper clippings. In a town where railroads represented vitality and romance, the latter could take on mythic proportions. As she wrote, Cather may have recalled the May 17, 1884, *Chief* story from Chicago in which a tramp threw a rock at a brakeman "and caused him to fall from the car to the ground beneath, where he was run over and killed" (7). Or she may have recalled the September 26, 1884, *Chief* that described the wreck of a freight train in Wabash in which "The head brakeman was killed" (2). Or she could have recalled the July 6, 1888, *Chief*: "Two boys were cut to pieces and two brakemen badly hurt by an accident to flat cars near Meadville, Mont., the other day" (5). Abutting this story was the report of a freight train crash in Indiana in which "the engine and ten cars were wrecked and a brakeman killed" (5). Here was material fit for Western arias, and Cather seized the opportunity.

The author deftly hints that she has been building toward this moment over the last several chapters. Ray tells the girl, "You were a regular brick to come, Thee" (163). The girl who carries a hot brick to bed has become the solid source of comfort for the dying man. Thanks to all his reading, Ray may even know that his proverbial compliment comes from King Lycurgus of Sparta, who explained the lack of walls around the city by saying, " 'There are Sparta's walls,' he replied, pointing at his soldiers, 'and every man is a brick.' "[12] Thea really does embody the best of Moonstone at this moment, and her words come right to the point: "I feel just as much at home with you as ever, now" (163). For Thea, it is a kind of epiphany: "It was the first time she had ever been conscious of that power to bestow intense happiness by simply being near any one" (163). Although Thea's story of emergence centers on her art, her growth as a friend and comrade were nearly as important for her creator.

Nowhere is this more evident than in Thea's relationship with Dr. Archie, deftly modeled on Cather's old friend Dr. McKeeby of Red Cloud. When the heroine complains to her friend about life in a country town, he imagines escape. "But you talk about going," she says, "and a body has to have something to go *to*" (92). Cather was thinking in precisely these terms when she was stuck at home in Red Cloud after graduating from college, eventually revisiting those sandy feelings in stories such as "El Dorado," "The Treasure of Far Island," and "The Sculptor's Funeral." At the same time, Thea is clearly feeling the typical restlessness of all young people on the verge of adulthood when she declares, "I wish there'd be a fire" (93). When she promises "to ring the fire-bell" for a bit of excitement, the dowdy doctor warns her that she will be arrested (93). It is a quintessential moment of youth and age sharing their discontent.

In her invention of this friendship, Cather transforms memory in fascinating ways. Active members of the Red Cloud Cooking Club, McKeeby and his wife participated in the social life of the community. In her portrait of Archie and his wife, Cather emphasizes the couple's isolation. As previously mentioned, McKeeby served as mayor of Red Cloud and found himself embroiled in vitriolic local politics with his friend Charles Cather and the other members of the so-called Big Eight. Cather looked on as the *Chief* mocked her mentor, calling him the Artful Dodger and Uriah Heep, taunting him with "Eh, Docky!" All the while, McKeeby was fighting back in public meetings and in the pages of his own newspaper. Cather elides all of these elements in her portrait of Archie. Perhaps there was no room for McKeeby's complexity in Cather's novel. She may have been writing a richly detailed novel, but she was not writing *War and Peace.*

In any event, one aspect of Cather's transformation deserves discussion. McKeeby and Cather seem to have had a richer relationship in Red Cloud than Archie and Thea in Moonstone. As Woodress points out, "she often went on calls with Dr. McKeeby" (*WCLL,* 52). And she shared in the work of townmaking with her mentor. When McKeeby took over the *Republican* during the political turmoil of the late 1880s, Cather was overjoyed to serve on the newspaper's "staff." She bragged to Helen Stowell on August 18, 1889, "you know I have a natural propensity for knowing the business of the town in general. Doctor McKeeby is editor and that insures the intellectual & political items as first class" (*SLWC,* 11). Where Thea sees Archie as a wise confidante who admires her, Cather viewed McKeeby as a collaborator.

But things changed. Cather left Red Cloud for college. McKeeby left Red Cloud in 1897, after Cather had settled in Pittsburgh. In 1901, he moved to Pueblo, CO, and died there on April 24, 1905. (Cather's *Troll Garden* had appeared in March.) A little item in the April 28, 1905, *Chief* reported that his wife and his son Fred had come back to town with the body and quickly returned to Pueblo (5). We have no letters between Cather and McKeeby, and only one letter in which Cather recalls the care of the doctor.[13] He does not seem to have helped Cather in the material ways that Archie helps Thea. They do not seem to have exchanged visits. The extant letters do not mention an adult friendship.

In the novel, by contrast, the author amplifies the doctor's influence. Indeed, she was so intent on this agenda that she envisioned Archie becoming the governor of Colorado—until her editor advised against the exuberant idea. Ultimately, Cather seems to have wanted to emphasize that Archie is an example of what Ray calls "halfway people . . . who help the winners win, and the failers fail" (137). Perhaps the author, who liked to explore alternative lives for herself, as she did in "The Treasure of Far Island" and "The Sculptor's Funeral," was indulging in a fantasy of enduring friendship.

Readers feel the importance of this vision near the end of the novel, when Archie visits Thea in New York after seeing her performance in *Lohengrin.* The old friends hesitate. Archie feels that the Thea he knew has vanished, and Thea would really rather live in her childhood memories. For Cather it was an autobiographical impasse that she knew only too well. As she often did in her short stories, the author uses fiction to envision a solution for life. Thea tells Archie that she "measures" the world by Moonstone "standards"—Ray Kennedy's six hundred dollars and the height of the country town standpipe (503). Archie tells Thea that she reminds him of her mother, and Thea accepts it as a high compliment. Archie confesses, "you've always been my romance. Those years when you were growing up were my happiest. When I dream about you, I always see you as a little girl" (503). Thea's response is apposite but in a different key: "Do you? Nearly all my dreams, except those about breaking down on the stage or missing trains, are about Moonstone" (503–04).

And the diva goes on and on, rehearsing dream fragments until Archie believes she may have forgotten about him. She talks about seeking something ineffable in art. He professes his undying belief in her. Common sense says the two old friends are not communicating. Archie is talking about Thea, and she is talking about the old days. But Thea may be speaking for both of them when she declares, "They save me: the old things, things like the Kohlers' garden. They are in everything I do" (506). In her Nebraska stories, Cather was always returning to old things, but as her work evolved it became clearer that these old things might save her.

The first words of the novel's Epilogue tell us everything we need to know about Cather's evolving relationship with Nebraska: "Moonstone again . . ." (531). With Thea's parents gone and Archie in Denver, the narrator follows Tillie around the country town, treating her as the old "genius of the place." In a letter to Katharine Foote on February 17, 1916, Cather admitted, "My theme was always her [Thea's] 'Moonstone-ness', and what she gave back to Moonstone in the end" (*SLWC,* 216). The final sentence of the novel spells out this gift: "So, into all the little settlements of quiet people, tidings of what their boys and girls are doing in the world bring real refreshment; bring to the old, memories, and to the young, dreams" (539). On March 15, 1916, she confessed to Canfield, "my point is always Moonstone" (*SLWC,* 218). As she always did, Cather was thinking in divided terms: "The book is done in two manners—one intimate, one remote. She goes on, but I stand still in Moonstone with Tillie, and I write from Moonstone" (*SLWC,* 218).

When *My Ántonia* appeared in 1918, Willa Cather moved beyond emergence to triumph. Her reviewers certainly felt it and, as Jewell and Stout observe, her "literary reputation was made" (*SLWC,* 271).Writing in the *Dial,* Randolph Bourne realized that the author's accomplishment had everything to do with the West: "Here at last is an American novel, redolent of the Western prairie, that our most irritated and exacting preconceptions can be content with."[14] With this novel, Bourne declared, Cather had "taken herself out of the rank of provincial writers."[15]

Cather was particularly touched by the distinctions Bourne was making. In a letter to her brother Roscoe on January 5, 1919, she referred to Bourne's review, contrasting her work with the writings of Kansas author William Allen White. "I knew," she explained, "that there was a common way of presenting common life, which is worthless, and a finer way of presenting it which would be much more true. Of course Antonia's story could be told in exactly the same jocular, familiar, grapenutsy way that Mr. White thinks is so American."[16] But Cather's territorial imagination was fired by loftier aims and long practice. She knew she had taken the high road, building upon all of her Nebraska fiction, its lessons and experiments, from "Peter" in 1892 to *O Pioneers!* and *The Song of the Lark,* to this story of Jim Burden and his Ántonia. She knew, as Thacker suggests, that White and Garland and other writers like them had followed "generic conventions," but she "struggled until she devised forms that spoke to her readers through the voices of prairie people and, by way of their perspective, seemingly, through the voice of the prairie landscape itself."[17]

How did she do it? Once again, an aggregate of processes and a mixture of ingredients engendered results that seemed to transcend their origins. Clues about this alchemy can be found in a letter to her brother Roscoe written during the summer of 1916. Reeling from a series of personal losses,[18] Cather complained, "I don't seem to have acquired a single new idea since Sandy Point" (*SLWC,* 226). When she read N. P. Dawson's flattering review of *My Ántonia,* she must have smiled at his description of the book "unfolding as a set of Chinese boxes."[19] Sandy Point had "unfolded" out of packing boxes from the Miner Brothers' store. Perhaps her triumph really did depend on her first new idea. As Wallace Stegner puts it, "If, as is often said, every novelist is born to write one thing, then the one thing that Willa Cather was born to write was first fully realized in *My Ántonia* (1918)."[20]

The first four sentences of *My Ántonia* encapsulate her recycling and repurposing. One after another, Cather invokes the "boxes" that form her imaginary Nebraska. Towns. Friends. Summer. Plains. Trains. Rivers. Pasture. Dust. Wind. Childhood. Corn. Harvest. Winter. The more a reader knows of the works that have preceded these sentences, the more one feels a profound sense of commencement. Willa Cather is the creator of "Jim Burden, as *we* still call him in the *West* [*italics mine*]" (ix). With magisterial authority, the artist was claiming her place in a region, among her people.

Having ghost-written McClure's *My Autobiography,* as she confided to Will Owen Jones in a letter on May 20, 1919, she "had a nagging wish to try the experiment again" (*SLWC,* 278). In convincing detail, Thacker has demonstrated that "the effects of Cather's act in *My Autobiography* define the contexts of *My Ántonia*" and the possibilities for a more modern sort of "autobiographical realism."[21] Recalling her male avatars in "The Way of the World," "The Treasure of Far Island," "The Sculptor's Funeral," and "The Wagner Matinee," Cather was using Jim Burden to envision yet another version of her own maturation on the long road from Nebraska to New York.

Beginning with her memories of Anna Sadilek (1869–1955), Cather invented Ántonia Shimerda. In the same way that Cather is not, simply, Jim, Ántonia is not, simply, Anna. From the first chapters of the novel, Cather transformed autobiographical materials. For instance, Cather first met Anna at the Miners' house in Red Cloud, not on the Sadilek farm. Murphy points out that Cather's fond memories of childhood adventures on the farm can be traced back to "Lydia (Leedy) Lambrecht [who] was Willa's age and explored the country with her, hunting for snakes."[22] Viewed in the context of Cather's early fiction, this revision is another attempt by the author to imagine an alternative version of her own life. What if, she seems to have wondered, I had known Anna as a child on the prairie? What if, to borrow the romantic terminology of "The Treasure of Far Island," we had *played* together? What would our adult relationship be like?

Suffice it to say, Cather had many questions on her mind. In a May 20, 1919 letter to Jones, she hinted at her experimental strategy: "I wished here to present the chief character through a man's memory, because the most interesting things I knew about the several women of whom she was made, were told me by men" (*SLWC,* 277). What if Cather was working on an experiment in gendered epistemology that she had begun to sketch in "The Way of the World"? What could a woman make out of what men know about women? After a century of response to the novel, it seems clear that the resulting work will continue to unsettle, in distinctly modern ways, certain prevailing assumptions about gender and knowledge.

I think Cather was working with this level of finesse when she decided to introduce Ántonia as "a central figure" with the power "to call up pictures of people and places, to set a quiet drama going in one's brain" (xi–xii). As Lindemann has pointed out, a figure is a sketch or an outline or perhaps a rhetorical figure of words: "Made of words, Ántonia generates words as readily as she generates children."[23] Once again, as they did in *The Song of the Lark,* Cather's experimental gambits—rooted in the West she remembered—produce novelistic fecundity.

As part of this autobiographical experiment in gendered knowledge, Cather returned to the territorial imagination. Inside the novel's complex frame,[24] Jim Burden returns to his boyhood: "I first heard of Ántonia on what seemed to me an interminable journey across the great midland plain of North America" (3). Signaling her experimental agenda, Cather imagines Jim reading a book about Jesse James (4). Drawing from a different array of territorial materials, Cather will offer an alternative to the Western.[25] As territorial folks used to do, Jim names his heroine, including a footnote on the pronunciation, and rechristens the region as "the great midland plain." When the kindly conductor tells Jake and Jim about the foreign family with the same destination, he reports: "They can't any of them speak English, except one little girl, and all she can say is 'We go Black Hawk, Nebraska'" (4). Cather, following a practice she began way back in "Tommy, the Unsentimental," renames the town by switching colors, substituting Black for Red before replacing Cloud with Hawk, a move that manages to appropriate the name of another Native American leader. "The only thing very noticeable about Nebraska," Jim remembers, "was that it was still, all day long, Nebraska" (5). When Jim and Jake arrive in Black Hawk at night, the author is townmaking again. This town is divided, thanks to the railroad, just like Red Cloud.[26]

Recalling the early promotional representations of the prairie by Gilpin, the paintings of Catlin, and the gardens of Mrs. Bergson and Alexandra, Mrs. Burden's garden is an enclosed world of cultivation. Echoing *O Pioneers!,* Chapter Three begins with a Sunday morning drive to see neighbors. Just as she did in her first Nebraska novel, the author passes over farm labor in order to map the countryside and engage immigrant neighbors. In doing so, she again borrows from *O Pioneers!* by having Jim recall "a wild place" (18), but Jim transitions quickly to the element that unites Cather's allegorical vision of her life: "The road ran about like a wild thing" (19). As the wagon approaches "Squaw Creek" (20), we realize that the natural features have already been renamed for the travelers. Cather is savoring the territorial pleasure of precisely marking and renaming Indian Creek near the Sadilek farm. When Jim visits the pumpkin patch and then eats melons with Ántonia, it is a kind of reunion with the Cucurbitaceae family that Cather had been cultivating in her short fiction. In all these ways, Cather was redeploying elements of the fiction that had come before.

More particularly, in "The Shimerdas," Cather wants to bring the prairie landscape to life. Ever since "Eric Hermannson's Soul," she had been paying painterly attention to matters of composition and light on the prairie, finally widening her approach in *O Pioneers!*. In this triumphant novel, she was intent on refining her previous experiments.[27] Recalling his first visit to the garden, Jim juxtaposes "the big yellow pumpkins" and "the red grass" (16). Jim recalls "the pale yellow cornfields" beside the "rich copper color" of the smartweed (28). Step by step, the author captures the timelessness of pastoral pleasure in the midst of so much openness: "All those fall afternoons were the same, but I never got used to them. As far as we could see, the miles of copper-red grass were drenched in sunlight that was stronger and fiercer than at any other time of the day. The blond cornfields were red gold, the haystacks turned rosy and threw long shadows" (39). When Cather wants to suggest the difficulties ahead, she switches deftly to a grayscale that seems to embody the idea of foreshadowing (41). A glance at Solomon D. Butcher's 1887 photograph of the Garness family alongside their abundant pumpkin harvest helps us appreciate Cather's accomplishment. Butcher did all he could with black and white composition. We grasp the topography, the pumpkin aesthetic, and even the character of the family. But no artist in any medium before Cather (and perhaps no writer since) has bound up so much feeling in the colors of the prairie landscape. With these passages, Cather became the brilliant painter of the prairie that Whitman had once imagined.

Against this painterly backdrop, Cather is telling an alternative story of masculinity in the West. Jim recalls his encounter with Otto Fuchs, a real live cowboy with "the face of a desperado" (6). Fuchs can manage his work around the farm and talks of "outlaws and desperate characters he had known" (66). The cowboy's best story is about taking care of a mother and her triplets (67). No desperado, Fuchs sings in "a good baritone voice," leads the singing at church, makes a sled, and cherishes Christmas ornaments (65). Readers familiar with Wister's *Virginian* will recall the comic battle between man and pony that opens the novel. In *My Ántonia,* Jim gets a new pony when he arrives out West. Cather's gentle cowboy pulls Jim aside at the first opportunity to tell him that this pony is "a 'perfect gentleman' " (12).

Jim sets off on his pony much as the author seems to have done (27–28), but readers fascinated by stories of boys living on the Great Plains such as Garland's *Boy Life on the Prairie* (1899) have probably found these passages a bit odd. What about Jim's chores? Late in the section, he mentions them. But what, exactly, did Jim *do* on the farm?[28] Of course, Cather had little interest in these Georgic matters, a fact that had been clear in her fiction from "On the Divide" to "A Wagner Matinee" to *O Pioneers!*. Here she was intent on adapting some of her own best memories of her days on the prairie (*WCP,* 19), and perhaps, as Timothy C. Blackburn points out, echoing McClure's loathing of chores in his *Autobiography.*[29] Faithful descriptions of boy life from the period seem, quite simply, beside the point.

By now it should be clear that melons, cucumbers, gourds, and squash occupy a special place in Cather's luminous imagination. Perhaps they did for all the early inhabitants of the Great Plains who longed to see plants grow and produce fruit in an environment that seemed to favor only grass. When Jim and Ántonia visit Peter and Pavel, they see "a big melon patch, and a garden where squashes and yellow cucumbers lay about on the sod" (34). Once again, Jim is remembering pastoral pleasure that has nothing to do with work: "Peter put the melons in a row on the oilcloth-covered table and stood over them brandishing a butcher knife. Before the blade got fairly into them, they split of their own ripeness" (35). The juicy red abundance is implicitly juxtaposed with the "corn and beans and fat yellow cucumbers" on the floor (35). Cather's newspaper aesthetic, her green vase juxtaposed with the yellow orange, has been perfectly realized on the Great Plains.

More grandly, Cather concludes "The Shimerdas" by hearkening back to the expansive voice of *O Pioneers!* and by anticipating her *Nation* essay "The End of the First Cycle." Jim declares: "July came on with that breathless, brilliant heat which makes the plains of Kansas and Nebraska the best corn country in the world" (131). Flying high over the old territorial boundaries with a cartographer's perspective, Jim explains, "If all the great plain from the Missouri to the Rocky Mountains had been under glass, and the heat regulated by a thermometer, it could not have been better for the yellow tassels" (132). Season merges with territory in an aerial view of prairie being inevitably transformed into farmland.

Narrowing his focus, Jim recalls how one night he and Ántonia "climbed up on the slanting roof of the chicken-house to watch the clouds" (133–34). For the author, the scene is laden with recollections, some real, some imagined. She is recalling the time she and her brother Roscoe climbed the windmill to watch a storm in 1893, and she is returning to a similar scene in "Eric Hermannson's Soul." Sounding like one of the early travelers crossing the prairie, Jim describes "the optical illusions, an implicit prairie/sea analogy, and the vast space that allows one to see both clear weather and violent storm at once."[30] The two old friends have discovered the panoramic view coveted by the first territorial settlers.

THE Garness family in front of their sod house in Custer County Nebraska by Solomon Butcher, 1887. Source: Nebraska State Historical Society.

When Jim and his grandparents move to Black Hawk, the same process of recycling and repurposing comes to brilliant life as Cather creates her definitive palimpsest of Red Cloud: "Black Hawk . . . was a clean, well-planted little prairie town, with white fences and good green yards about the dwellings, wide, dusty streets, and shapely little trees growing along the wooden sidewalks. In the center of the town there were two rows of new brick 'store' buildings, a brick schoolhouse, the court house, and four white churches" (141). The term "well-planted" echoes the early townmaking literature. As the editors of the Red Cloud newspapers had done in the 1880s, Jim draws his readers' attention to the sidewalks. But the term "little prairie town" does not imitate the boosting language that Red Cloud newspapers used in the early 1880s.[31] In ways the newspapers did not attempt, Cather's sense of color animates the description. White is set against green in yards that are simply "good." Bricks are the *center* of the town, representing prosperity, novelty, and Red Cloud. In sum, Jim is neither boosting nor condemning the town he remembers as a boy. His language suggests a simple description of a live western town that has much in common with the Red Cloud of Cather's youth.

With this picture in mind, Cather is unusually precise in her depiction of the Miner family. Indeed, after the novel's publication, both Cather and her Red Cloud friends were quite clear that Harling was another name for Miner. In any event, Cather and the Miners were delighted by their fictional roles.

Carrie took great pride in being the prototype for Frances and even claimed to have been consulted on her fictional name, which she (in territorial fashion) had changed as a youth.[32] Perhaps for the Miner children, their recasting represented the ultimate extension of Sandy Point. Decades after their childhood collaboration, they continued to play a part in their gifted comrade's town-making. The road was truly circular and shared, a sentiment Cather made clear by dedicating the novel to Carrie and her sister Irene.[33]

Old Red Cloud stories of boy life, already transformed in "The Treasure of Far Island," "The Way of the World," and "The Enchanted Bluff," flicker behind Jim's recollection of arriving in town: "I was quite another boy, or thought I was. Suddenly put down among boys of my own age, I found I had a great deal to learn. Before the spring term of school was over I could fight, play 'keeps,' tease the little girls, and use forbidden words as well as any boy in my class" (141). Fighting, playing keeps, teasing girls, and swearing constitute Jim's "education," but Jim never bothers to tell any of these stories. He simply recalls, "I was restrained from utter savagery only by the fact that Mrs. Harling, our nearest neighbor, kept an eye on me" (141).

Many readers of *My Ántonia* probably think they know what Jim means when he says that he nearly escaped "utter savagery," but a return to Red Cloud newspapers and their fascination with "the natural history of a boy," as the *Argus* called it in 1881, suggests that we should not take Jim's metamorphosis for granted. Contrasted with the real "savagery" of Red Cloud boys who were stealing melons and finding skeletons, Jim's playing keeps and teasing girls seem decidedly tame and *story-less.*

In fact, as the section unfolds, Jim seems like a boy without a life. As Judith Fetterley puts it in her compelling discussion of Cather as a lesbian writer, "We have seen no part of this boys' world. Instead, we have seen Jim hanging out with the Harlings, participating in female-centered family life" (141). Cather was exploring, as she first did in "Tommy" back in 1896, alternative versions of her own life, all the while experimenting with the way gender is constructed in the West.

In doing so, the author offers insights into her own story of emergence. Take for instance Jim's recollection of "the painted glass window" in the Methodist Church: "Without knowing why, we used to linger on the sidewalk outside the church when the lamps were lighted early for the choir practice or prayer-meeting, shivering and talking until our feet were like lumps of ice. The crude reds and greens and blues of that colored glass held us there" (169). It is no coincidence that every time the author looked out of the north windows of the house on Seward Street during one of her visits to Red Cloud, she saw the Methodist Church that inspired the passage. The particular proximities of Red Cloud platting kept memories of winter and color alive for the author long after she had moved away.[34] The phenomenon had something to do with memory, minimalism, and color. Somehow extreme cold, night, and clarity of consciousness mattered to the equation. As she wrote this scene for *My Ántonia,* the "fine colorist" that Whitman once imagined was consciously meditating on past and present while marveling over the way a town could "make" an author.

I would be tempted to see this allegory as central to the section, but Cather's title, "Hired Girls," suggests something different. What matters most in this part of the novel is how Ántonia and the other country girls became town people, a theme Cather first noted in "On the Divide." When Ambrosch brings his sister to Black Hawk to work for the Harlings, she tells Jim: "Maybe I be the kind of girl you like better, now I come to town" (150). Lena Lingard embodies yet another version of country town metamorphosis. She demands: "Ain't you crazy about town, Tony?" (159). Far from a revolt from the village, Lena is ready to lead a revolt *to* the village.

For Ántonia, the revolt begins at the Harlings' house. Nodding back to the all-important church window, Jim remembers, "On winter nights, the lights in the Harlings' windows drew me like the painted glass. Inside that warm, roomy house there was color, too. After supper I used to catch up my cap, stick my hands in my pockets, and dive through the willow hedge as if witches were after me" (169). Jim's exuberance is particularly contagious because, in part, we know it is Cather who is racing toward the bright windows that symbolize imagination in a little town on the prairie. And so we come to focus on Jim's "Winterreise," and that is nothing less than a perfect Saturday night at the Harlings' house. In Jim's mind, Ántonia takes center stage, telling her story of the tramp who threw himself into the threshing machine. As Funda, Millington, and Woolley suggest, Ántonia embodies a mythic sort of storytelling that exceeds the narrative practices of the novel that contains it.[35] Hearkening back to the many tramp stories that appeared in the columns of the Red Cloud newspapers and to the memorable episode in *The Song of the Lark,* Cather's celebration of Western domesticity and the side-by-sidedness of storytelling is striking.

Of course, "The Hired Girls" might have turned on stories of youth indebted to "The Way of the World," "The Treasure of Far Island," or "The Enchanted Bluff," but the author's different agenda is apparent: "The Harling children and I were never happier, never felt more contented and secure, than in the weeks of spring which broke that long winter" (187). With a few more brushstrokes, childhood is suggested: "Yet the summer which was to change everything was coming nearer every day. When boys and girls are growing up, life can't stand still, not even in the quietest of country towns; and they have to grow up, whether they will or no" (187).

Readers familiar with Cather's long road to *My Ántonia* will probably think of the poem Cather used to preface "The Way of the World": "O! the world was full of the summer time." The lines add a melancholy frame of mature perspective to a story of childhood imagination. Here, Cather's more prosaic intervention creates the same effect, even though the story remains untold. Yet the concluding lines of the poem haunt this pivotal chapter:

> When I could believe in the fairies still,
>   And our elf in the cottonwood tree,
> And the poet of gold at the rainbow's end
>   And you could believe in me.

In *My Ántonia,* there is no elf in the cottonwood tree, no opportunity for Jim and Ántonia to engage in the kind of imaginative play that binds Douglass to Margie in "The Treasure of Far Island." So it should come as no surprise that Jim cannot continue to believe in Ántonia at the end of "The Hired Girls."

In this section, Cather replaces stories of playtime with more mature stories of music and dancing. Nowhere is this more apparent than in Jim's recollection of Blind d'Arnault's performance in Black Hawk, which reveals a great deal about the author's experimentation. For instance, the novelist could easily have stitched an Opera House event into her narrative, but she changed the setting to the Boys' Home, Black Hawk's "comfortable hotel" that looks a lot like the old Boys' Home of Red Cloud.[36] With this change, Jim tells a story of stealth, how he "ran downtown to the hotel and slipped quietly into the parlor" (176). He remarks the "atmosphere of unusual freedom" (176). "Side by side," as Cather would put it, the stories of music and dance at the Harlings' house and at the Boys' Home "produce a reaction which neither of them will produce alone." The stories whisper of the transgression implicit in performance and endorsed ambiguously by Black Hawk citizens.

The appearance of the dancing pavilion in Black Hawk plays an important part in this theme. Jim reports to Mrs. Harling and Ántonia that "three cheerful-looking Italians" have opened a dancing pavilion on a vacant lot (188). "That vacant lot," Jim declares, "soon became the most cheerful place in town. Even on the hottest afternoons the cottonwoods made a rustling shade . . ." (189). No elf waits in these cottonwood trees. Elaborating on the change in the townscape, Jim lists details that could have come from a glance at the "City News" or "The Local Department": "Dancing became popular now, just as roller skating had been the summer before. The Progressive Euchre Club arranged with the Vannis for the exclusive use of the floor on Tuesday and Friday nights. At other times any one could dance who paid his money and was orderly; the railroad men, the Round House mechanics, the delivery boys, the iceman, the farmhands who lived near enough to ride into town after their day's work was over" (190–91).

More than ever before in her fiction, more than she did in *The Song of the Lark,* Cather was snipping and rearranging elements from the pages of the *Argus* and the *Chief* for her fiction. Although there were people such as Jim's Baptist grandparents who did not approve of dancing, the local newspapers reported such events with general approbation.[37]

The author, who had once danced the night away in Blue Hill during her winter of discontent after college, remembered this context vividly in all sorts of ways that the local newspapers would never have discussed, namely, how dancing in a country town might transform a young woman's life. Jim recalls: "It was at the Vannis' tent that Ántonia was discovered" (198). The sentence echoes Cather's own cherished memories of being discovered in Red Cloud. What elocution and theater did for the author, dancing does (more or less) for Ántonia—*more* because dancing is no intermediate activity for the heroine and *less* because her dancing could never be worthy of reportorial comment in the town newspapers. Cather clearly cares about such distinctions. Jim moralizes: "Ántonia's success at the tent had its consequences. The iceman lingered too long now." (199). Towns make town people, but the translation has "consequences."

Like Cather's recollections, Jim's memories of Nebraska are often inflected by morality and moralizing. In this mood, he rehearses the awkward position of the country girls who worked to help their fathers pay off their farms. The girls were enchanting objects of desire and admirable models of industry, but Jim explains how they were also "considered a menace to the social order" (195). The Black Hawk newspapers do not tell their stories, but Jim recalls their transformation: "Physically they were almost a race apart, and out-of-door work had given them a vigor which when they got over their first shyness on coming to town, developed into a positive carriage and freedom of movement, and made them conspicuous among Black Hawk women" (192). As

Prchal points out, Cather seems to be "implying that Americans of the dominant culture should emulate immigrants rather than pressure immigrants to assimilate to their culture."[38]

In Jim's mind, memories and moralizing go together, but so do moods. "I was moody and restless that winter," he recalls, "and tired of the people I saw every day" (209–10). Unlike Thea in *The Song of the Lark,* he has no Dr. McKeeby with whom he can share his feelings. So he prowls—over to the saloon of Anton Jelinek, clearly modeled on John Polnicky's South Side Sample Rooms, which opened in 1892 on 4th Avenue in Red Cloud. In the novel, Jim reports another case of the farmer becoming the town person: "Handsome Anton Jelinek, who had rented his homestead and come to town, was the proprietor" (210). Jim remembers how he "liked to drop into his barroom and listen to the talk" until his grandfather put an end to his visits (210–11). Jim recalls his moody vision of country town life: "One could hang about the drug store, and listen to the old men who sat there every evening, talking politics and telling raw stories" (211). "One could," Jim muses, "go to the cigar factory and chat with the old German who raised canaries for sale, and look at his stuffed birds. But whatever you began with him, the talk went back to taxidermy" (211).[39] Jim recalls heading for the depot, which, as it was in Red Cloud, is "down" from the center of town (211). Such are the taxidermal feelings of a solitary teenager in a Western town.

On the heels of this frustrating trip down memory lane, Jim's famous diatribe spills out in a long paragraph that deserves careful attention because it comes at a pivotal time in the novel and because it must affect the way we value the town life at the heart of *My Ántonia.* Jim recalls: "On starlight nights I used to pace up and down those long, cold streets, scowling at the little, sleeping houses on either side" (212). The townscape about to be described is seen through the eyes of the scowling high school senior who detects "jealousy and envy and unhappiness" everywhere (212). As Jim *saw* it, these houses were infested with hypocrisy: "The life that went on in them seemed to me made up of evasions and negations" (212). Lest we miss the point, Cather has included the phrase "seemed to me" in this attack. Seen through the eyes of the high school senior who is smart enough not to study and who will one day complete law school, the town deserved condemnation. It would, therefore, be a mistake to take Jim's critique in this section as a compelling indictment of life in Black Hawk, as a passionate and final repudiation of town life in general—just as it would be a mistake to collect all such condemnations of tyranny authored by intelligent high school seniors and cite them as definitive.

The real point of Jim's tirade is that he had reached a turning point, and it is here that we reach the limits of a life in town on the Great Plains. Black Hawk can hardly satisfy when Lena lets him kiss her, when dancing with Lena is "like coming in with the tide" (215). Jim shares these feelings with Ántonia, and she bristles over Lena's behavior because she envisions greater things for Jim than boy life in a country town: "Now, don't you go and be a fool like some of these town boys. You're not going to sit around here and whittle store-boxes and tell stories all your life. You are going away to school and make something of yourself" (217). Many people, then and now, have made something of themselves by staying put, but many more have left town in order to complete the transformation. The problem for such towns over the last century or so has been that so few return after their "making." The author, who once arranged "store-boxes" in order to invent Sandy Point, has her heroine state the case emphatically—*you are going away.*

Just as it did for Cather, Jim's high school commencement signals the end of his town life. Once again, the author was orchestrating layers of memory, private and public. For instance, Cather certainly remembered her own speech and must have also recalled the June 13, 1890, *Chief.* Side by side with a note about boys catching channel cats in the Republican, the newspaper declared: "Miss Willa Cather treated the audience to a fine oration on 'Superstition vs. Investigation,' which was a master piece of oratory" (5). Such praise might have been sufficient, but the editor concludes, "Her line of thought was well carved out and a great surprise to her many friends."

Cather had to be chagrined by the editor's inelegant prose and back-handed compliment. When she invented Jim Burden's memories, she worked out of this recollection. Mrs. Harling tells the graduate: "You surprised me, Jim" (222). Ántonia tells of meeting Jim's grandfather: "He won't tell you, but he told us he was awful surprised himself, didn't he, girls?" (223). Mrs. Harling and Jim's grandfather effectively "quote" the *Chief* with their "surprise." In this way, Cather transforms the Red Cloud newspaper notice into an intimate moment of self-discovery for Jim that just happens to echo her own past triumph. The old story of community surprise becomes a personal memento, a priceless effect of the author's re-composition. Jim testifies: "I have had no other success that pulled at my heartstrings like that one" (223).

Cather engages in another sort of re-composition in the following chapter. Red Cloud newspapers reported church picnics, school picnics, and holiday picnics. They touted the first picnic of the season and the last. They described the annual Old Settlers' Picnics and the annual Ohio Picnic in Lincoln. A story from the August 30, 1883, *Argus* describes the particular pleasures of such an event: "The day was pleasant and the drive was delightful. Late in the afternoon tables were spread with all the delicacies of the season, to which a hungry crowd of village picnickers did ample justice. The young folks tarried during the evening to trip the light fantastic" (4). Set side-by-side with stories of mercantile change, political dispute, births, and deaths, picnic tales emphasize youthful pleasure that resists the passage of time. The natural rhythms of the good life appear as an effect on the newspaper page.

In Cather's novel, Jim is writing through this newspaper genre, but his story is no ordinary account of a Nebraska picnic. In a grand prologue of prairie pastoral, Jim is botanist and painter as he catalogs and juxtaposes "pink bee-bush," "flaming orange-colored milk-weed, rare in that part of the state" (225). He foregrounds "the gaillardia [that] came up year after year and matted over the ground with the deep, velvety red that is in Bokhara carpets" (225). In passing, he recalls "the dogwood bushes, all overgrown with wild grapevines" (225). Warren and Hosmer never reported in this way. Professor Bessey, who had died in 1915, would probably have been delighted.

As Jim undresses for a swim, Cather revisits one of her most cherished settings, sketching it with a new sense of purpose: "The sandbars, with their clean white beaches and their little groves of willows and cottonwood seedlings, were a sort of No Man's Land, little newly-created worlds that belonged to the Black Hawk boys. Charley Harling and I had hunted these woods, fished from the fallen logs, until I knew every inch of the river shores and had a friendly feeling for every bar and shallow" (226). With obvious fidelity, Cather seems to nod back to "The Treasure of Far Island" and "The Enchanted Bluff," stories that celebrated childhood imagination unfolding along the Republican River. Needless to say, the difference between Jim's memories and the short stories is profound. Jim recounts none of the river adventures he seems to have had with Charley. Although he can name shrubs and flowers, he cannot muster a single reference to an adventure he had with the larger group of "Black Hawk boys." Jim swims alone, "playing about indolently," already sighing over the loss of his youth (226).

Quite in keeping with the conventions of pastoral, the solitary swimmer eventually spies his central figure in a bower—"Ántonia, seated alone under the pagoda-like elders" (228). He leaps up and in doing so recalls the warm spontaneity of Douglass Burnham, the mature Speckle from "The Way of the World," as he sits with Margie in "The Treasure of Far Island." In the older sketch, Douglass and Margie develop a theory of imagination rooted in childhood. Inspired by their vision, they refuse to leave the sandbar to meet the expectations of the town.

Cather aims for something else in this novel. The young friends experience the kind of prairie mirage that used to captivate territorial folk. The magnified plow, the trick of light that Jim describes as "a picture writing on the sun," surprises the picnickers. Cather juxtaposes the happenstance with the young folks' stories of the past, engendering an elegiac mood tinged with irony. Like Yorick's skull in *Hamlet,* the plow in *My Ántonia* has come to stand for the classic text, a synecdoche that seems to capture the essence of the work, an enduring mood that early modern writers called *mutability.* At the same time, as Stout points out, it "redefines the saga of the West from one of adventure and violence to one of cultivation and family survival."[40]

What remains after picnics on sand? In "The Enchanted Bluff," the boys share a story they pass down to their children. And this, as any fan of literature recognizes, is the real treasure of all sandy adventures because, as Joan Didion so elegantly declares, "we tell ourselves stories in order to live."[41] By contrast, at the end of "The Hired Girls," Jim is at a loss. When he takes Ántonia's place at Wick Cutter's house and finds himself wrestling in bed with the despicable money lender, Jim confronts an abyss. Hiding behind his bedroom door, Jim hears his friend crying: "I felt that I never wanted to see her again" (242). Because he could no longer believe in Ántonia, he was either unable or unwilling to tell a story he could live with. Or perhaps it was a failure in storytelling that undermined his belief? Regardless of which part of the relationship we emphasize, it seems certain that Jim finally writes his narrative in order to remedy the old impasse.

As she did in *The Song of the Lark,* Cather telescopes her narrative in *My Ántonia.* "The Hired Girls" is shorter than "The Shimerdas," and the final two sections are shorter still. Turning to Jim's university days, she imagined an alternative version of her own career with its own satisfactions and limitations. Owing to his solitary ways and narrow focus, Jim never stirs up enmity with his journalism, but he does discover, while reading Virgil, a rationale for the use of Old World allusions out West. The autobiographical experiment is evident here. He never seems to return home, and he has no summer adventures to rival Cather's trip to Brownville. His months in Lincoln fairly fly by. Because he never falls for a fellow student, he avoids the pain Cather felt when her relationship with Pound ended. And, perhaps most important, because he follows Gaston Cleric back East to complete his education, he never suffers the intense personal doubt that threatened to crush Cather after she graduated.

It must be said that Jim's life is a pale imitation of Cather's lively vigor during these years. The woman on the wheel embraced her own physical prowess, whereas Jim merely refers to a few tennis matches with his professor. Through all of her ups and downs, Cather was writing, fiction and non-fiction, earning recognition for the former, and money and public praise for the latter. Through the turbulence of these times, Cather shared her feelings with Mariel Gere and with her beloved brothers.

Readers familiar with all of the fiction that preceded this novel will recognize that "Cuzak's Boys" stands as a "coda" for this portion of the author's career. Employing techniques she had been experimenting with for decades, the author shaped the fraught reunion. As Jim walks up to the Cuzak house, the scene is immediately softened: "Ducks and geese ran quacking across my path. White cats were sunning themselves among yellow pumpkins on the porch steps. I looked through the wire screen into a big, light kitchen with a white floor" (320). The juxtaposition of the cats, pumpkins, and kitchen, yellow and white, transforms the farm into a genre painting. Beauty stands in for anxiety. Simultaneously, all the important elements echo Jim's first impressions of his grandparents' farm. As Jim steps through the orderly composition, the past lives elegantly on in a present filled with anxious questions.

Then, with no preparation on either side, no changes by either old friend to prepare for the meeting, Ántonia suddenly stands before him. Jim takes care to point out that the painterly encounter of artist and subject has not come easily: "the miracle happened; one of those quiet moments that clutch the heart, and take more courage than the noisy, excited passages in life" (321). Ántonia, Jim recalls, "was there, in the full vigor of her personality, battered but not diminished, looking at me, speaking to me in the husky, breathy voice I remembered so well" (321–22). If a hard life need not diminish the person who lives it, then memory may not be the idealist's only salvation. If a bright being could be, in certain ways that matter most, impervious to time, then the idealist would not need to flee from human contact. By envisioning such possibilities in fiction, a great novelist, like Willa Cather, might feel that she had transcended the eternal and inevitable cycle of life and death.

Having worked on the novel in New Hampshire, writing each morning in a tent pitched in the middle of a meadow, Cather must have felt compelled to improve upon this epiphany in a green enclosure, a pastoral bower undisturbed by the erotic passion of *O Pioneers!*. Jim recalls, "There was the deepest peace in that orchard" (330). He goes on to paint a luminous picture of the place from within: "The orchard seemed full of sun, like a cup, and we could smell the ripe apples on the trees. The crabs hung on the branches as thick as beads on a string, purple-red, with a thin silvery glaze over them" (331). The old territorial mapmakers had envisioned such spaces as naturally occurring oases in the vast prairie openness.

Gathering up the threads of her previous Nebraska novels, the author returns with precision to the Epilogue of *The Song of the Lark* and to this novel's central focus on how Western towns shape people. When Ántonia explains that she belongs on a farm and not in a town, Jim declares, "You ought never to have gone to town, Tony" (333). Ántonia quickly corrects him: "Oh, I'm glad I went! I'd never have known anything about cooking or housekeeping if I hadn't" (333). In her mind, the town offered a chance to "learn" (333). With everything else that is at stake in this finale, the heroine's relationship to the town must be settled.

And her portrait must be completed. In the early decades of the novel's existence, Ántonia was simply the Nebraska pioneer woman with great heart. As readers became more skeptical, she was a mere "figure" used by the selfish narrator to explain himself. Reconsidering her abilities, other readers saw her as the rival artist in the novel, the storyteller who achieves effects that Jim cannot. There is truth, of course, in each of these portraits.

Because Ántonia has often seemed synonymous with the early history of Nebraska, another version of her final portrait deserves attention here. Reviewing his memories of the heroine as "a succession of such pictures," Jim puzzles: "She was a battered woman now, not a lovely girl; but she still had that something which fires the imagination" (342). What is "that something"? Jim suggests, "She had only to stand in the orchard, to put her hand on a little crab tree and look up at the apples, to make you feel the goodness of planting and tending and harvesting at last" (342). This person is no mere figure, but neither is she a Wagnerian heroine of action. She is neither visionary farmer nor diva. Instead, she is a Nebraska heroine who can make the goodness of the country's planting and tending palpable. In certain other worlds, say deep in a Bohemian forest of her ancestors, Ántonia would be called a saint. Simply telling her story would be enough to make a life worth living. With this in mind, Rosowski urges us to view the heroine as "Earth Mother."[42] Yet, as Funda argues, over the course of the novel, Ántonia has become a powerful storyteller in her own right, and her emergence in this regard completes the novel every bit as much as Jim's.[43]

Any summing up of Jim Burden will inspire more heated debate. Aiming for a balanced verdict, Murphy suggests: "As a true Romantic Jim imagines and constructs his history with Ántonia into a miniature of man's, fills his emptiness, and enables himself to carry on. Such is the essence of the novel's optimism. What is pessimistic is the need for the effort, that so much was missed in Jim's life and in his relationships with Ántonia and Lena."[44] Some readers will accept this summation, but others will continue to see Jim as the sexually repressed misogynistic failure described by Blanche H. Gelfant and Lindemann.[45] Other eyes, for various reasons, will follow Randall, who sees an inspired Jim at the novel's end and so believes that *My Ántonia* is "the most affirmative book Willa Cather ever wrote."[46] Perhaps, as Blackburn argues, we should note the allusions to the *Odyssey* and *Rip Van Winkle* in the novel and view Jim "as a restless Odyssean traveler living without despair in an America that has failed its great cultural opportunity."[47] One thing seems certain: in a great novel, divergent readings will always be possible.

Here is one more. We know Jim Burden is not Willa Cather, even as we recognize that he shadows some important elements of the author's life. If at the end of the novel, as Thacker points out, we have "misgivings" about Jim's success, our doubts "are directed toward the character, not his creator" (*GPF,* 161). Perhaps what matters most at the end of the novel is the way Jim allows Cather to confirm her own emergence?

It was a triumph that could not endure the way the author wished. With each passing year, Cather was more concerned with memory than with emergence. As she grew older, she simply could not sustain her commitment to the territorial imagination and its assurance that things can always be otherwise. The old delight in creating palimpsests, alternative and layered versions of her own life, faded along with her attachment to Bergsonian becoming. These shifts explain, in many ways, the difference between the three great prairie novels and the later fiction set in Nebraska.

But to truly understand the aging author, we need to remember how much she had in common with the emerging author. Writing under her familiar banner "The Passing Show" for the *Courier* in Lincoln on August 24, 1895, the woman on the wheel assayed the talents of Jean de Reszke, the famous Polish opera star. "De Reszke is a great artist," she wrote with the cold certainty of her critic's pen, "a perfect singer, and he still makes, in spite of his fifty odd years, as graceful and charming a lover as any prima could wish for. But after all age is age and art cannot quite conceal it. Youth's candles are burnt out" (6). Reszke was, in fact, forty-five at the time, but Cather knew what she knew. Age is age. And it would not be surprising if the author, who turned forty-five the year she published *My Ántonia,* remembered Reszke on her birthday that December.

World War I also had something to do with Cather's graying disposition. Moved by the death of her cousin G. P. Cather on the battlefield, the author explored a version of his Nebraskan life "at the end of the First Cycle" in *One of Ours* (1922). But her hero Claude is a case of arrested development unfolding on another farmstead setting that Cather could not fully embrace. His boy life is merely mentioned. Like Nils in "The Bohemian Girl," he flees the prairies in search of a European destiny. If he achieves a kind of fulfillment, it is on the battlefield far from the farms of Nebraska.[48]

On the heels of this novel, *A Lost Lady* (1923) looks back at a Nebraska that has much in common with the settings of *The Song of the Lark* and *My Ántonia* but the style is Modern, minimal, and elegiac. "Thirty or forty years ago," the novel begins, "in one of those grey towns along the Burlington railroad, which are so much greyer to-day than they were then, there was a house well known from Omaha to Denver for its hospitality and for a certain charm of atmosphere" (7). At first blush, the novel seems like another Bildungsroman punctuated by boy life, with Neil Herbert at the center; but Neil's story is far less important than his function as a lens for remembering Mrs. Forrester. Cather's take on the old "Far Country" was evolving. With good reason, Sinclair Lewis called it "about the finest thing that has ever appeared in American fiction."[49]

Although something was fading in Cather's Nebraskan landscapes, her desire for experimentation remained indomitable. In 1925, while working on the page proofs of *The Professor's House,* she was tinkering with the book's design, a process that felt like an "experiment."[50] In 1931, a laudatory review by Wilbur Cross of *Shadows on the Rock* in the *Saturday Review of Literature* triggered a letter from the author. Echoing her description of the "different process" of *O Pioneers!* nearly two decades earlier, Cather thanked Cross for recognizing her "different kind of method" in this novel, musing, "surely you'll agree with me that our writers experiment too little, and produce their own special brand too readily."[51] In an August 26, 1940, letter to her brother Roscoe, Cather confessed that in *Sapphira and the Slave Girl,* she had "tried an experiment in form which most people will not like" (*SLWC,* 587). Three years later, she was complaining about "unfortunate experiments" with domestic help.[52]

Obscure Destinies (1932), *Lucy Gayheart* (1935), and "The Best Years" (1945) represent the final phase of Cather's writing about the West. They have much in common with their predecessors. In "Neighbour Rosicky," Cather is still trying to tell a farm story and get the Georgic elements right. Once more she offers a loving tribute to the Czech neighbors she remembered and to John Pavelka, who had already served as the prototype for Ántonia's husband in the earlier novel. In "Old Mrs. Harris" and "Two Friends," she indulges once more in territorial renaming. The first story is set in a hybrid place called "Colorado" that recalls the setting of *The Song of the Lark.* In the second story, the narrator begins, "Long ago . . . in a little wooden town in a shallow Kansas river valley, there lived two friends" (*CSP,* 673). Feeling no need to use Kansas as the territorial "other" as she had done in "El Dorado" and "The Sculptor's Funeral" so many years before, the author readily turns to the kind of mythical time that Jim Burden invokes in the famous novel: "Every evening in winter, when I went to the post-office after supper, I passed through Dillon's store . . . for the warmth and cheerfulness" (675).[53] More than anything else, the reader recognizes Cather's enduring passion for townmaking. The red bricks in "Two Friends" counterpoint the electric lights and Methodist lawn party in "Old Mrs. Harris," which complement the river skating in *Lucy Gayheart* and the snowy walk up the hill in "The Best Years."

But these late works ultimately have more in common with *A Lost Lady* than with the first Nebraska novels. The elegiac tone is palpable and so is the missing emphasis on emergence. Cather's father died of a heart attack on March 3, 1928, and Cather recast the event in "Neighbor Rosicky." We glimpse Vickie Templeton's childhood in "Old Mrs. Harris," but not her transformation. At first glance, Lucy Gayheart seems like another version of Thea Kronborg, but her relationship with her hometown smells of the grave: "She loved her own little town, but it was a heart-breaking love, like loving the dead who cannot answer back" (144). Lucy lacks Thea's artistic talent and dies suddenly.

The mood of these stories is perhaps summed up by Mrs. Ferguesson at the end of "The Best Years": "Our best years are when we're working hardest and going right ahead when we can hardly see our way out" (756). The best years are rooted in youth, talent, struggle, and emergence. What we make of the later, lesser years has everything to do with memory, or so Cather seemed to feel in the later years of her life.

Writing to Irene Miner Weisz on March 12, 1931, Cather headed the letter "Crossing Kansas" (*SLWC,* 442). In territorial motion on the Santa Fe Californian Limited, Cather had been dreaming. In her late poem "Going Home," she describes the sensation:

How smoothly the trains run beyond the Missouri;
Even in my sleep I know when I have crossed the river.
The wheels turn as if they were glad to go;
They run like running water,
Like Youth, running away. . . .[54]

Now, in this latest dream, Cather had been traveling with Irene on the way to her parents' golden wedding celebration back in 1922. Then she awoke: "At first I felt sad—then very happy. I did not really deserve that happy time. I had never been a very thoughtful daughter. My mind and heart were always too full of my one all-absorbing passion. I took my parents for granted. But, deserving or not, I had it, and there is no one in the round world whom I would have chosen before you to share it with me."

With so much life behind her, Cather was still aiming for understanding and reconciliation. At what cost had she become a major American author, and could it all be redeemed in some way? In her late stories of memory, she tried to respond by creating a West that would endure the vicissitudes of time, but her immediate answer in this letter came straight from the pages of *O Pioneers!*. Crossing the old Kansas-Nebraska Territory, Cather wanted more than anything else the kind of understanding she shared with her childhood friend. "I want," she wrote, "somebody from Sandy Point to go along with me to the end."

Notes

1. Bergson, *Creative Evolution*, 7.
2. Giannone, *Music in Willa Cather's Fiction*, 83, 85.
3. At the beginning of the novel, Thea is eleven. Ronning, in the Scholarly Edition, explains, "The chronological parallel to Cather's life is important here. Born on December 7, 1873, Cather was eleven in late December 1884 . . ." (624–25).
4. See also Ann Moseley, "Editing the Scholarly Edition of *Song of the Lark:* The Legacy of Cather's Journalism in the Social and Literary History of the Novel," *American Literary Realism* 41.2 (2009): 133–53. Bennett offered the first comprehensive gathering of these references, and readers interested in such connections will also want to consult March and Arnold.
5. Shaw, *Willa Cather and the Art of Conflict*, 42.
6. Robert Thacker, "It's through Myself That I Knew and Felt Her': S. S. McClure's 'My Autobiography' and the Development of Willa Cather's Autobiographical Realism," *American Literary Realism* 33.2 (2001): 123–42.
7. Tony R. Magagna, "A Place Apart: Transcending Social Topographies in *The Song of the Lark,*" *Willa Cather's* The Song of the Lark, ed. Debra L. Cumberland (Amsterdam and New York: Rodopi, 2010), 108.
8. "To H. W. Boynton," December 6, 1915, *SLWC*, 211.
9. Moseley, "Editing the Scholarly Edition of *Song of the Lark*," 145.
10. For an excellent discussion of Cather's understanding of Mexican communities, see Sarah Clere, "Locating Mexicans in *The Song of the Lark*," Willa Cather's *The Song of the Lark*, ed. Debra L. Cumberland (Amsterdam and New York: Rodopi, 2010), 149–63.
11. See Ronning, Scholarly Edition, 648; March and Arnold, *A Reader's Companion*, 267–68.
12. Robert Hendrickson, *The Facts on File Encyclopedia of Word and Phrase Origins*, 4th ed. (New York: Facts on File, 2008), 119.
13. "To Virginia Cather," February 13, [1914], University of Nebraska–Lincoln Libraries, Archives and Special Collections, Susan J. and James Rosowski Cather Collection (MS228).
14. Randolph Bourne, "Morals and Art from the West," *The Dial* (December 14, 1918): 557.
15. Ibid.
16. (*SLWC*, 272). Cather had more harsh things to say about White in this letter. In retrospect, she seems to be echoing the furious terms of Bourne, who had condemned White's recent novel before reviewing hers. Cather seems to have changed her mind about White four years later. In a letter to Sergeant on October 4, 1922, she described a tea she had recently had with the "Will Whites—aren't they *nice*, and jolly?" (326).
17. Thacker, *GPF*, 158.
18. In the summer of 1916, before she began writing *My Ántonia*, Cather was at a loss. In fact, she was reeling from a series of losses, none more painful than the rather sudden marriage of Isabelle McClung to Jan Hambourg, a well-known violinist. The event more or less coincided with the death of Isabelle's father and the selling of the McClung mansion in Pittsburgh. For years, McClung and Cather had maintained an intimate relationship that clearly meant a great deal to both women. Cather had lived with the McClungs for several years and then later returned from time to time to enjoy their hospitality. Over the years, McClung was both support and inspiration for the author, who dedicated books to her. McClung's marriage ended that intimacy.
19. N. P. Dawson, *New York Globe and Commercial Advertiser* (January 11, 1919), n.p.
20. Wallace Stegner, "The West Authentic: Willa Cather," *The Sound of Mountain Water* (Lincoln: University of Nebraska Press, 1985), 237.
21. Thacker, "It's Through Myself That I Knew," 123–24.

22. John J. Murphy, *My Ántonia: The Road Home* (Boston: Twayne, 1989), 26.
23. Marilee Lindemann, "'It Ain't My Prairie': Gender, Power, and Narrative in *My Ántonia*," *New Essays on* My Ántonia, ed. Sharon O'Brien (Cambridge: Cambridge University Press, 1999), 115. For more on Ántonia's character, see also Murphy, My Ántonia: *The Road Home,* 116; Funda, "'The Breath Vibrating Behind It,'" *Western American Literature,* 198; Paula Woolley, "'Fire and Wit': Storytelling and the American Artist in Cather's *My Ántonia,*" *Cather Studies* 3 (1996), 150.
24. On the problems presented by the novel's frame, see Rosowski, "Willa Cather's Subverted Endings," *Cather Studies,* 79, who proceeds to describe some of the complexity of the identification; Wilhite, "Unsettled Worlds," *Studies in the Novel,* 271–74; Goggans, "Social (Re)Visioning in the Fields of *My Ántonia,*" *Cather Studies,* 168;
25. Rosowski, *Birthing a Nation,* 12.
26. *My Ántonia,* Scholarly Edition, n. 10.
27. Murphy, My Ántonia: *The Road Home,* 45–56. On the influence of Ruskin and Turner in this novel, see Joseph C. Murphy, "Cather's Ruskinian Landscapes: Typologies of the New World," *Cather Studies: Willa Cather: A Writer's Worlds* 8 (2010): 229–32.
28. Jim's strange version of a boy's life on the farm comes into focus when contrasted with a comparable passage in Garland's *Boy Life on the Prairie* (New York: Macmillan, 1899): "It was time for vacation, and as a matter of fact the boys on the farm found a little leisure between corn-ploughing and haying for base-ball, swimming, fishing, and berrying. . . . They knew from dear experience that from the time the sickle set into the timothy there was no vacation till the snow fell" (106). For an extended discussion of the many similarities between Garland's book and Cather's book, see Randall L. Popken, "From Innocence to Experience in *My Ántonia* and *Boy Life on the Prairie,*" *North Dakota Quarterly* 46.2 (1978): 73–81.
29. Timothy C. Blackburn, "'Have I Changed So Much?': Jim Burden, Intertextuality, and the Ending of *My Ántonia,*" *Cather Studies: Willa Cather as Cultural Icon* 7 (2007): 158, n. 13.
30. *GPF,* 166.
31. The February 15, 1883, *Argus* was typical: "It is no idle claim to say that Red Cloud is the 'boss' town in southwestern Nebraska" (4).
32. Like Cather, Carrie Miner was not satisfied with her given name. Bennett, *WWC,* 238, tells how Miner chose the name "Frances," which Cather then used in her novel.
33. But not all Miner children were equal. Although her name figures so prominently in the fiction that preceded the novels, Margie (Sally) plays a small and shadowy role in the novel. For a discussion of Cather's ambiguous relationship to Margie in her short fiction, see Chapter Two.
34. If Red Cloud continues to conjure up this magic, it is because visitors can still stand in the dining room on Seward Street and look out at the window that made children linger so long ago.
35. Funda, "'The Breath Vibrating Behind It,'" 199; Richard Millington, "Willa Cather and 'The Storyteller': Hostility to the Novel in *My Ántonia,*" *American Literature* 66 (1994): 689–717; Woolley, "'Fire and Wit,'" 150.
36. For more on the hotel's history, see March and Arnold, *A Reader's Companion to the Fiction of Willa Cather,* 87. For an elaborate (by Red Cloud newspaper standards) account of Boys' Home hospitality on the occasion of Seward Garber's twenty-first birthday, see the *Argus* (November 24, 1881): 4.
37. On January 4, 1883, the venerable G.A.R. hosted a successful oyster supper and dance. The January 29, 1885, *Argus* reported: "Miss Anna Hawkins, of Lincoln, will arrive here Friday and be present at the Pleasant Hour Club hop on that evening. During her stay an effort will be made to organize a class in dancing" (3). It seems appropriate that the prototype for Cather's "lost lady" sponsored this event. The February 25, 1886, *Argus* captured the dancing scene in Red Cloud when it reported a "brilliant affair" hosted by the Knights of Pythias and, on the same page, a "knock-down,

drag-out" out at the skating rink dance (8). But the invitation of the July 23, 1886, *Chief* was typical: "Don't forget the pleasant dance at the rink tonight" (3).

38. Prchal, "The Bohemian Paradox," 11.
39. Cather was certainly thinking of Jacob Nustein and his factory across the street from the hotel in Red Cloud.
40. Stout, *Picturing a Different West,* 125.
41. Joan Didion, *The White Album* (1979; New York: Farrar, Strauss and Giroux, 1990), 11.
42. Rosowski, *Birthing a Nation,* 82.
43. Funda, " 'The Breath Vibrating Behind It,' " 214.
44. Murphy, My Ántonia: *The Road Home,* 103. For Murphy's analysis of this "pessimistic" side of Jim, see "The Respectable Romantic and the Unwed Mother: Class Consciousness in *My Ántonia,*" *Colby Quarterly* 10 (1973): 149–56. Stouck, *Willa Cather's Imagination,* 58, offers a compatible reading in terms of pastoral.
45. Blanche H. Gelfant, "The Forgotten Reaping-hook: Sex in *My Ántonia,*" *American Literature* 43 (1971): 81–82; Lindemann, " 'It Ain't My Prairie': Gender, Power, and Narrative in *My Ántonia,*" 115.
46. John H. Randall, *The Landscape and the Looking Glass: Willa Cather's Search for Value* (Boston: Houghton Mifflin, 1960), 149. Richard Harris, "Renaissance Pastoral Conventions," *Markham Review* 8 (1978), 11, cites Randall and concurs. Approaching the novel through a Freudian lens, Shaw, *Willa Cather and the Art of Conflict,* 64, concludes, "the Ántonia-Jim union represents an expression of Cather's most optimistic impulses."
47. Blackburn, " 'Have I Changed So Much?,' " 140. For a complementary reading, see also Handley, "Willa Cather," 90–91.
48. Palmer, "Ripening Claude," 130.
49. Qtd. in Stout, *Willa Cather,* 186.
50. To Robert Josephy, June 26, [1925], *SLWC,* 371.
51. To Wilbur Cross, August 25, [1931], *SLWC,* 451, 452.
52. To Irene Miner Weisz, December 31, 1943, *SLWC,* 624.
56. For more on the evolving place of Kansas in Cather's imagination, see Palmer, "Kansas-Nebraska3Acts," 31–35.
54. Willa Cather, "Going Home," *April Twilights and Other Poems,* 148.

Texts and Abbreviations

References to the novels of Willa Cather come from the following Willa Cather Scholarly Editions and are cited parenthetically in the text.

A Lost Lady. Willa Cather Scholarly Edition. Ed. Charles W. Mignon and Frederick M. Link with Kari Ronning. Historical Essay by Susan J. Rosowski with Kari A. Ronning. Explanatory Notes by Kari A. Ronning. Lincoln: University of Nebraska Press, 1997.

Lucy Gayheart. Willa Cather Scholarly Edition. Historical Essay by David Porter. Explanatory Notes by Kari A. Ronning and David Porter. Textual Essay and Editing by Frederick M. Link and Kari A. Ronning. Lincoln: University of Nebraska Press, 2015.

My Ántonia. Willa Cather Scholarly Edition. Ed. Charles W. Mignon with Kari A. Ronning. Historical Essay by James Woodress. Lincoln: University of Nebraska Press, 1994.

O Pioneers!. Willa Cather Scholarly Edition. Ed. Susan J. Rosowski and Charles W. Mignon with Kathleen Danker. Historical Essay and Explanatory Notes by David Stouck. Lincoln: University of Nebraska Press, 1992.

The Professor's House. Willa Cather Scholarly Edition. Ed. Frederick M. Link. Historical Essay by James Woodress. Explanatory Notes by James Woodress with Kari Ronning. Lincoln: University of Nebraska Press, 2002.

The Song of the Lark. Willa Cather Scholarly Edition. Ed. Kari A. Ronning. Historical Essay and Explanatory Notes by Ann Moseley. Lincoln: University of Nebraska Press, 2012.

CSF *Willa Cather's Collected Short Fiction.* Intro. Mildred R. Bennett. Lincoln: University of Nebraska Press, 1965.

CSP *Cather: Stories, Poems, and Other Writings.* Ed. Sharon O'Brien. New York: Library of America, 1992.

KA *The Kingdom of Art: Willa Cather's First Principles and Critical Statements, 1893–1896.* Ed. Bernice Slote. Lincoln: University of Nebraska Press, 1966.

GPF *The Great Prairie Fact and Literary Imagination.* By Robert Thacker. Albuquerque: University of New Mexico Press, 1989.

OD *Obscure Destinies.* Historical Essay and Explanatory Notes by Kari A. Ronning. Textual Essay by Frederick M. Link, with Kari A. Ronning and Mark Kamrath. Lincoln: University of Nebraska Press, 1998.

SLWC *The Selected Letters of Willa Cather.* Ed. Andrew Jewell and Janis Stout. New York: Knopf, 2013.

WCAT *April Twilights.* Ed. Bernice Slote. Lincoln: University of Nebraska Press, 1968.

WCEV *Willa Cather: The Emerging Voice.* By Sharon O'Brien. New York: Fawcett Columbine, 1987.

WCL *Willa Cather Living.* By Edith Lewis. 1953; Lincoln: University of Nebraska Press, 1976.

WCLL *Willa Cather: A Literary Life.* By James Woodress. Lincoln: University of Nebraska Press, 1987.

WCP *Willa Cather in Person.* Ed. L. Brent Bohlke. Lincoln: University of Nebraska Press, 1986.

WCW *Willa Cather on Writing: Critical Studies on Writing as an Art.* By Willa Cather. 1949; Lincoln: University of Nebraska Press, 1988.

WP *The World and the Parish: Willa Cather's Articles and Reviews, 1893–1902.* 2 vols. Ed. William M. Curtin. Lincoln: University of Nebraska Press, 1970.

WWC *The World of Willa Cather.* By Mildred Bennett. 1951; Lincoln: University of Nebraska Press, 1961.

Works Cited

Abate, Michelle Ann. "Constructing Modernist Lesbian Affect from Late Victorian Masculine Emotionalism: Willa Cather's 'Tommy, the Unsentimental' and J. M. Barrie's *Sentimental Tommy.*" *Women's Writing* 18:4 (2014): 468–485.

Acocella, Joan. *Willa Cather and the Politics of Criticism.* Lincoln: University of Nebraska Press, 2000.

Ahearn, Amy. "Full-Blooded Writing and Journalistic Fictions: Naturalism, the Female Artist and Willa Cather's *The Song of the Lark.*" *American Literary Realism* 33.2 (2001): 146–47.

Albertini, Virgil. "Willa Cather and Baseball: Some Personal and Literary Connections." *Platte Valley Review* 17.2 (1989): 16–24.

———. "Willa Cather and the Bicycle." *Platte Valley Review* (Spring, 1987): 12–22.

An Ordinance for the Government of the Territory of the United States Northwest of the River Ohio. www.ourdocuments.gov/doc.php?doc=8&page=transcript. July 14, 2014.

Anderson, P. W. "More is Different." *Science* 177.4047 (1972): 393–96.

Arnold, Marilyn. "The Allusive Cather." *Cather Studies* 3 (1996): 137–48.

———. "Poses of the Mind, Paeans of the Heart: Cather's Letters of Life in the Provinces." *Willa Cather: Family, Community, and History.* Ed. John J. Murphy. Provo: Brigham Young University Humanities Center, 1999. 3–17.

———. *Willa Cather's Short Fiction.* Athens: Ohio University Press, 1984.

Baker, Bruce P. "'The Enchanted Bluff': Dream and Disillusion." *Nebraska English and Language Arts Journal* 37.1 (1991): 28–33.

———. "Nebraska's Cultural Desert: Nebraska's Early Short Stories." *Midamerica: The Yearbook of the Society for the Study of Midwestern Literature* 14.1 (1987): 12–17.

———. "Nebraska Regionalism in Selected Works of Willa Cather." *Western American Literature* 3.1 (1968): 19–35.

———. "'Old Mrs. Harris' and the Intergenerational Family." *Willa Cather: Family, Community, and History.* Ed. John J. Murphy. Provo: Brigham Young University Humanities Center, 1999. 33–40.

———. "*O Pioneers!: The Problem of Structure.*" *Great Plains Quarterly* 2.4 (1982): 218–23.

Baym, Nina. *Women Writers of the American West,* 1833–1927. Champaign: University of Illinois Press, 2011.

Beecher, Lyman. *A Plea for the Nation.* Cincinnati: Truman and Smith, 1835.

Bennett, Mildred R. "The Childhood Worlds of Willa Cather." *Great Plains Quarterly* 10.1 (1982): 204–09.

———. *The World of Willa Cather.* 1951; Lincoln: University of Nebraska Press, 1961.

Bergson, Henri. *Creative Evolution.* Trans. Arthur Mitchell. 1911; Mineola: Dover, 1998.

Bintrim, Timothy W. "The Outlandish Hands of Fred Demmler: Pittsburgh Prototypes in *The Professor's House.*" *Cather Studies* 11 (2017): 188–213.

Burgess, Cheryll. "Willa Cather's Homecomings: A Meeting of Selves." *Willa Cather: Family, Community, and History.* Ed. John J. Murphy. Provo: Brigham Young University Humanities Center, 1999. 49–56.

Blackburn, Timothy C. "'Have I Changed So Much?': Jim Burden, Intertextuality, and the Ending of *My Ántonia.*" *Cather Studies: Willa Cather as Cultural Icon* 7 (2007): 140–64.

Bloom, Edward, and Lillian Bloom. *Willa Cather's Gift of Sympathy.* Carbondale: Southern Illinois University Press, 1964.

Boag, Peter. "Sexuality, Gender, and Identity in Great Plains History and Myth." *Great Plains Quarterly* 18 (1998): 327–40.

Bourne, Randolph. "Morals and Art from the West." *Dial* (December 14, 1918): 556–57.

Bradley, Jennifer. "To Entertain, To Educate, To Elevate: Cather and the Commodification of Manners at the *Home Monthly.*" *Willa Cather and Material Culture: Real-World Writing, Writing the Real World.* Ed. Janis P. Stout. Tuscaloosa: University of Alabama Press, 2005. 37–65.

Brown, E. K. *Rhythm in the Novel.* Toronto: University of Toronto Press, 1950.

———. *Willa Cather: A Critical Biography.* 1953; New York: Avon, 1980.

Butler, Judith. *Bodies That Matter: On the Discursive Limits of "Sex."* New York and London: Routledge, 1993.

———. "'Dangerous Crossing': Willa Cather's Masculine Names." *Bodies That Matter: On the Discursive Limits of Sex.* New York and London: Routledge, 1993. 143–66.

Cather, Willa. *Alexander's Bridge,* ed. Frederick M. Link. Lincoln: University of Nebraska Press, 2007.

———. *A Lost Lady.* Willa Cather Scholarly Edition. Ed. Charles W. Mignon and Frederick M. Link with Kari Ronning. Historical Essay by Susan J. Rosowski, with Kari A. Ronning. Explanatory Notes by Kari A. Ronning. Lincoln: University of Nebraska Press, 1997.

———. *Cather: Stories, Poems, and Other Writings.* Ed. Sharon O'Brien. New York: Library of America, 1992.

———. *Lucy Gayheart.* Willa Cather Scholarly Edition. Historical Essay by David Porter. Explanatory Notes by Kari A. Ronning and David Porter. Textual Essay and Editing by Frederick M. Link and Kari A. Ronning. Lincoln: University of Nebraska Press, 2015.

———. *My Ántonia.* Willa Cather Scholarly Edition. Ed. Charles W. Mignon, with Kari A. Ronning. Historical Essay by James Woodress. Lincoln: University of Nebraska Press, 1994.

———. *O Pioneers!.* Willa Cather Scholarly Edition. Ed. Susan J. Rosowski and Charles W. Mignon, with Kathleen Danker. Historical Essay and Explanatory Notes by David Stouck. Lincoln: University of Nebraska Press, 1992.

———. *Obscure Destinies.* Historical Essay and Explanatory Notes by Kari A. Ronning. Textual Essay by Frederick M. Link, with Kari A. Ronning and Mark Kamrath. Lincoln: University of Nebraska Press, 1998.

———. *The Professor's House.* Willa Cather Scholarly Edition. Ed. Frederick M. Link. Historical Essay by James Woodress. Explanatory Notes by James Woodress, with Kari Ronning. Lincoln: University of Nebraska Press, 2002.

———. *The Song of the Lark.* Willa Cather Scholarly Edition. Ed. Kari A. Ronning. Historical Essay and Explanatory Notes by Ann Moseley. Lincoln: University of Nebraska Press, 2012.

———. *The Selected Letters of Willa Cather.* Ed. Andrew Jewell and Janis Stout. New York: Knopf, 2013.

———. *Willa Cather's Collected Short Fiction.* Intro. Mildred R. Bennett. Lincoln: University of Nebraska Press, 1965.

———. *Willa Cather in Person.* Ed. L. Brent Bohlke. Lincoln: University of Nebraska Press, 1986.

———. *Willa Cather on Writing.* New York: Knopf, 1949.

———. *The World and the Parish: Willa Cather's Articles and Reviews,* 1893–1902. 2 vols. Ed. William M. Curtin. Lincoln: University of Nebraska Press, 1970.

Cherny, Robert W. "Nebraska, 1883–1925: Cather's Version and History's." *Willa Cather: Family, Community, and History.* Ed. John J. Murphy. Provo: Brigham Young University Humanities Center, 1999. 229–38.

———. "Willa Cather and the Populists." *Great Plains Quarterly* 10.1 (1983): 206–18.

Clere, Sarah. "Locating Mexicans in *The Song of the Lark*," *Willa Cather's The Song of the Lark*. Ed. Debra L. Cumberland. Amsterdam and New York: Rodopi, 2010. 149–63.

Conlogue, William. "Managing the Farm, Educating the Farmer: *O Pioneers!* and the New Agriculture." *Great Plains Quarterly* 21.1 (2001): 3–15.

Cochran, Robert. *Louise Pound: Scholar, Athlete, Feminist Pioneer.* Lincoln: University of Nebraska Press, 2009.

Danker, Kathleen. "The Influence of Willa Cather's French Canadian Neighbors in Nebraska in *Death Comes for the Archbishop* and *Shadows on the Rock*." *Great Plains Quarterly* 20 (2000): 35–54.

Dick, Everett. *Sod-House Frontier: 1854–1890.* 1937; Lincoln: University of Nebraska Press, 1979.

Dickinson, Emily. *The Complete Poems of Emily Dickinson.* Ed. Thomas H. Johnson. Boston: Back Bay Books, 1976.

Didion, Joan. *The White Album.* 1979; New York: Farrar, Strauss and Giroux, 1990.

Dillon, Sarah. "Reinscribing De Quincey's Palimpsest: The Significance of the Palimpsest in Contemporary Literary and Cultural Studies." *Textual Practice* 19.3 (2005): 243–63.

Documents of the Coronado Expedition, 1539–1542. Trans. and Annotated Richard Flint and Shirley Cushing Flint. Dallas: Southern Methodist University Press, 2005.

Downs, M. Catherine. *Becoming Modern: Willa Cather's Journalism.* Selinsgrove, PA: Susquehanna University Press; London: Associated University Presses, 1999.

Duryea, Polly Patricia. "Paintings and Drawings in Willa Cather's Prose: A Catalogue Raisonne." PhD diss. University of Nebraska, Lincoln, Nebraska, 1993.

Facknitz, Mark A. R. "Changing Trains: Metaphors of Transfer in Willa Cather." *Cather Studies: Willa Cather and Modern Cultures* 9 (2011): 67–92.

———. "Character, Compromise, and Idealism in Willa Cather's Gardens." *Cather Studies* 5 (2003): 291–307.

Faragher, John Mack. *Women and Men on the Overland Trail.* New Haven and London: Yale University Press, 1979.

Farris, Sara. "American Pastoral in the Twentieth-Century *O Pioneers!, A Thousand Acres,* and *Merry Men*." 5 *ISLE* (1998): 27–48.

Fetterley, Judith. "*My Ántonia,* Jim Burden and the Dilemma of the Lesbian Writer." *Major Literary Characters: Ántonia.* Ed. Harold Bloom. New York: Chelsea House, 1991.

Fischer, Mike. "Pastoralism and Its Discontents: Willa Cather and the Burden of Imperialism." *Mosaic* 23.1 (1990): 31–44.

Forster, E. M. *Aspects of the Novel.* New York: Houghton Mifflin, 1956.

Friedman, Susan Stanford. *Mappings: Feminism and the Cultural Geographies of Encounter.* Princeton: Princeton University Press, 1998.

Fryer, Judith. *Felicitous Space: The Imaginative Structures of Edith Wharton and Willa Cather.* Chapel Hill: The University of North Carolina Press, 1986.

Funda, Evelyn I. "'The Breath Vibrating behind It': Intimacy in the Storytelling of Ántonia Shimerda." *Western American Literature* 29.3 (1994): 195–216.

———. "Womanhood Distorted: Mrs. Archie as Thea's Foil in *The Song of the Lark*." *Willa Cather Pioneer Memorial Newsletter* 39.2-3 (1995): 30–33.

Garland, Hamlin. *Boy Life on the Prairie.* New York: Macmillan, 1899.

Gelfant, Blanche H. "The Forgotten Reaping-Hook: Sex in *My Ántonia*." *American Literature* 43 (1971): 60–82.

Giannone, Richard. *Music in Willa Cather's Fiction.* Lincoln: University of Nebraska Press, 1968.

Gilpin, William. *The Central Gold Region.* Philadelphia: Sower, Barnes, and Co., 1860.

Goggans, Jan. "Social (Re)Visioning in the Fields of *My Ántonia*." *Cather Studies* 5 (2003): 153–72.

Goldberg, Jonathan. *Willa Cather and Others.* Durham: Duke University Press, 2001.

———. "Willa Cather and Sexuality." *The Cambridge Companion to Willa Cather.* Ed. Marilee Lindemann. Cambridge: Cambridge University Press, 2005. 86–100.

Gridley, Roy E. "Some Versions of the Primitive and the Pastoral on the Great Plains of America." *Survivals of Pastoral.* Ed. Richard F. Hardin. Lawrence: University of Kansas Publications, 1979. 61–85.

Griffith, Jean C. "How the West Was Whitened: 'Racial' Difference on Cather's Prairie." *Western American Literature* 41.4 (2007): 393–417.

Gross, Barry. "In Another Country: The Revolt from the Village." *Midamerica* 4.4 (1977): 101–11.

Hallenbeck, Sarah. *Claiming the Bicycle: Women, Rhetoric, and Technology in Nineteenth-Century America.* Carbondale: Southern Illinois University Press, 2016

Handley, William R. "Willa Cather: 'The West Authentic,' the West Divided." *True West: Authenticity and the American West.* Ed. William R. Handley and Nathaniel Lewis. Lincoln: University of Nebraska Press, 2004. 72–94.

Handley, William R., and Nathaniel Lewis. "Introduction." *True West: Authenticity and the American West.* Ed. William R. Handley and Nathaniel Lewis. Lincoln: University of Nebraska Press, 2004. 1–17.

Hardin, Richard F. "The Pastoral Moment." *Survivals of Pastoral.* Ed. Richard F. Hardin Lawrence: University of Kansas Publications, 1979. 1–17.

Harris, Jeane. "A Code of Her Own: Attitudes Toward Women in Willa Cather's Short Fiction." *Modern Fiction Studies* 36.1 (1990): 81–89.

Harris, Richard C. "Barbusse's L'Enfer: A Source for 'Coming, Aphrodite' and 'The Novel Démeublé." *Cather Studies* 7 (2007): 106–18.

———. "Peck, Turner, and Willa Cather's *O Pioneers!*." *Midwest Review* 7 (1985): 41–49.

———. "Renaissance Pastoral Conventions." *Markham Review* 8 (1978): 8–11.

Haywood, C. Robert. *Victorian West: Class and Culture in Kansas Cattle Towns.* Lawrence: University Press of Kansas, 1991.

Hendrickson, Robert. *The Facts on File Encyclopedia of Word and Phrase Origins.* 4th ed. New York: Facts on File, 2008.

Highfill, Juli. *Modernism and Its Merchandise: The Spanish Avant-Garde and Material Culture, 1920–1930.* University Park: Pennsylvania State University Press, 2014.

Hillman, James. *The Force of Character.* New York: Random House, 1999.

Homestead, Melissa J., and Anne L. Kaufman. "Willa Cather and Edith Lewis's Creative Partnership." *Western American Literature* 43.1 (2008): 41–69.

Horace. *The Odes and Epodes.* Trans. C. E. Bennett. London: Heinemann, 1921.

Hudson, John C. *Plains Country Towns.* Minneapolis: University of Minneapolis Press, 1986.

Hull, Ron. "Mildred Bennett." *The Willa Cather Foundation,* accessed January 31, 2015. www.willa-cather.org/about-us/mildred-bennett.

Irving, Katrina. *Immigrant Mothers: Narratives of Race and Maternity, 1890–1925.* Urbana and Chicago: University of Illinois Press, 2000.

James, Edwin. *Early Western Travels.* Ed. Reuben Gold. Vol. 17. Cleveland: Clark, 1905.

Jameson, Elizabeth. "Women as Workers, Women as Civilizers: True Womanhood in the American West." *The Woman's West.* Ed. Susan Armitage and Elizabeth Jameson Norman and London: University of Oklahoma Press, 1987. 145–64.

Jeffrey, Julie Roy. *Frontier Women: 'Civilizing' the West? 1840–1880.* Rev. ed. 1979; New York: Hill and Wang, 1998.

———. " 'There Is Some Splendid Scenery': Women's Responses to the Great Plains Landscape, *Great Plains Quarterly* 8 (1988): 69–78.

Jewett, Sarah Orne. *Letters of Sarah Orne Jewett.* Ed. Annie Fields. Boston: Houghton Mifflin, 1911.

Jones, Stephen R., and Ruth Carol Cushman. *A Field Guide to the North American Prairie.* New York: Houghton Mifflin, 2004.

Kinbacher, Kurt E. "Imagining Place: Nebraska Territory, 1854–1867." *Regionalism and the Humanities.* Ed. Timothy R. Mahoney and Wendy J. Katz. Lincoln: University of Nebraska Press, 2008. 251–73.

Kolodny, Annette. *The Lay of the Land.* Chapel Hill: The University of North Carolina Press, 1975.

———. *The Land Before Her: Fantasy and Experience of the American Frontiers, 1630–1860.* Chapel Hill and London: University of North Carolina Press, 1984.

Laegreid, Renee M. "The Good, The Bad, and the Ignored: Immigrants in Willa Cather's *O Pioneers!,*" *Great Plains Quarterly* 27 (2007): 101–15.

Lee, Hermione. *Willa Cather: Double Lives.* New York: Pantheon Books, 1989.

Lewes, G. H. *Problems of Life and Mind.* London: Trübner, 1875.

Lewis, Edith. *Willa Cather Living.* Lincoln: University of Nebraska Press, 1976.

Lewis, Nathaniel. "Truth or Consequences: Projecting Authenticity in the 1830s." *True West: Authenticity and the American West.* Ed. William R. Handley and Nathaniel Lewis Lincoln: University of Nebraska Press, 2004. 21–37.

Lewis, Pericles. *Cambridge Introduction to Modernism.* Cambridge: Cambridge University Press, 2007.

Limerick, Patricia Nelson. *The Real West.* Denver: Civic Center Cultural Complex, 1996.

Lindemann, Marilee. "'It Ain't My Prairie': Gender, Power, and Narrative in *My Ántonia." New Essays on* My Ántonia. Ed. Sharon O'Brien. Cambridge: Cambridge University Press, 1999. 111–35.

———. *Willa Cather and the Queering of America.* New York: Columbia University Press, 1999.

Lutes, Jean Marie. *Front Page Girls: Women Journalists in American Culture and Fiction, 1880–1930.* Ithaca and London: Cornell University Press, 2006.

MacMurphy, John A. "Part of the Making of a Great State." *Here You Have My Story: Eyewitness Accounts of the Nineteenth-Century Central Plains.* Ed. Richard E. Jensen. Lincoln: University of Nebraska Press, 2009. 234–56.

Madigan, Mark J. "Cather and the Short Story." *The Cambridge Companion to Willa Cather.* Ed. Marilee Lindemann. Cambridge: Cambridge University Press, 2005. 131–45.

———. "Willa Cather and Dorothy Canfield Fisher." *Cather Studies* 1. Ed. Susan J. Rosowski. Lincoln and London: University of Nebraska Press, 1990. 115–29.

Magagna, Tony R. "A Place Apart: Transcending Social Topographies in *The Song of the Lark.*" *Willa Cather's* The Song of the Lark. Ed. Debra L. Cumberland. Amsterdam and New York: Rodopi, 2010. 107–25.

March, John, and Marilyn Arnold, with Debra Lynn Thornton. *A Reader's Companion to the Fiction of Willa Cather.* Westport: Greenwood, 1993.

Marcy, Randolph Barnes. *The Prairie Traveler, Kansas Collection Books,* www.kancoll.org/books/marcy/index.html. February 3, 2013.

Middleton, Jo Ann. *Willa Cather's Modernism: A Study of Style and Technique.* Rutherford: Fairleigh Dickinson University Press and London: Associated University Presses, 1990.

Millington, Richard. "Willa Cather and 'The Storyteller': Hostility to the Novel in *My Ántonia,*" *American Literature* 66 (1994): 689–717.

———. "Willa Cather's American Modernism." *The Cambridge Companion to Willa Cather.* Ed. Marilee Lindemann. Cambridge: Cambridge University Press, 2005. 51–65.

Milner II, Clyde A. "National Initiatives." *The Oxford History of The American West.* Ed. Clyde A. Milner II, Carol A. O'Connor, and Martha A. Sandweiss. New York and Oxford: Oxford University Press, 1994. 155–93.

Miner, Craig. *West of Wichita: Settling the High Plains of Kansas 1865–1890.* Lawrence: University Press of Kansas, 1986.

Montrie, Chad. " 'Men Alone Cannot Settle a Country': Domesticating Nature in the Kansas-Nebraska Grasslands." *Great Plains Quarterly* 25.4 (2005): 245–58.

Morgan, Ted. *A Shovel of Stars: The Making of the American West 1800 to the Present.* New York: Touchstone, 1995.

Moseley, Ann. "Editing the Scholarly Edition of *Song of the Lark:* The Legacy of Cather's Journalism in the Social and Literary History of the Novel." *American Literary Realism* 41.2 (2009): 133–53.

———. "A New World Symphony: Cultural Pluralism in *Song of the Lark* and *My Ántonia." Willa Cather Pioneer Memorial Newsletter* 39.1 (1995): 7–12.

———. "Willa Cather's Transitional Novel: *The Song of the Lark* as a Romantic-Naturalistic Novel with a Modernist Center." *Willa Cather's* The Song of the Lark. Ed. Debra L. Cumberland. Amsterdam and New York: Rodopi, 2010. 225–40.

Murphy, John J. My Ántonia*: The Road Home.* Boston: Twayne, 1989.

———. "Nebraska Naturalism in Jamesian Frames." *Great Plains Quarterly* 10.1 (1984): 231–37.

———. "The Green Vase, the Yellow Orange, and the White Chapel: Trying to Define an Art." *Cather Studies: Willa Cather: A Writer's Worlds* 8 (2010): 428–443.

———. "The Respectable Romantic and the Unwed Mother: Class Consciousness in *My Ántonia."* *Colby Quarterly* 10 (1973): 149–56.

Murphy, Joseph C. "Cather's Ruskinian Landscapes: Typologies of the New World." *Cather Studies: Willa Cather: A Writer's Worlds* 8 (2010): 228–45.

Myres, Sandra L. *Westering Women and the Frontier Experience, 1800–1915.* Albuquerque: University of New Mexico Press, 1982.

Nash, Roderick. *Wilderness and the American Mind.* New Haven: Yale University Press, 1967.

Nichols, Roy F. "The Territories: Seedbeds of Democracy." *Nebraska History* 35 (1954): 159–72.

O'Brien, Sharon. *Willa Cather: The Emerging Voice.* New York: Fawcett Columbine, 1987.

Olson James C. and Ronald C. Naugle. *History of Nebraska.* 3rd ed. Lincoln: University of Nebraska Press, 1997.

Palmer, Daryl W. "'The Bohemian Girl,' 'Old Mrs. Harris,' and the Hospitalities of Red Cloud," *Willa Cather Newsletter and Review* 54.2 (2010): 48–51.

———. "Kansas-Nebraska Acts: Territorial Imagination in 'El Dorado,' *Song of the Lark,* and *The Professor's House.*" *Willa Cather Newsletter and Review* 53.2 (2009): 31–35.

———. "Quivira, Coronado, and Kansas: A Formative Chapter in the Story of Kansans' Collective Memory." *Kansas History* 35.4 (2012–13): 250–65.

———. "Recomposing Nineteenth-Century Nebraska: Red Cloud Newspapers and Cather's 'Hired Girls' in *My Ántonia." Willa Cather Newsletter and Review* 55.3 (2012): 2–9.

———. "Ripening Claude: Willa Cather's *One of Ours* and the Philosophy of Henri Bergson," *American Literary Realism* 41.2 (2009): 114–19.

Parkman, Francis. *The Oregon Trail.* Ed. William Ellery Leonard. Boston: Ginn and Company, 1910.

Peck, Demaree C. *The Imaginative Claims of the Artist in Willa Cather's Fiction: "Possession Granted By a Different Lease."* Selinsgrove: Susquehanna University Press and London: Associated University Presses, 1996.

———. " 'Possession Granted by a Different Lease': Alexandra Bergson's Imaginative Conquest of Cather's Nebraska." *MFS: Modern Fiction Studies* 36.1 (1990): 5–22.

Peck, John Mason. *A New Guide for Emigrants to the West.* Boston: Gould, Kendall and Lincoln, 1836.

Pfeiffer, Benjamin. "The Role of Joseph E. Johnson and His Pioneer Newspapers in the Development of Territorial Nebraska." *Nebraska History* 40.2 (1956): 119–36.

Pike, Zebulon Montgomery. *The Expeditions of Zebulon Montgomery Pike.* Ed. Elliott Coues. Vol. 2. New York: Harper, 1895.

Plato. *The Collected Dialogues of Plato*. Ed. Edith Hamilton and Huntington Cairns. Princeton: Princeton University Press, 1961.

Popken, Randall L. "From Innocence to Experience in *My Ántonia* and *Boy Life on the Prairie*." *North Dakota Quarterly* 46.2 (1978): 73–81.

Porter, David. *On the Divide: The Many Lives of Willa Cather*. Lincoln: University of Nebraska Press, 2008.

Prchal, Tim. "The Bohemian Paradox: *My Ántonia* and Popular Images of Czech Immigrants," *MELUS* 29.2 (2004): 3–25.

———. "Reimagining the Melting Pot and the Golden Door: National Identity in Gilded Age and Progressive Literature," *MELUS* 32.1 (2007): 29–51.

Quantic, Diane Dufva. *The Nature of the Place: A Study of Great Plains Fiction*. Lincoln: University of Nebraska Press, 1995.

———. "The Revolt from the Village and Middle Western Fiction, 1870–1915." *Kansas Quarterly* 5.6 (1973): 5–16.

Quirk, Tom. *Bergson and American Culture: The Worlds of Willa Cather and Wallace Stevens*. Chapel Hill: University of North Carolina Press, 1990.

Rabin, Jessica G. "'Honey, do we really need five copies of this?': *April Twilights* Revisited." *Willa Cather: New Facts, New Glimpses, Revisions*. Ed. John J. Murphy and Merrill Maguire Skaggs. Madison: Fairleigh Dickinson University Press, 2008. 117–37.

Randall, John H. *The Landscape and the Looking Glass: Willa Cather's Search for Value*. Boston: Houghton Mifflin, 1960.

———. "Willa Cather and the Pastoral Tradition." *Five Essays on Willa Cather: The Merrimack Symposium*. Ed. John J. Murphy. North Andover, MA: Merrimack College, 1974. 75–96.

Reynolds, Guy. "Willa Cather as Progressive: Politics and the Writer." *The Cambridge Companion to Willa Cather*. Ed. Marilee Lindemann. Cambridge: Cambridge University Press, 2005. 19–34.

———. *Willa Cather in Context: Progress, Race, and Empire*. New York: St. Martin's Press, 1996.

Reynolds, Guy, ed. *Willa Cather: Critical Assessments*. Vol. 1. Mountfield: Helm Information, 2003.

Riley, Glenda. *The Female Frontier: A Comparative View of Women on the Prairie and the Plains*. Lawrence: University Press of Kansas, 1988.

———. "Women's Responses to the Challenges of Plains Living," *Great Plains Quarterly* 9 (1989): 174–84.

Robinson, Phyllis. *Willa: The Life of Willa Cather* (New York: Holt, Rinehart and Winston, 1983), 71.

Romines, Ann. *At Willa Cather's Tables: The Cather Foundation Cookbook*. Ed. Ann Romines. Red Cloud: Willa Cather Foundation, 2010.

———. "Historical Essay." *Sapphira and the Slave Girl*. Ed. Charles W. Mignon, Kari A. Ronning, and Frederick M. Link. Lincoln: University of Nebraska Press, 2009. 297–404.

———. *The Home Plot: Women, Writing, and Domestic Ritual*. Amherst: University of Massachusetts Press, 1992.

———. "Kolache Controversies." *Willa Cather Newsletter and Review* 49.2 (2005): 46–47.

———. "Willa Cather: A Life with Quilts." *Willa Cather and Material Culture: Real-World Writing, Writing the Real World*. Ed. Janis Stout. Tuscaloosa: University of Alabama Press, 2004. 15–36.

Rosowski, Susan J. *Birthing a Nation: Gender, Creativity, and the West in American Literature*. Lincoln: University of Nebraska Press, 1999.

———. "Cather's Manifesto for 'Coming, Aphrodite!'" *Willa Cather Pioneer Memorial Newsletter* 38.3 (1994): 51–56.

———. *The Voyage Perilous*. Lincoln: University of Nebraska Press, 1986.

———. "Willa Cather and the French Rural Tradition of Breton and Millet: *O Pioneers!*, *The Song of the Lark,* and *My Ántonia.*" *The Rural Vision: France and America in the Late Nineteenth Century.* Ed. Hollister Sturges. Omaha: Joslyn Art Museum, 1987. 53–61.

———. "Willa Cather Editing Willa Cather: From Houghton Mifflin to the House of Knopf." *Studies in the Literary Imagination* 29.2 (1996): 9–25.

———. "Willa Cather's Ecology of Place." *Western American Literature* 30.1 (1995): 37–51.

———. "Willa Cather and the Fatality of Place: *O Pioneers!, My Ántonia,* and *A Lost Lady.*" *Geography and Literature: A Meeting of the Disciplines.* Ed. William E. Mallory and Paul Simpson-Housley. Syracuse: Syracuse University Press, 1987. 81–94.

———. "Willa Cather's Female Landscapes: *The Song of the Lark* and *Lucy Gayheart.*" *Women's Studies* 11.3 (1984): 233–46.

Ross, Alex. "A Walk in Willa Cather's Prairie." *New Yorker* (October 2, 2017): xx.

Rowse, A. L. "On the Track of Willa Cather in Nebraska." *Blackwood's Magazine* 328 (August–September, 1980): 84–92, 164–71.

Rule, Jane. *Lesbian Images.* Garden City: Doubleday, 1975.

Ryan, Melissa. "The Enclosure of America: Civilization and Confinement in Willa Cather's *O Pioneers!.*" *American Literature* 75.2 (2003): 275–303.

Ryder, Mary R. "'Looking for Love in All the Wrong Places': Voyeurism in Cather's 1920s Fiction." *Willa Cather Newsletter and Review* 49.1 (2005): 3–8.

Sandburg, Carl. *The American Song Bag.* New York: Harcourt, Brace, and Company, 1927.

Sedgwick, Eve Kosofsky. "Across Gender, Across Sexuality: Willa Cather and Others." *South Atlantic Quarterly* 88.1 (1989): 53–72.

Seibel, George. "Willa Cather from Nebraska." *New Colophon* 2.7 (1949): 195–208.

Seivert, Debra. "Responding to Romance with Realism in Cather's 'Tommy, the Unsentimental.'" *American Literary Realism* 33.2 (2001): 104–09.

Schubnell, Matthias. "Religion and Ecology on the Divide: Ivar's Monasticism in *O Pioneers!,*" *Willa Cather and the Culture of Belief.* Ed. John J. Murphy, with Linda Hunter Adams and Jesse S. Crisler. Provo: Brigham Young University Press, 2002. 41–49.

Schulten, Susan. *The Geographical Imagination in America, 1880–1950.* Chicago: University of Chicago Press, 2001.

Sergeant, Elizabeth Shepley. *Willa Cather: A Memoir.* 1953; Lincoln: University of Nebraska Press, 1963.

Shakespeare, William. *The Riverside Shakespeare,* 2nd ed. Ed. G. Blakemore Evans and J. J. M. Tobin. Boston: Houghton Mifflin, 1997.

Shaw, Patrick. *Willa Cather and the Art of Conflict: Re-Visioning Her Creative Imagination.* Troy: Whitston, 1992.

———. "Short Story: Art and Artifice." *Nation* (September 25, 1920): 352–53.

Sims, Sally. "The Bicycle, the Bloomer and Dress Reform in the 1890s." *Dress and Popular Culture.* Ed. Patricia A. Cunningham and Susan Voso Lals. Bowling Green: Bowling Green State University Popular Press, 1991. 125–45.

Skaggs, Merrill Maguire. *After the World Broke in Two: The Later Novels of Willa Cather.* Charlottesville and London: University of Virginia Press, 1990.

Slote, Bernice. "An Exploration of Cather's Early Writing," *Great Plains Quarterly* (1982): 210.

———. "Willa Cather and Her First Book." *April Twilights (1903)* by Willa Cather. Ed. Bernice Slote. Rev. ed. (Lincoln: University of Nebraska Press, 1968). ix–xlv.

———. "Willa Cather and Plains Culture." *Vision and Refuge: Essays on the Literature of the Great Plains.* Lincoln: University of Nebraska Press, 1982. 93–105.

———. "Willa Cather as a Regional Writer," *Kansas Quarterly* 2.2 (1970): 8.

———. "Willa Cather: The Secret Web." *Five Essays on Willa Cather: The Merrimack Symposium.* Ed. John Murphy. North Andover, MA: Merrimack College, 1974. 1–19.

Slote, Bernice, ed. *The Kingdom of Art: Willa Cather's First Principles and Critical Statements, 1893–1896.* Lincoln: University of Nebraska Press, 1966.

Smith, Henry Nash. *Virgin Land: The American West as Symbol and Myth.* Cambridge: Harvard University Press, 1950.

Southwick, Helen Cather. "Memories of Willa Cather in Red Cloud." *Willa Cather Pioneer Memorial Newsletter* 29.3 (1985): 11–13.

Stegner, Wallace. *The American West as Living Space.* Ann Arbor: University of Michigan, 1987.

———. "The West Authentic: Willa Cather." *The Sound of Mountain Water.* Lincoln: University of Nebraska Press, 1985. 237–49.

Stevenson, Robert Louis. *A Child's Garden of Verses.* London: Longmans, Green, and Co., 1885.

Stouck, David. *Willa Cather's Imagination.* Lincoln: University of Nebraska Press, 1975.

Stout, Janis P. *Picturing a Different West: Vision, Illustration, and the Tradition of Cather and Austin.* Lubbock: Texas Tech University Press, 2007.

———. *Through the Window and Out the Door: Women's Narratives of Departure, from Austin and Cather to Tyler, Morrison, and Didion.* Tuscaloosa: University of Alabama Press, 1998.

———. *Willa Cather: The Writer and Her World.* Charlottesville: University Press of Virginia, 2000.

Swift, John. "Willa Cather in and out of Zane Grey's West." *Cather Studies* 9 (2011): 1–20.

Thacker, Robert. "Foreword." *April Twilights and Other Poems* by Willa Cather. Ed. RobertThacker. New York: Everyman, 2013. 11–20.

———. *The Great Prairie Fact and Literary Imagination.* Albuquerque: University of New Mexico Press, 1989.

———. " 'It's Through Myself That I Knew and Felt Her': S. S. McClure's *My Autobiography* and the Development of Willa Cather's Autobiographical Realism." *American Literary Realism* 33.2 (2001): 123–42.

Toliver, Harold E. *Pastoral: Forms and Attitudes.* Berkeley: University of California Press, 1971.

Trenton, Patricia. "Preface and Acknowledgements." *Independent Spirits: Women Painters of the American West, 1890–1945.* Los Angeles: Autry Museum of Western Heritage and Berkeley: University of California Press, 1995. ix–xiii.

Trout, Steven. "From 'The Namesake' to 'One of Ours': Willa Cather on War." *American Literary Realism* 37.2 (2005): 117–40.

———. *Memorial Fictions: Willa Cather and the First World War.* Lincoln: University of Nebraska Press, 1999.

Tuan, Yi-Fu. *Space and Place: The Perspective of Experience.* Minneapolis: University of Minnesota Press, 1977.

Turner, Frederick Jackson. *The Frontier in American History.* New York: Henry Holt and Company, 1921.

Unruh, John D. *The Plains Across: The Overland Emigrants and the Trans-Mississippi West, 1840–60.* Urbana: University of Illinois Press, 1979.

Urgo, Joseph. *Willa Cather and the Myth of American Migration.* Urbana: University of Illinois Press, 1995.

Van Doren, Carl. *Contemporary American Novelists: 1900–1920.* New York: Macmillan, 1922.

Wasserman, Loretta. "The Music of Time: Henri Bergson and Willa Cather," *American Literature* 57 (1985): 227–28.

Webb, Walter Prescott. *The Great Plains.* Lincoln: University of Nebraska Press, 1931.

Welsch, Roger L., and Linda K. *Cather's Kitchens: Foodways in Literature and Life.* Lincoln: University of Nebraska Press, 1987.

Welty, Eudora. "The House of Willa Cather." *Miracles of Perception: The Art of Willa Cather.* Charlottesville: Alderman Library, University of Virginia, 1980. 66–81.

West, Elliott. *The Contested Plains: Indians, Goldseekers, and the Rush to Colorado.* Lawrence: University of Kansas Press, 1998.

Westling, Louise H. *The Green Breast of the New World: Landscape, Gender, and American Fiction.* Athens and London: University of Georgia Press, 1996.

Whitman, Walt. *Specimen Days, Prose Works 1892*. Vol. 1. Ed. Floyd Stovall. New York: New York University Press, 1963.

———. "O Me! O Life!," *The Complete Poems*, ed. Francis Murphy. 1975; London: Penguin, 2004, 298.

Wilhite, Keith. "Unsettled Worlds: Aesthetic Emplacement in Willa Cather's *My Ántonia.*" *Studies in the Novel* 42.3 (2010): 269–86.

Willard, Frances. *How I Learned to Ride the Bicycle.* New York: Fleming H. Revell, 1895.

Wolff, Cynthia Griffin. "Dressing for the Part: [What's] the Matter with Clothes." *Willa Cather's Southern Connections: New Essays on Cather and the South.* Ed. Ann Romines. Charlottesville and London: University Press of Virginia, 2000. 198–220.

Wood, Gardner W. "Books of the Day." *McClure's Magazine* 41 (1913): 199.

Woodress, James. "A Dutiful Daughter: Willa Cather and Her Parents." *Willa Cather: Family, Community, and History.* Ed. John J. Murphy. Provo: Brigham Young University Humanities Center, 1999. 19–31.

———. *Willa Cather: A Literary Life*. Lincoln: University of Nebraska Press, 1987.

———. "Willa Cather: American Experience and European Tradition." *The Art of Willa Cather*. Ed. Bernice Slote and Virginia Faulkner. Lincoln: University of Nebraska Press, 1974. 43–62.

Woolley, Paula. "'Fire and Wit': Storytelling and the American Artist in Cather's *My Ántonia.*" *Cather Studies* 3 (1996): 149–81.

Index

Acknowledgments

On November 12, 2013, the heart attack I never anticipated happened. Many things have seemed different since then, including this book. The project that had begun as a simple study of Willa Cather and Nebraska became more personal. Reading Andrew Jewell and Janis Stout's marvelous *Selected Letters of Willa Cather,* I realized that my interest in the author's prairie roots was wider and deeper than I had envisioned. Slowly but surely, the project shifted toward a focus on Cather's growth as an artist and a human being, on her capacity for creation and its roots in the West. I would write about Cather's heart, about the kindheartedness and the coldheartedness, the heartlands, the heartthrobs, the heartaches, and the heart attacks. And, in keeping with the alliterative pattern, I would write about "the halfway people," as Ray Kennedy calls them in *The Song of the Lark,* "who help the winners win, and the failers fail." Many halfway people have played a part in the finishing of this book, and this is the place to acknowledge their big hearts.

Two Cather friends deserve special thanks. Before I really knew him, Steven Trout inspired me, through his *Memorial Fictions,* to write about Cather. Later on, after many long conversations about literature and life, he encouraged me to write this book before I knew I could do it. When I felt more like a "failer" than a winner, he offered support. Ann Romines has been a heartening friend and colleague for what seems like forever. More than anyone else, she has woven me into the Cather community. She knows all the best recipes for food, scholarship, and friendship.

Three crucial readers made this book possible. Author of the still-definitive *Great Prairie Fact and Literary Imagination*, Robert Thacker read three versions of the manuscript. When another scholar would have given up on the Sisyphean labor, he worked with Herculean faith in the project. I know the book would not exist without his wisdom, expertise, and bigheartedness. With extraordinary attention to detail and a generous spirit, Timothy Bintrim helped me to improve the manuscript in many ways. Philosopher, teacher, friend, tennis rival, and hero, Alan (aptly named, for this document) Hart read versions of this manuscript with his usual wisdom and good cheer. I wish I knew how to thank a "reader" who has always believed that I am better than I am.

The world of Cather studies is filled with halfway people. Many years ago, when I was beginning my career as a Shakespeare scholar but had a notion to present a little paper on Cather at a major conference, Sue Rosowski took me aside after the panel. She encouraged me to keep working on Cather, inviting me to present at future conferences. Although it took a while for me to come around, the kindhearted welcome stuck. Many a Cather scholar will tell you a similar story about Sue. I am fortunate indeed that Andy Jewell, Chuck Peek, and Steve Shively have offered both wisdom and encouragement on many occasions when I needed it most.

When it comes to telling stories in Cather studies, I think of Tracy Tucker, education director and archivist at the National Willa Cather Center in Red Cloud. A superb storyteller with a hearty devotion to archives, Tracy inspired many a twist and turn in this manuscript. Everything I write about Cather these days is better because of her influence.

At this juncture, I should thank everyone connected with the National Willa Cather Center. Their hospitality and annual programing have offered ideas, inspiration, and community. Particular thanks go to Ashley Olson, Cheryl Wilson, Dorothy Mattison, and Tom Gallagher, who wears many hats in his successful life, but helped me visualize the earliest iterations of this project in print. Finally, I offer warm thanks to Antonette Willa Skupa Turner for her wisdom, faith, and support of my work and all things Cather.

Regis University made this book possible in many ways. I thank my warmhearted colleagues in the Department of English for all their support: Mark Bruhn, Scott Dimovitz, David Hicks, Alyse Knorr, Frank McGill, Nick Myklebust, and Lara Narcisi. Former director of honors and now dean, Tom Bowie has been a mentor, friend, and collaborator for years. Quoting Joan Didion, he reminds me over and over again that we tell ourselves stories in order to live. If this book succeeds, it is because Tom showed me how to tell a better story. My colleagues at Dayton Memorial Library supported my work in many ways. I could and should thank many more colleagues at Regis University, but in this limited space I must thank Karen Adkins and Dan Clayton. It was in their brilliant company, teaching a course for the Regis College Core, that I rediscovered Willa Cather.

Three very different doctors have watched over my heart as I worked on this project. Indeed, I find it hard to imagine having survived some of the more challenging days without the care of Jim Sparandeo, Lara Narcisi, and Jerry Miklin.

Any writer is fortunate indeed to acknowledge dear friends who also play and have played the parts of halfway people. Some are close. Some are far away. Because no words on the page will ever capture their many gifts to me, I will simply name them here: Tom Averill, Bette and Rick Bohn, Dianna and Richard Cooper-Ribner, Harry, Wendy, and Avery Davidson, Spencer Evans, Connie Gates, Alan and Judy Hart, Abby and Matt Heller, Juli Highfill, Rol Hoverstock, Judy and Sandy Kahn, Trudy Morron, Fred Terry, Olivia Tracy, Brad, Jenny, Campbell, and Elise Tuininga, and Dick Wiens.

Justin Race, at the University of Nevada Press, guided the initial stages of the editorial process with a graciousness and professional acumen that I have rarely encountered. At an important stage, Alrica Goldstein made this book better. Willa Cather would be impressed.

Like Cather's famous professor, Godfrey St. Peter, I was once a Kansas boy. I know that I have lived two lives, practiced eliminations and combinations, and been utterly attached to my house. Unlike the professor, I had no dress forms to inspire me. Whenever I climbed the stairs to write this book, Miranda, the black cat who adopted us fourteen years ago, was there to help.

Books come, of course, from heads and hearts. Nina Molinaro, more than anyone else I have ever known, has cared for my head and heart. Having endured so many years of my writerly obsessions, she shows me every day that books, like life, depend on love.

About the Author

Daryl W. Palmer is a professor of English at Regis University in Denver, CO. He is the author of *Hospitable Performances: Dramatic Genre and Cultural Practices in Early Modern England* and *Writing Russia in the Age of Shakespeare.*